CODING IPHONE APPS FOR KIDS

A PLAYFUL INTRODUCTION TO SWIFT

BY GLORIA WINQUIST
AND MATT MCCARTHY

**no starch
press**

San Francisco

CODING IPHONE APPS FOR KIDS. Copyright © 2017 by Gloria Winquist and Matt McCarthy.

Printed in Canada

Second printing

21 20 19 18 17   2 3 4 5 6 7 8 9

ISBN-10: 1-59327-756-3
ISBN-13: 978-1-59327-756-7

Publisher: William Pollock
Production Editors: Alison Law and Riley Hoffman
Cover Illustration: Josh Ellingson
Illustrator: Keiko Satoh
Additional Illustrations: Max Burger
Developmental Editors: Tyler Ortman, Jan Cash, and Hayley Baker
Technical Reviewer: Mark H. Granoff
Copyeditor: Rachel Monaghan
Compositors: Alison Law and Riley Hoffman
Proofreader: Shannon Waite

For information on distribution, translations, or bulk sales, please contact No Starch Press, Inc. directly:

No Starch Press, Inc.
245 8th Street, San Francisco, CA 94103
phone: 1.415.863.9900; info@nostarch.com
www.nostarch.com

Library of Congress Cataloging-in-Publication Data

Names: Winquist, Gloria, author. | McCarthy, Matt (Software engineer), author.
Title: Coding iPhone apps for kids : a playful introduction to swift / Gloria
    Winquist and Matt McCarthy.
Description: San Francisco : No Starch Press, Inc., [2017] | Audience: Age 10
    plus.
Identifiers: LCCN 2017002199 (print) | LCCN 2017015717 (ebook) | ISBN
    9781593278373 (epub) | ISBN 1593278373 (epub) | ISBN 9781593278380 (mobi)
    | ISBN 1593278381 (mobi) | ISBN 9781593277567 (pbk.) | ISBN 1593277563
    (pbk.)
Subjects: LCSH: Swift (Computer program language)--Juvenile literature. |
    iPhone (Smartphone)--Programming--Juvenile literature. | Application
    software--Development--Juvenile literature.
Classification: LCC QA76.73.S95 (ebook) | LCC QA76.73.S95 W56 2017 (print) |
    DDC 004.1675--dc23
LC record available at https://lccn.loc.gov/2017002199

To Dagmar, Jude, Gretchen, Colin, Brenna, and Jackie

ABOUT THE AUTHORS

Gloria Winquist is a longtime Apple enthusiast and has fond memories of playing Zork on her family's Apple III home computer. Her first programming languages were Logo and BASIC, and then she learned C while getting her mechanical engineering degree. She worked for a while as a mechanical engineer but realized all she really wanted to do at work was write code. So she went to night school and learned Java, then Lisp, then JavaScript, and finally iOS programming and Objective-C. She found that she loved writing apps and has been doing it ever since!

Matt McCarthy first learned to program in BASIC on an Apple II+ at the age of 10. He still remembers his first program; it was just two lines of code, but he was instantly hooked. He's programmed professionally (and for fun) in many computer languages. But when the iOS App Store launched in 2008, he was immediately drawn to it and soon started publishing iOS apps through his company, Tomato Interactive LLC. Matt has worked professionally as an iOS engineer since 2012, developing healthcare apps for doctors and patients.

Gloria and Matt live in Concord, Massachusetts, and are the parents of a blended family of six kids. *Coding iPhone Apps for Kids* is their first book.

ABOUT THE TECHNICAL REVIEWER

Mark H. Granoff is an iOS developer and professional software engineer. For more than 30 years Mark has developed all kinds of software, but in 2009 he switched his focus to iOS and founded Hawk iMedia (*www.hawkimedia.com*). He's developed more than two dozen iOS applications and has reviewed several iOS programming books on a variety of topics. Mark lives outside Boston, Massachusetts, with his wife, two daughters, and one Cairn terrier named Kenzie.

ABOUT THE ILLUSTRATOR

Keiko Satoh has been drawing ever since she could hold a pencil, and her doodling skills came in handy when she had to move England not knowing a word of English. Besides always finding some excuse to draw, Keiko has worked in botanical gardens, hospitals, and even a cemetery, organizing archives, setting up websites, and helping people understand their health and the environment. These days she can be seen doodling with her Apple Pencil while in transit between the three cities she considers her homes—Tokyo, Boston, and London.

BRIEF CONTENTS

CONTENTS IN DETAIL

PART 1: XCODE AND SWIFT

7
FUNCTIONS ARE A PARTY, AND YOU'RE INVITED   81

8
CUSTOM CLASSES AND STRUCTS   95

PART 2: BIRTHDAY TRACKER

9
CREATING BUTTONS AND SCREENS
ON THE STORYBOARD 121

10
ADDING A BIRTHDAY CLASS AND
HANDLING USER INPUT 141

11
DISPLAYING BIRTHDAYS 155

PART 3: SCHOOLHOUSE SKATEBOARDER

18
GAME STATE, MENUS, SOUNDS, AND
SPECIAL EFFECTS

RESOURCES

INDEX

ACKNOWLEDGMENTS

First and foremost, we would like to thank the amazing staff at No Starch Press for working with us. Tyler Ortman was immediately enthusiastic when first approached and made this book possible. He gave us great tips on how to write for a younger audience when editing the early chapters of the book. Jan Cash brought our book across the finish line with her editing expertise, and Hayley Baker helped immensely in the editing process. We want to thank our production editors, Alison Law and Riley Hoffman, for their patience and hard work in polishing our words and perfecting the layouts that make the book look fantastic. Serena Yang—a big thanks for dealing with code coloring, illustrations, the cover, and lots of screenshots!

Thank you to Keiko Satoh, our illustrator. She read through all of our examples and came up with the witty drawings that you see scattered throughout the book's pages. Gloria has loved Keiko's artwork ever since they went to school together long ago in Brighton, England, and is thrilled that Keiko came on board to illustrate her first book!

We would also like to thank Josh Ellingson for the cover illustration and Max Burger for additional illustrations inside the book.

Thanks to Mark H. Granoff for the technical review. Swift is a new language, and we appreciate the time and effort that he spent familiarizing himself with Swift and for carefully and thoroughly reviewing our book.

Finally, we are so grateful to Gloria's dad, Floyd Winquist, for his patient and careful review of the book. He tested all the examples, read through several versions of all of the chapters, and provided much valuable feedback.

INTRODUCTION

Have you ever heard someone say, "I wish there was an app for that?" Maybe they were talking about a holiday card organizer or an app that can turn someone into a kitten. Well, you can be the person who makes that app! In this book, you'll learn how to program in Swift, the language used for mobile applications that run on all Apple devices. By the time you've finished reading, you'll have developed apps you can run on your iPhone, iPad, or iPod touch.

If you're new to programming, Swift is a great first programming language. It's modern and powerful, yet fun and easy to learn. You can write Swift in Xcode's playground, which lets you see the results of your code immediately. Once you have the basics down, you can go from using the playground to creating mobile apps in Xcode that you can carry everywhere—right in your pocket!

Learning a programming language will give you skills in problem solving, communication, and creativity. For these reasons and many more, programming is a highly useful skill to have. Even if you don't intend to become a professional programmer, if you regularly use a computer or a mobile device, then learning to program can improve your life.

WHO SHOULD READ THIS BOOK?

If you're interested in learning how to program, this book is a great place to start! *Coding iPhone Apps for Kids* is targeted toward kids, but it is also a good resource for adults who are new to programming. You should find this book useful whether you have no programming experience or are an experienced programmer who wants to learn how to develop apps.

If you're new to programming, we recommend that you start at the beginning and then work your way forward, chapter by chapter, through Part 1: Xcode and Swift. These chapters teach you basic programming skills that will build upon each other. As you read, test out the examples and try writing your own code.

If you have some experience programming in another language, we recommend starting with Chapter 1, which shows you how to download and install Xcode and then walks you through creating a simple "Hello, world!" app. You may feel comfortable skimming through Chapters 2 to 4 and 6 to 8, but don't skip Chapter 5. It covers optionals, which are an important programming feature that is unique to Swift.

WHAT'S IN THIS BOOK?

Chapter 1 covers installing Xcode on your computer and includes a simple tutorial to make a "Hello, world!" app that you can run on your iPhone, iPad, or iPod touch.

Chapter 2 delves into programming in an Xcode playground environment and shows you how to create variables and constants of different data types.

Chapters 3 and **4** teach you how to control the flow of a computer program. Chapter 3 covers if statements and conditionals, and Chapter 4 covers for-in and while loops.

Chapter 5 covers optionals, which are variables or constants that can either have a value or no value. Optionals are an important concept that's unique to the Swift programming language, so be sure to read this chapter carefully.

In **Chapter 6**, you'll learn how to work with two Swift collection types: arrays and dictionaries.

Chapter 7 covers writing functions, which are blocks of code that can be called repeatedly to perform specific tasks.

In **Chapter 8**, you'll learn how to make a custom class, which is a blueprint for creating objects that represent real-world items, such as a backpack, a car, a cat, or anything else that you can imagine.

Part 2: Birthday Tracker includes Chapters 9 to 13. These five chapters walk you through creating an app that lets you save your friends' birthdays on your phone and sends you reminders to wish them a happy birthday.

Part 3: Schoolhouse Skateboarder includes Chapters 14 to 18. These chapters walk you through the development of a game in which the player controls a skateboarder that jumps over cracks in the sidewalk and collects gems to increase their score.

Finally, the **Resources** provide information that will help you as you make your own apps, including tips for troubleshooting errors, where to find useful documentation, handy keyboard shortcuts, and information about Xcode versions.

THE COMPANION WEBSITE

Swift is an evolving language, and it gets updated often. We'll keep track of those updates and how they affect this book on the book's website (*https://www.nostarch.com/iphoneappsforkids/*). There, you can also find all the downloads for the examples we use.

HAVE FUN!

Programming is fun for so many reasons—you get to solve puzzles, impress people with your code creations, and feel pretty powerful once you know how to control a device. So, above all, don't forget to have fun!

PART 1

XCODE AND SWIFT

1

HELLO, WORLD!

In this chapter, we'll walk you through creating your very first app. But what exactly is an app? Short for *application*, an *app* is a computer *program*, which is a set of written instructions for a computer to follow. An app performs a task for the user, like giving driving directions, predicting the weather, or even just providing entertainment with a game. The apps that run on a phone or a tablet, often called *mobile apps*, have a lot in common with the programs that run on regular computers. After reading this book, you'll be able to use your new programming skills on way more than an iPhone or iPad! A computer is a computer, after all—whether it's in your pocket, on your lap, or on your desk. You're sure to impress your friends and family with the unique and fun new apps you'll create!

Besides being a cool thing to show to your loved ones, however, your apps can be submitted to the Apple App Store and shared with users all over the world. Over 140 billion apps have been downloaded from Apple so far. You don't need to own a company or be a big shot to get an app into the App Store. Anyone with a good idea and some decent programming skills can have a best-selling app.

This book is going to teach you how to develop an app for iOS, the mobile operating system developed by Apple that makes the iPhone and all of its apps work. Some other common operating systems are Apple's macOS and Microsoft Windows, which both run on desktop computers. iOS is designed specifically for Apple devices like the iPhone, iPod touch, and iPad.

iOS and macOS programs have long been written in a language called *Objective-C*. In the summer of 2014, Apple introduced a new and exciting language for writing apps called *Swift*. This is the language you'll learn in this book. Apple engineers have spent years making Swift a fast and powerful computer language that's also fun and easy to use. Swift is a great first computer language to learn because it works like the English language. For example, you can output the words "Hello, world!" with just one line of code:

```
print("Hello, world!")
```

We're excited to teach you Swift, but first we'll need to get your tools ready. Then we'll walk you through creating your first app, which will display "Hello, world!" onscreen.

INSTALLING XCODE, YOUR CODE EDITOR

To write your first iOS app, you'll need a relatively recent Mac computer. Specifically, you'll need a Mac running macOS 10.12.6 or newer. To find out which version of macOS you're running, click the Apple icon in the top-left corner of your Mac's screen, and then select **About This Mac**.

You'll also need Xcode and the iOS Software Development Kit (SDK). Xcode is a fancy code editor known as an *integrated development environment (IDE)*. It lets you write code and also includes a *simulator* that you can use to see how your code will run on any type of Apple device. The iOS SDK is a suite of prebuilt programming libraries that help you write apps quickly and in a way that Apple expects. A programming *library* is a collection of related software modules that you can use in your programs. The iOS SDK is included with Xcode, so a single download will get you both. To open the App Store, click the Apple icon in the top-left corner of the screen and then select **App Store**. Search for Xcode, which should be the first search result, and click the **Get** button to install it (see Figure 1-1).

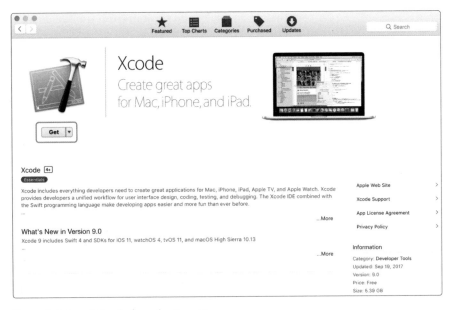

Figure 1-1: Install Xcode from the App Store.

You'll need to sign in with your Apple ID to install Xcode. If you've bought anything on iTunes or installed an app on your iPhone, you already have an Apple ID. If you don't already have an Apple ID, create one by clicking the **Create Apple ID** button. Installing Xcode may be the trickiest part of this process, so don't be shy—ask an adult for help if you need it.

YOUR FIRST APP!

Now you can get started creating your first app. Open Xcode by double-clicking the Xcode icon in the *Applications* folder in your Finder window. The first time you do this, you might see Xcode and iOS Terms and Conditions. If you do, click **Agree** and then wait for Xcode to install its components (Figure 1-2). It may take a little while, so be patient.

Figure 1-2: The first time Xcode launches, it needs to install its components.

Select **Create a new Xcode project** from the Welcome to Xcode dialog shown in Figure 1-3.

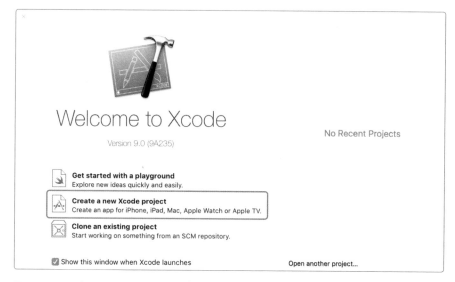

*Figure 1-3: Select **Create a new Xcode project**. When you start working on your projects, you'll also see a list of projects to choose from here.*

Select **iOS** in the upper-left corner of the dialog, and then select the **Single View App** template on the main screen (Figure 1-4). Click **Next**.

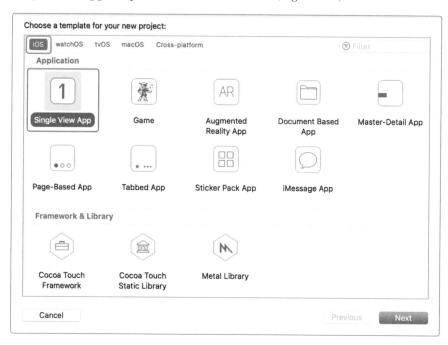

*Figure 1-4: Select **Single View App**. This is the simplest kind of project.*

Next, Xcode will ask you to set a few options for your new app (see Figure 1-5).

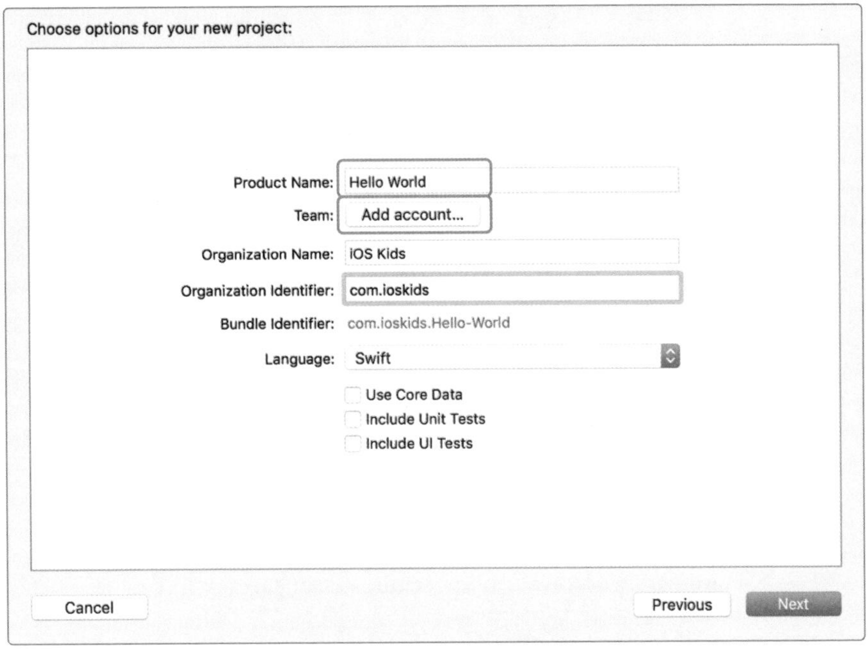

Choose options for your new project:

Product Name:	Hello World
Team:	Add account...
Organization Name:	iOS Kids
Organization Identifier:	com.ioskids
Bundle Identifier:	com.ioskids.Hello-World
Language:	Swift

  Use Core Data
  Include Unit Tests
  Include UI Tests

Cancel   Previous   Next

Figure 1-5: You can change these options in the Project Settings menu even after you set them here.

For Product Name, give your app the name *Hello World*.

If you have an iPhone, iPod touch, or iPad and would like to run the app on that device, Xcode needs to know the information for your Apple account. Click the **Add account...** button, and you'll see the sign-in form shown in Figure 1-6.

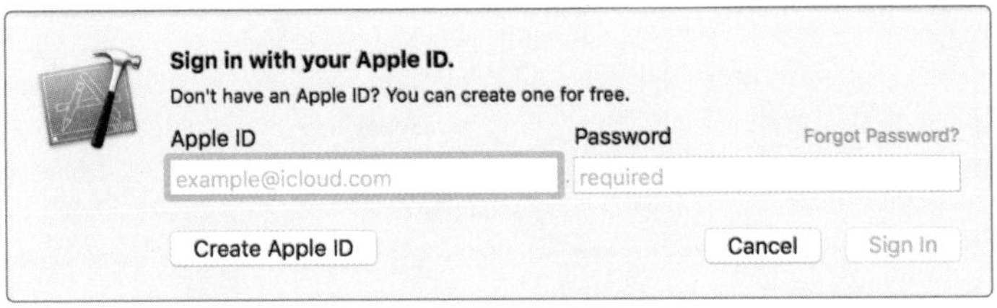

Sign in with your Apple ID.
Don't have an Apple ID? You can create one for free.

Apple ID   Password   Forgot Password?

example@icloud.com   required

Create Apple ID   Cancel   Sign In

Figure 1-6: Sign in to Xcode using an Apple ID to allow your apps to run on a real device.

Enter your Apple ID and password. If you created an Apple ID earlier, you can use that here. Or, if you use iCloud on your iPhone, iPod touch, or iPad, you can use that login information.

Once you've successfully signed in with your Apple ID, you'll see the Accounts window, as shown in Figure 1-7.

Figure 1-7: After signing in, you'll see your account under Apple IDs in the Accounts window.

Close this window by clicking the red close button in the upper-left corner, and you'll see the New Project window again. But now it shows your Apple account under Team, as you can see in Figure 1-8.

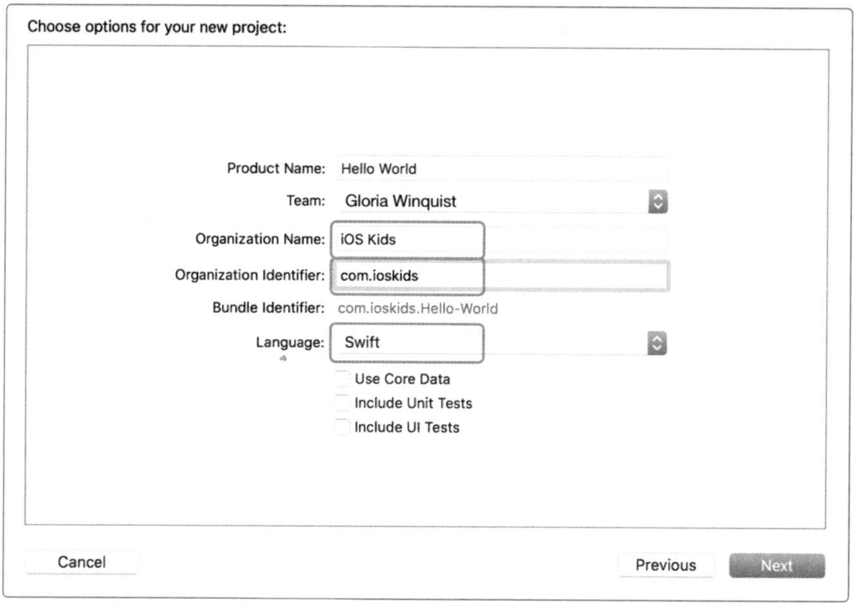

Figure 1-8: The New Project window now shows your Apple account under Team.

Next, add an Organization Name. You can invent your own company name, use your real name, or choose anything else you want. The Organization Identifier needs to be a unique name, so it's common to format this like a backward website address. (Don't worry—an actual website is not required!) The Bundle Identifier combines the names you entered in the Organization Identifier and the Product Name fields, and it is created automatically.

Set the Language option to **Swift**. Make sure the checkboxes for Use Core Data, Include Unit Tests, and Include UI Tests are not selected. Click **Next** and then **Create**, which will save the application and launch Xcode.

Your new *Hello World* Xcode project will open.

INTRODUCING THE STORYBOARD

On the left side of the Xcode window, you'll see a pane that contains the files and folders that make up your project. This is called the *Navigator pane*. Select *Main.storyboard* from the Navigator pane. This will open the project's *storyboard*, which gives us a picture-book view of the device screens when we run our app (see Figure 1-9). We can use the storyboard to design all of the screens and the connections between them. You don't necessarily have to use a storyboard when building an app, since you can write all of your app's design elements in code. However, using the storyboard is much easier, so that's what we'll do in this book.

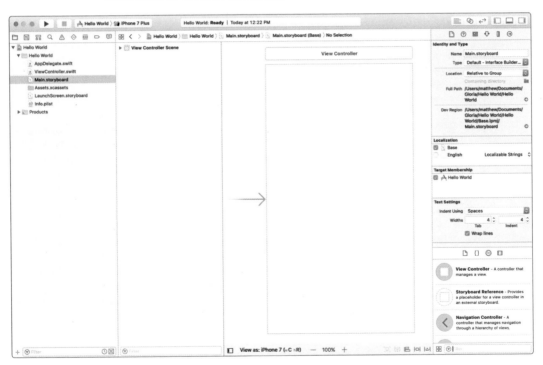

Figure 1-9: The project's main storyboard

When we created this project, we selected the Single View App template. This starts us off with an app that displays one empty, white screen. You can see this screen in the storyboard in Figure 1-9—it's the box with an arrow pointing to its left side. That arrow indicates that it's the starting screen of the application. This box is called the *view controller scene*. In Swift, a *view controller* manages the views that are displayed on the screen when an app is running. A *scene* in the storyboard is a visual representation of a view controller and all the views it contains.

You can hide or show the different parts of Xcode using the three buttons in the upper-right corner. Each button represents a different part of the screen that you can toggle on or off by clicking it. When the button is gray, that part of Xcode is hidden. When the button is blue, that part of Xcode is shown. Click these buttons until they look like Figure 1-10, where the two left buttons are gray and the right button is blue.

Figure 1-10: These buttons are used to show or hide different parts of Xcode.

This hides the Navigator pane (the list of files on the left) and the *debug area* (the bottom area that shows us messages about the app while it's running) and gives us a little more screen space to work with on the storyboard. The pane on the right side of the screen that we left on (represented by the blue button) is the *Utilities pane*. We'll use this to find objects to add to our storyboard.

ADDING USER INTERFACE ELEMENTS WITH THE OBJECT LIBRARY

Inside the Utilities pane, select the Object Library icon, which is a square inside a circle, as shown in Figure 1-11.

Scroll up and down inside the Object Library to see the kinds of *user interface elements* you can use in your app. You'll see labels, buttons, text fields, image views, and also elements that aren't visible to the user, such as gesture recognizers. If you want additional information on any of these objects, just double-click one and a dialog will pop up.

Let's start by adding a label to the screen. Select **Label** from the Object Library and drag it onto the view controller in the editor (see Figure 1-12).

Figure 1-11: The Object Library contains the elements you can drag into your storyboard to design your user interface.

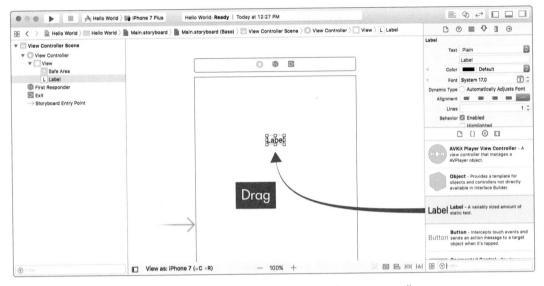

Figure 1-12: Drag a label from the Object Library and drop it onto the view controller.

Once you've placed the label, click the Size Inspector icon (it looks like a ruler) at the top of the Utilities pane, as shown in Figure 1-13. The Size Inspector allows us to change the size of an object in the storyboard.

The label you added to your view controller isn't big enough to display a nice "Hello, world!" message, so let's make it bigger. In the Size Inspector, change the Width of the label to **200** pixels and the Height to **40** pixels.

Now move the label to the upper-left area of the view controller screen. You can do this by clicking the label and dragging it to the desired position or by entering the x- and y-coordinates in the Size Inspector. The *x-coordinate* specifies the label's horizontal position, and the *y-coordinate* specifies the label's vertical position. Set values of **80** for X and **40** for Y. Now your values should match those shown in Figure 1-13.

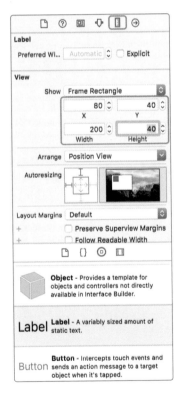

Figure 1-13: Setting new width, height, and x- and y-coordinates for our label with the Size Inspector

To change the text of the label, switch to the Attributes Inspector, as shown in Figure 1-14.

Enter `Hello, world!` into the Label text field. You can also enter text directly into the label by double-clicking the label on the storyboard and typing the text you want it to display. Let's also make our "Hello, world!" message bigger and bolder by changing the font. Click the T icon in the Font field, select **Bold** from the Style drop-down menu, enter **30** into the Size field, and then click **Done**. Figure 1-14 shows all of these settings.

Finally, choose center alignment for the text, as shown in Figure 1-15, by selecting the second icon next to Alignment.

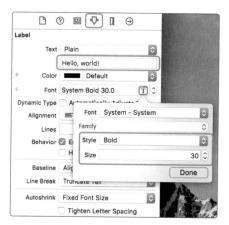

Figure 1-14: Change the label so it reads "Hello, world!" Make it bold and set the font size to 30.

Figure 1-15: Center-align the text of the label.

Try running the app and see what happens. You can run your app in a lot of different ways. You can click the play button in the upper-left corner of Xcode, choose the menu option Product ▶ Run, or use the keyboard shortcut ⌘-R.

The first time you run the app, it takes a while for the simulator to turn itself on and load. Be patient. You may also find that the iPhone simulator is too large to fit on your screen. If this is the case, you can adjust the size using the simulator menu, as shown in Figure 1-16. Go to **Window ▶ Scale** and then select a smaller size that will fit on your screen.

Figure 1-16: Sizing down the simulator so that it fits on your computer screen

When your app loads and is running, you'll see something like Figure 1-17.

Not only are there a lot of ways to run your app, but there are also several ways to stop it. You can click the square stop button in the upper-left corner of Xcode, go to Product ▸ Stop, or use the keyboard shortcut ⌘-period.

Figure 1-17: This is what success looks like!

SAVING YOUR WORK

Xcode will autosave your work every time you run your app, but you can also save your project at any time by pressing ⌘-S. To open your project again, you have two options. The first is just to launch Xcode. Your recent projects will show up on the right side of the Welcome to Xcode dialog, and you can open your app directly from there. The second is to find and double-click the *Hello World. xcodeproj* project in Finder (see Figure 1-18).

Figure 1-18: Double-click the Hello World.xcodeproj file in Finder to open your app in Xcode.

RUNNING THE APP ON A REAL DEVICE

If you own an iPhone, iPod, or iPad and would like to run your app on it, you'll learn how to do that in this section. Otherwise, you can skip to Chapter 2 and test and run your apps on the Xcode simulator.

In order to run an app that you've developed on a real device, you need to do a couple of things: you need to let Xcode know about your device so it can keep track of which devices it's allowed to run apps on, and you need to tell your device to trust Xcode so it will allow Xcode to install apps to it.

To let Xcode know about your device, log in with your Apple ID in Xcode, and then connect your device to your computer's USB port. You should have already logged in to Xcode earlier in this chapter when you created the Hello World project. If you didn't, go to **Xcode ▸ Preferences...**, select the **Accounts** tab, click the + button in the lower-left corner, and then select **Apple ID** and click **Continue**, as shown in Figure 1-19.

Figure 1-19: Adding an Apple ID to Xcode in Preferences under the Accounts tab

Once you've logged in with your Apple ID in Xcode (you should only have to do that once because Xcode will remember your login info from now on), plug your device into your computer. The very first time you plug your device in, your device will ask if you trust your computer, as seen in Figure 1-20. Tap **Trust**.

Figure 1-20: Your device will ask if you trust the computer you've plugged into.

Note that you have to unlock your device to get this message. Once you've tapped Trust, you'll need to wait about 30 seconds, unplug your device from your computer, and then plug it back in again. When you plug it in the second time, the Trust This Computer? alert shouldn't come up. This means that your device already knows to trust this computer when it's connected to it.

Now take a look at Xcode. The status bar at the top of Xcode should tell you that it's processing symbols for your device. This is a one-time process that Xcode has to complete before it can run an app on your device. You just have to sit tight for a couple of minutes while this is done. Once the process is complete, change Xcode's run option to your device by clicking the iPhone simulator label next to Hello World and the play button in the upper-left toolbar. This will bring up a menu where you can choose what to run your app on. Your device will be at the top of the list of simulators, as shown in Figure 1-21.

Now click the play button in Xcode (or press ⌘-R) to run the app on your device. If you see a message saying the iPhone is busy, ignore it and allow the app to keep running. The iPhone is processing files and will run the app automatically once it is done.

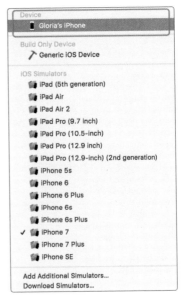

Figure 1-21: Selecting your device so you can run the app on it

If you see a message like the one shown in Figure 1-22, there's one more step you need to take to get your phone to trust your computer.

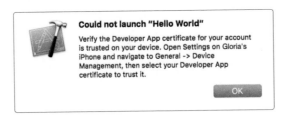

Figure 1-22: This message means your phone isn't quite ready to install apps yet.

If you got this message, go into the Settings app on your device, choose **General**, and then choose **Device Management** (see Figure 1-23).

Inside the Device Management settings, you'll see a message that apps from your developer account are not trusted on your device. Tap the **Trust *"email"*** button, and then tap **Trust** again in the pop-up that appears (see Figure 1-24).

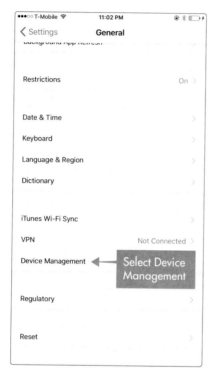

Figure 1-23: Selecting Device Management in the General settings on your device

Figure 1-24: The final step in making your device trust your computer so you can install apps

That should do it! Now go back to Xcode and click the play button again. This time, after a minute or so, the Hello World app should run on your device.

WHAT YOU LEARNED

You installed Xcode and created your first app. In doing so, you learned how to add a label to a view controller in the storyboard and how to run your app in a simulator or on a real device. In Chapter 2, you'll learn how to create expressions in Swift, which is just like writing sentences.

2

LEARNING TO CODE IN
A PLAYGROUND

A "Hello, world!" app is no small accom-
plishment, but now it's time to really learn
how to write some code. Xcode provides a
special type of document called a *playground*,
which is a great place to learn how to program. In a
playground, you can write and run code immediately
to see the results, without going through the trouble
of writing a whole app, as we did in Chapter 1.

Let's open a playground. Open Xcode and select **Get started with a
playground**, as shown in the Welcome to Xcode dialog in Figure 2-1. If this
window doesn't automatically open, select **Welcome to Xcode** from the
Window option in the menu or press ⌘-SHIFT-1.

Figure 2-1: Getting started with a playground

You'll be asked to choose a template for your new playground (Figure 2-2). Select **iOS** and the **Blank** template, and then click **Next**. Name your playground *MyPlayground.playground* and click **Create**.

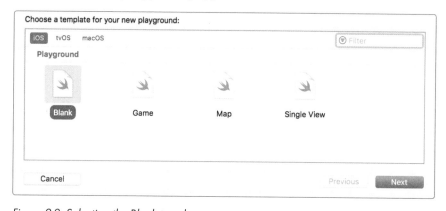

Figure 2-2: Selecting the Blank template

When the playground first opens, you'll see two panels in the window, just like in Figure 2-3. On the left is the playground editor, where you'll write your code. On the right is the results sidebar, which displays the results of your code.

The line var str = "Hello, playground" in Figure 2-3 creates a variable named str. A *variable* is like a container; you can use it to hold almost anything—a simple number, a string of letters, or a complex object (we'll explain what that is later). Let's take a closer look at how variables work.

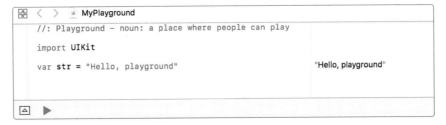

Figure 2-3: Playground editor and results sidebar

CONSTANTS AND VARIABLES

Here's the line of code from Figure 2-3 again:

`var str = "Hello, playground"`	`"Hello, playground"`

It does two things. First, it creates a variable named `str`. This is called a *declaration* because we are declaring that we would like to create a variable. To create a variable, you type the word var and then type a name for your variable—this case, `str`. There are some rules when naming variables, which we'll go over later, so for now stick with this example.

Second, this line of code gives a value of `"Hello, playground"` to `str` using the = operator. This is called an *assignment* because we are assigning a value to our newly created variable. Remember, you can think of a variable as a container that holds something. So now we have a container named `str` that holds `"Hello, playground"`.

You can read this line of code as "the variable `str` equals `Hello, playground`." As you can see, Swift is often very readable; this line of code practically tells you in English what it's doing.

Variables are handy because if you want to print the words "Hello, playground" all you have to do is use the command print on `str`, like in the following code:

`print(str)`	`"Hello, playground\n"`

This prints `"Hello, playground\n"` in the results sidebar. The \n is added automatically to the end of whatever you print. It is known as the *newline* character and tells the computer to go to a new line.

To see the results of your program as it would actually run, bring up the debug area, which will appear below the two panels, as shown in Figure 2-4. To do this, go to **View ▸ Debug Area ▸ Show Debug Area** in the Xcode menu or press ⌘-SHIFT-Y. When `str` is printed in the console of the debug area, you can see that the quotes around `Hello, playground` and the newline character don't appear. This is what `str` would really look like if you were to officially run this program!

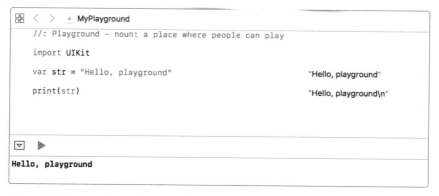

```
⊞ ⟨ ⟩ ↴ MyPlayground
    //: Playground – noun: a place where people can play

    import UIKit

    var str = "Hello, playground"                    "Hello, playground"

    print(str)                                        "Hello, playground\n"


 ▽  ▶
Hello, playground
```

Figure 2-4: Viewing the real output of your program in the debug area

Variables can change (or *vary*!) in your programs, so you can change the value of a variable to hold something else. Let's try that now. Add the following lines to your playground.

❶ `str = "Hello, world"`	`"Hello, world"`
`print(str)`	`"Hello, world\n"`

To change the value of a variable, type its name and use the = operator to set it to a new value. We do this at ❶ to change the value of str to "Hello, world". The computer throws away whatever str used to hold, and says, "Okay, boss, str is now Hello, world" (that is, it would say that if it could talk!).

Notice that when we change the value of str, we don't write var again. The computer remembers that we declared str in a previous line of code and knows that str already exists. So we don't need to create str again. We just want to put something different in it.

You can also declare *constants*. Like variables, constants hold values. The big difference between a constant and a variable is that a constant can never change its value. Variables can vary, and constants are, well, constant! Declaring a constant is similar to declaring a variable, but we use the word let instead of var:

`let myName = "Gloria"`	`"Gloria"`

Here we create a constant called myName and assign it the value of "Gloria".

Once you create a constant and give it a value, it will have that value until the end of time. Think of a constant as a big rock into which you've carved your value. If you try to give myName another value, like "Matt", you'll get an error like the one in Figure 2-5.

```
//: Playground - noun: a place where people can play

import UIKit

var str = "Hello, playground"                          "Hello, playground"
print(str)                                             "Hello, playground\n"

str = "Hello, world"                                    "Hello, world"
print(str)                                             "Hello, world\n"

let myName = "Gloria"                                   "Gloria"
  myName = "Matt"        Cannot assign to value: 'myName' is a 'let' constant  "Matt"
```

Figure 2-5: Trying to change the value of a constant won't work.

NOTE *In the playground, an error will appear as a red circle with a tiny white circle inside it. Clicking the error mark will show the error message and tell you what's wrong. If you have your debug area showing, you should also see information describing what happened and sometimes even how to fix it.*

WHEN TO USE CONSTANTS VS. VARIABLES

Now you've successfully created a variable and a constant—good job! But when should you use one over the other? In Swift, it's best practice to use constants instead of variables unless you expect the value will change. Constants help make code "safer." If you know the value of something is never going to change, why not etch it into stone and avoid any possible confusion later?

For example, say you want to keep track of the total number of windows in your classroom and the number of windows that are open today. The number of windows in your classroom isn't going to change, so you should use a constant to store this value. The number of windows that are open in your classroom will change depending on the weather and time of day, however, so you should use a variable to store this value.

```
let numberOfWindows = 8              8
var numberOfWindowsOpen = 3          3
```

We make `numberOfWindows` a constant and set it to 8 because the total number of windows will always be 8. We make `numberOfWindowsOpen` a variable and set it to 3 because we'll want to change that value when we open or close windows.

Remember: use `var` for variables and `let` for constants!

NAMING CONSTANTS AND VARIABLES

You can name a variable or constant almost anything you want, with a few exceptions. You can't name them something that is already a word in Swift. For example, you can't name a variable var. Writing var var would just be confusing, to you and the computer. You'll get an error if you try to name a variable or constant using one of Swift's reserved words. You also can't have two variables or constants with the same name in the same block of code.

In addition to these rules, there are some other good programming guidelines to follow when naming things in Swift. Your names should always start with a lowercase letter. It's also a good idea to have *very* descriptive names (they can be as long as you want). When you use a descriptive name, it's a lot easier to figure out what that variable or constant is supposed to be. If you were looking at someone else's code, which variable name would you find easier to understand: numKids or numberOfKidsInMyClass? The first one is vague, but the second one is descriptive. It's common to see variables and constants that are a bunch of words strung together, like numberOfKidsInMyClass. This capitalization style, where the first letter of each word is capitalized when multiple words are joined together to make a variable name, is called *camel case*. That's because the pattern of lowercase and uppercase letters looks like the humps on a camel's back.

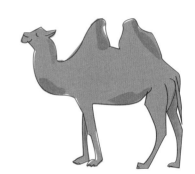

DATA TYPES

In Swift, you can choose what kind of data—the *data type*—you want a variable or constant to hold. Remember how we said you can think of a variable as a container that holds something? Well, the data type is like the container type. The computer needs to know what kind of things we'll put in each container. In Swift programming, once you tell the computer you want a variable or constant to hold a certain data type, it won't let you put anything but that data type in that variable or constant. If you have a basket designed to hold potatoes, it'd be a bad idea to fill that basket with water— unless you like water leaking all over your shoes!

DECLARING DATA TYPES

When you create a variable or a constant, you can tell the computer what type of data it will hold. In our example about classroom windows, we know this variable will always be an *integer* (that is, a whole number—you can't really have half a window), so we could specify an integer data type, like this:

`var numberOfWindowsOpen: Int = 3`	`3`

The colon means "is of type." In plain English, this line of code says, "the variable `numberOfWindowsOpen`, which is an integer, is equal to 3." So this line of code creates a variable, gives it a name, tells the computer its data type, and assigns it a value. Phew! One line of code did all that? Did we mention that Swift is a very *concise* language? Some languages might require several lines of code to do this same thing. Swift is designed so that you can do a bunch of things with just one line of code!

You only have to declare the data type once. When we tell the computer that a variable will hold integers, we don't have to tell it again. In fact, if we do, Xcode will give us an error. Once the data type is declared, a variable or constant will hold that type of data forever. Once an integer, always an integer!

There's one more thing you need to know about data types: a variable or constant can't hold something that isn't its data type. For example, if you try to put a decimal number into `numberOfWindowsOpen`, you'll get an error, as shown in Figure 2-6.

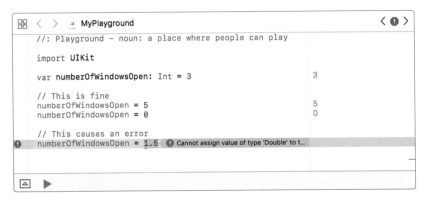

Figure 2-6: You can't put a decimal number into a variable that is supposed to hold an integer.

Setting `numberOfWindowsOpen = 5` and `numberOfWindowsOpen = 0` is valid and works. But you can't set `numberOfWindowsOpen = 1.5`.

COMMON DATA TYPES

As you just learned, a data type lets the computer know what *kind* of data it is working with and how to store it in its memory. But what are the data types? Some common ones include `Int`, `Double`, `Float`, `Bool`, and `String`.

Let's dig in and see what each one of these actually is!

Int (Integers)

We already talked a little bit about integers, but let's go over them in more detail. An integer, called an `Int` in Swift, is a whole number that has no decimal or fractional part. You can think of them as counting numbers. Integers are *signed*, meaning that they can be negative or positive (or zero).

Double and Float (Decimal Numbers)

Decimal numbers are numbers that have digits after the decimal point, like 3.14. (An integer like 3 would be written as 3.0 if you wanted it to be a decimal number.) There are two data types that can store decimal numbers: a `Double` and a `Float` (short for *floating-point number*). The `Double` data type is more common in Swift because it can hold bigger numbers, so we'll focus on those.

When you assign a `Double`, you must always have a digit to the left of the decimal place or you will get an error. For example, suppose bananas cost 19 cents each:

❶ `var bananaPrice: Double = .19 // ERROR`	
❷ `var bananaPrice: Double = 0.19 // CORRECT`	`0.19`

The code at ❶ will result in an error because it doesn't have a digit to the left of the decimal point. The code at ❷ works fine because it has a leading zero. (The phrases `// ERROR` and `// CORRECT` are *comments*, which are notes in a program that are ignored by the computer. See "A Few Quick Comments About Comments" on page 32.)

Bool (Booleans, or True/False)

A *Boolean value* can only be one of two things: true or false. In Swift, the Boolean data type is called a `Bool`.

`let swiftIsFun = true`	`true`
`var iAmSleeping = false`	`false`

Booleans are often used in `if-else` statements to tell the computer which path a program should take. (We'll cover Booleans and `if-else` statements in more detail in Chapter 3.)

String

The `String` data type is used to store words and phrases. A *string* is a collection of characters enclosed in quotation marks. For example, `"Hello, playground"` is a string. Strings can be made up of all sorts of characters: letters, numbers, symbols, and more. The quotation marks are important because they tell the computer that everything in between the quotes is part of a string that you're creating.

You can use strings to build sentences by adding strings together in a process called string *concatenation*. Let's see how it works!

`let morningGreeting = "Good Morning"`	`"Good Morning"`
`let friend = "Jude"`	`"Jude"`
`let specialGreeting = morningGreeting + " " + friend`	`"Good Morning Jude"`

By adding strings together with the plus sign (+), this code creates a variable called `specialGreeting` with the string `"Good Morning Jude"` as its value. Note that we need to add a string containing a space character (`" "`) between `morningGreeting` and `friend` here or else `specialGreeting` would be `"Good MorningJude"`.

TYPE INFERENCE

You may have noticed that sometimes when we declare a variable, we include the data type:

`var numberOfWindowsOpen: Int = 3`	3

And sometimes we do not include the data type:

`var numberOfWindowsOpen = 3`	3

What gives? The computer is actually smart enough to figure out the data type, most of the time. This is called *type inference*—because the computer will *infer*, or guess, the type of data we are using based on clues that we give it. When you create a variable and give it an initial value, that value is a big clue for the computer. Here are some examples:

- If you assign a number with no decimal value (like 3), the computer will assume it's an `Int`.
- If you assign a number with a decimal value (like 3.14), the computer will assume it's a `Double`.
- If you assign the word *true* or *false* (with no quotes around it), the computer will assume it's a `Bool`.
- If you assign one or more characters with quotes around them, the computer will assume it's a `String`.

When the type is inferred, the variable or constant is set to that data type just as if you had declared the data type yourself. This is done purely for convenience. You can include the data type every time you declare a new constant or variable, and that's perfectly fine. But why not let the computer figure it out and save yourself the time and extra typing?

TRANSFORMING DATA TYPES WITH CASTING

Casting is a way to temporarily transform the data type of a variable or constant. You can think of this as casting a spell on a variable—you make its value behave like a different data type, but just for a short while. To do this, you write a new data type followed by parentheses that hold the variable you are casting. Note that this *doesn't actually change the data type.* It just gives you a temporary value for that one line of code. Here are a few examples of casting between Int and Double. Take a look at the results of your code in the results sidebar.

`let months = 12`
`print(months)`
❶ `let doubleMonths = Double(months)`
`print(doubleMonths)`
	`12`
	`"12\n"`
	`12`
	`"12.0\n"`

At ❶, we cast our Int variable months to a Double and store it in a new variable called doubleMonths. This adds a decimal place, and the result of this casting is 12.0.

You can also cast a Double to an Int:

`let days = 365.25` ❶ `Int(days)`	`365.25` `365`

At ❶, we cast our Double, days, to an Int. You can see that the decimal place and all the digits following it were removed: our number became 365. This is because an Int is not capable of holding a decimal number—it can contain only whole numbers, so anything after the decimal point is chopped off.

Again, casting doesn't actually change a data type. In our example, even after casting, days is *still* a Double. We can verify this by printing days:

`print(days)`	`"365.25\n"`

The results sidebar shows that days is still equal to 365.25.

In the next section, we'll cover some examples of where and when you would use casting. So if it's not clear right now why you would cast a variable, just hold on a bit longer!

OPERATORS

There are a number of arithmetic operators in Swift that you can use to do math. You have already seen the basic assignment operator, =. You're probably also familiar with addition (+), subtraction (-), multiplication (*), and division (/).

You can use these operators to perform math on the Int, Float, and Double data types. The numbers being operated on are called *operands*. Experiment with these math operators in your playground by entering code like the following:

`6.2 + 1.4`	7.6
`3 * 5`	15
`16 - 2`	14
`9 / 3`	3

If you enter this code in your playground, you'll see the results of each math expression in the sidebar. Writing math expressions in code is not that different from writing them normally. For example, 16 minus 2 is written as 16 - 2.

You can even save the result of a math expression in a variable or constant so you can use it somewhere else in your code. To see how this works, enter these lines in your playground:

`var sum = 6.2 + 1.4`	7.6
❶ `print(sum)`	"7.6\n"
`let threeTimesFive = 3 * 5`	15

When you print sum ❶, you'll see 7.6 in the sidebar.

So far, we've used only numbers in our math expressions, but math operators also work on variables and constants.

Add the following code to your playground:

`let three = 3`	3
`let five = 5`	5
`let half = 0.5`	0.5
`let quarter = 0.25`	0.25
`var luckyNumber = 7`	7
`three * luckyNumber`	21
`five + three`	8
`half + quarter`	0.75

As you can see, you can use math operators on variables and constants like you did on numbers.

SPACES MATTER

In Swift, the spaces around an operator are important. You can either write a blank space on both sides of the math operator or leave out the spaces altogether. But you cannot just put a space on one side of the operator and not the other. That will cause an error. Take a look at Figure 2-7.

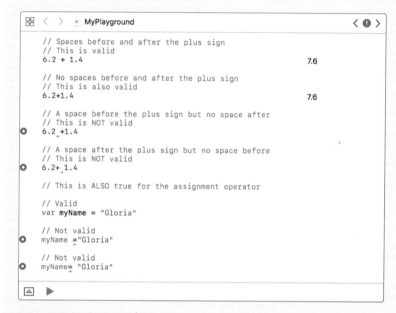

```
⊞  <  >   ⊿ MyPlayground                                    < ● >

// Spaces before and after the plus sign
// This is valid
6.2 + 1.4                                               7.6

// No spaces before and after the plus sign
// This is also valid
6.2+1.4                                                 7.6

// A space before the plus sign but no space after
// This is NOT valid
6.2 +1.4

// A space after the plus sign but no space before
// This is NOT valid
6.2+ 1.4

// This is ALSO true for the assignment operator

// Valid
var myName = "Gloria"

// Not valid
myName ="Gloria"

// Not valid
myName= "Gloria"

⊿  ▶
```

Figure 2-7: Make sure that you have the same number of spaces on each side of your operators.

There is one important thing to note: you can only use a math operator on variables or constants that are the *same* data type. In the previous code, three and five are both Int data types. The constants half and quarter are Double data types because they are decimal numbers. If you try to add or multiply an Int and a Double, you'll get an error like the one in Figure 2-8.

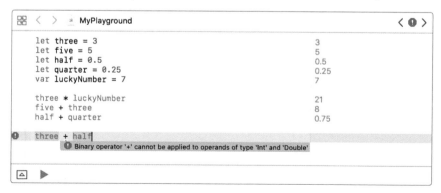

```
⊞  <  >   ⊿ MyPlayground                                    < ● >

let three = 3                                           3
let five = 5                                            5
let half = 0.5                                          0.5
let quarter = 0.25                                      0.25
var luckyNumber = 7                                     7

three * luckyNumber                                     21
five + three                                            8
half + quarter                                          0.75

● three + half
         ● Binary operator '+' cannot be applied to operands of type 'Int' and 'Double'

⊿  ▶
```

Figure 2-8: In Swift, you cannot do math on mixed data types.

But what if you really want to do math on mixed data types? For example, let's say you want to calculate one-tenth of your age:

`var myAge = 11 // This is an Int`
`let multiplier = 0.1 // This is a Double`
`var oneTenthMyAge = myAge * multiplier`
	`11`
	`0.1`

The last line will result in an error because we're attempting to multiply an Int by a Double. But don't worry! You have a couple of options to make sure your operands are the same data type.

One option is to declare myAge as a Double, like this:

`var myAge = 11.0 // This is a Double`
`let multiplier = 0.1 // This is a Double`
`var oneTenthMyAge = myAge * multiplier`
	`11.0`
	`0.1`
	`1.1`

This code works because we're multiplying two Double data types.

The second option is to use casting. (I told you we would come back to this!) Casting is a great solution in this case because we don't want to permanently change myAge to a Double, we just want to be able to perform math with it as if it were a Double. Let's take a look at an example:

`var myAge = 11 // This is an Int`
`let multiplier = 0.1 // This is a Double`
❶ `var oneTenthMyAge = Double(myAge) * multiplier`
❷ `oneTenthMyAge = myAge * multiplier`
	`11`
	`0.1`
	`1.1`

At ❶, we cast myAge to a Double before multiplying it. This means we no longer have mixed types, so the code works. But at ❷ we will get an error. That's because myAge is still an Int. Casting it to a Double at ❶ did not permanently change it to a Double.

Could we cast multiplier to an Int? You bet! Then we are doing math on two integers, which works fine. However, this results in a less precise calculation because we'll lose the decimal place. When you cast a variable from a Double to an Int, the computer simply removes any digits after the decimal to make it a whole number. In this case, your multiplier of 0.1 would cast to an Int of 0. Let's cast some variables in the playground and see what we get:

❶ `Int(multiplier)` ❷ `Int(1.9)`	`0` `1`

At ❶, casting our Double, multiplier, to an Int gives us 0. This value is quite different after casting, because we lost the decimal place: 0.1 became 0. This could be a very bad thing in our code if we were not expecting it to happen. You must be careful when casting to make sure you aren't unexpectedly changing your values. At ❷, there's another example of casting a Double to an Int, and as you can see, 1.9 does not get rounded up to 2. Its decimal value just gets removed and we are left with 1.

There's another math operator, the *modulo operator* (%), which might not be as familiar to you. The modulo operator (also called *modulus*) gives the remainder after division. For example, 7 % 2 = 1 because 7 divided by 2 has a remainder of 1. Try out the modulo operator in your playground, as follows.

`10 % 3`	1
`12 % 4`	0
`34 % 5`	4
`var evenNumber = 864`	864
❶ `evenNumber % 2`	0
`var oddNumber = 571`	571
❷ `oddNumber % 2`	1

As you can see, the modulo operator is useful for determining whether a number is even (`evenNumber % 2` equals 0) ❶ or odd (`oddNumber % 2` equals 1) ❷.

ORDER OF OPERATIONS

So far we've only done one math operation on each line of code, but it's common to do more than one operation on a single line. Let's look at an example.

How much money do you have if you have three five-dollar bills and two one-dollar bills? Let's calculate this on one line:

`var myMoney = 5 * 3 + 2`	17

This assigns a value of 17 to `myMoney`. The computer multiplies 5 times 3 and then adds 2. But how does the computer know to multiply first and *then* add 2? Does it just work from left to right? No! Take a look at this:

`myMoney = 2 + 5 * 3`	17

We moved the numbers around and the result is still 17. If the computer just went from left to right, it would add 2 + 5 and get 7. Then it would multiply that result, 7, times 3, and get 21. Even though we changed the order of the numbers in our math expression, the computer still multiplies first (which gives us 15) and then adds the 2 to get 17. *The computer will always do multiplication and division first, then addition and subtraction.* This is called the *order of operations.*

ORDERING OPERATIONS WITH PARENTHESES

You don't have to rely on the computer to figure out which step to do first like we did in the money example. You, the programmer, have the power to decide! You can use parentheses to group operations together. When you put parentheses around something, you tell the computer to do that step first:

❶ myMoney = 2 + (5 * 3)	17
❷ myMoney = (2 + 5) * 3	21

At ❶, the parentheses tell the computer to multiply 5 times 3 first and then add 2. This will give you 17. At ❷, the parentheses tell the computer to add 2 plus 5 first and then multiply that by 3, which gives you 21.

You can make your code even more specific by using parentheses inside of other parentheses. The computer will evaluate the inside parentheses first and then the outside ones. Try this example:

myMoney = 1 + ((2 + 3) * 4)	21

First the computer adds 2 and 3 between the inner parentheses. Then it multiplies the result by 4, since that's within the outer set of parentheses. It will add the 1 last because it's outside both sets of parentheses. The final result is 21.

COMPOUND ASSIGNMENT OPERATORS

Another category of operators that you'll use is the *compound assignment operators*. These are "shortcut" operators that combine a math operator with the assignment operator (=). For example, this expression

```
a = a + b
```

becomes

```
a += b
```

You can use these operators to update the value of a variable or constant by performing an operation on it. In plain English, an expression like a += b says "add b to a and store the new value in a." Table 2-1 shows math expressions using compound assignment operators and the same expressions in their longer forms.

Table 2-1: Short Form Assignment Operators vs. Long Form Expressions

Short form	Long form
a += b	a = a + b
a -= b	a = a - b
a *= b	a = a * b
a /= b	a = a / b

Let's see the += operator in action. Imagine that we're trying to write a program to calculate the number of animals on an ark. First we create a variable called `animalsOnArk` and set it to 0 because there aren't animals on the ark yet. As the different types of animals board the ark, we want to increase `animalsOnArk` to count all of the animals. If two giraffes board the ark, then we need to add 2 to `animalsOnArk`. If two elephants board the ark, then we need to add 2 again. If four antelope board the ark, then we need to increase `animalsOnArk` by 4.

`var animalsOnArk = 0`	0
`let numberOfGiraffes = 2`	2
`animalsOnArk += numberOfGiraffes`	2
`let numberOfElephants = 2`	2
`animalsOnArk += numberOfElephants`	4
`let numberOfAntelope = 4`	4
`animalsOnArk += numberOfAntelope`	8

After two giraffes, two elephants, and four antelope board the ark, the final value for `animalsOnArk` is 8. What a zoo!

A FEW QUICK COMMENTS ABOUT COMMENTS

Most programming languages come with a way to write comments inline with the code. Comments are notes that are ignored by the computer and are there to help the humans reading the code understand what's going on. Although a program will run fine without any comments, it's a good idea to include them for sections of code that might be unclear or confusing. Even if you're not going to show your program to anybody else, your comments will help you remember what you were doing or thinking when you wrote that code. It's not uncommon to come back to a piece of code you wrote months or years ago and have no idea what you were thinking at the time.

There are two ways to add comments in Swift. The first way is to put two forward slashes (//) in front of the text you want to add. These comments can be placed on their own line, like this:

```
// My favorite things
```

Or they can be placed on the same line as a line of code—as long as the comment comes *after* the code:

```
var myFavoriteAnimal = "Horse" // Does not have to be a pet
```

The second way is used for long comments, or *multiline* comments, where the start and end of the comment is marked by /* and */. (Note that we'll use *--snip--* in this book to show where there are more code lines that we've omitted for space.)

```
/*
  This block of code will add up the animals
  that walk onto an ark.
*/
{
  var animalsOnArk = 0
  let numberOfGiraffes = 2
  animalsOnArk += numberOfGiraffes
  --snip--
}
```

Multiline comments are useful when you debug your code. For example, if you don't want the computer to run part of your code because you're trying to find a bug, but you also don't want to delete all of your hard work, you can use multiline comments to *comment out* sections of code temporarily. When you format a chunk of code as a comment, the computer will ignore that code just like it ignores any other comment.

WHAT YOU LEARNED

In this chapter you learned how to write code in a Swift playground, which lets you see results right away. You created variables and constants and learned how to use the basic data types and operators that you will be seeing again and again as you write your own computer programs.

In Chapter 3, you will be using conditional statements, which tell the computer which code path you want it to go down. The code path is chosen based on a condition's value.

3

MAKING CHOICES

Now that we've covered how to create constants and variables, you're ready to learn how to tell your computer to make choices. This chapter is about controlling the flow of a computer program by telling the computer which path to take. When we talk about *flow*, we're referring to the order in which the statements of the program are executed.

Up to this point, you've only seen statements performed in the order you've typed them. You've done some cool things with this, but by telling the computer how to make choices about the order of executing statements, you can do even more. To get the computer to make a choice, we'll use *conditional statements* that tell the computer to run some code based on a condition's value.

You already use conditional statements to make choices every day! For example, before you leave home in the morning, you check the weather. If it's sunny, you may put on a pair of sunglasses. If it's raining, you grab your umbrella. In each case, you're checking a condition. If the condition "it is raining" is true, then you take your umbrella when you leave the house. When the condition could be true or false, it's called a *Boolean expression*. The Bool data type that you learned about in Chapter 2 is used to represent the value true or false.

BOOLEAN EXPRESSIONS

A common type of Boolean expression is one that compares two values using a *comparison operator*. There are six comparison operators. Let's start with two simple ones: *is equal* and *is not equal*.

IS EQUAL AND IS NOT EQUAL

You'll use the *is equal* and *is not equal* comparison operators a lot. *Is equal* is written with two equal signs next to each other, like this: ==. *Is not equal* is written with an exclamation mark and one equal sign, like this: !=.

Let's try them both out in the playground!

❶ `3 + 2 == 5`	true
`4 + 5 == 8`	false
❷ `3 != 5`	true
`4 + 5 != 8`	true
`// This is wrong and will give you an error`	
❸ `3 + 5 = 8`	error

In plain English, the line at ❶ says, "three plus two equals five," which is a true statement, and the output in the right pane will confirm this as soon as you finish typing it. At ❷, the line says, "three is not equal to five," which is also a true statement. Note that ❸ is an error. Do you know why? While = and == look a lot alike, remember that a single equal sign (=) assigns values. That statement reads, "Put the value of 8 into something called 3 + 5," which doesn't work.

In Swift, the == operator also works with other data types, not just numbers. Let's try making some other comparisons.

```
// Comparing strings
let myName = "Gloria"                              "Gloria"
myName == "Melissa"                                false
myName == "Gloria"                                 true
❶ myName == "gloria"                               false
var myHeight = 67.5                                67.5
myHeight == 67.5                                   true
// This is wrong and will give you an error
❷ myHeight == myName                               error
```

The line at ❶ is a tricky one; did you expect it to be true? Those two strings are close but not exactly the same, and an *is equal* comparison is true only if the two values match exactly. The constant myName has a value of "Gloria" with a capital *G*, which is not the same as "gloria" with a lowercase *g*.

Remember in Chapter 2 when we said that you can't use math operators like + and * on things that aren't the same data type? The same is true for comparisons. You can't compare things that are different types. The line at ❷ will cause an error because one is a String and the other is a Double.

GREATER THAN AND LESS THAN

Now let's look at four other comparison operators. We'll start with *greater than* (written as >) and *less than* (written as <). You probably already have a good idea of how these work. A Boolean expression like 9 > 7, which reads "9 is greater than 7," is true. Often, you'll also want to know if something is greater than or equal to something or less than or equal to something. There are two more operators that cover those cases: *greater than or equal to* (which looks like >=) and *less than or equal to* (which looks like <=). Let's try these out with some more examples:

```
// Greater than
9 > 7                                              true
// Less than
9 < 11                                             true
// Greater than or equal to
❶ 3 + 4 >= 7                                       true
❷ 3 + 4 > 7                                        false
// Less than or equal to
❸ 5 + 6 <= 11                                      true
❹ 5 + 6 < 11                                       false
```

Note the difference between *greater than or equal to* at ❶ and *greater than* at ❷. The sum of 3 + 4 is not greater than 7, but it is greater than or equal to 7. Similarly, 5 + 6 is less than or equal to 11 ❸, but it's not less than 11 ❹.

Table 3-1 summarizes the six comparison operators.

Table 3-1: Comparison Operators

Symbol	Definition
==	Is equal to
!=	Is not equal to
>	Is greater than
<	Is less than
>=	Is greater than or equal to
<=	Is less than or equal to

You'll find yourself using these operators often when you write conditional statements.

COMPOUND BOOLEAN EXPRESSIONS

Compound Boolean expressions are simple Boolean expressions that have been joined together. It's a lot like making compound sentences in English with the words *and* and *or*. In programming, there is a third case: *not*. In Swift, we call these words *logical operators*. A logical operator either combines a Boolean expression with another one or negates it. The three logical operators in Swift are shown in Table 3-2.

Table 3-2: Logical Operators

Symbol	Definition
&&	Logical AND
||	Logical OR
!	Logical NOT

With logical operators, you can write statements that test if a value falls within a range, such as, "Is this person's age between 10 and 15?" You would do this by testing if the age is greater than 10 *and* less than 15 at the same time, like this:

var age = 12 age > 10 && age < 15	12 true

The statement age > 10 && age < 15 is true because both the conditions are true: age is greater than 10 and less than 15. An AND statement is true only if both conditions are true.

Try changing the value of age to 18 to see what happens:

`var age = 18` `age > 10 && age < 15`	`18` `false`

Because we changed age to 18, only one side of the statement is true. The variable age is still greater than 10, but it's no longer less than 15, so our expression evaluates to false.

Now test out OR by entering this code in your playground:

`let name = "Jacqueline"`
`name == "Jack"`
❶ `name == "Jack" || name == "Jacqueline"`
	`"Jacqueline"`
	`false`
	`true`

First, we make up a person named Jacqueline by setting the constant name to "Jacqueline". Next, we test some conditions to see if they are true or false. Because name == "Jacqueline" is true, the OR statement at ❶ is true even though name == "Jack" is false. In English, this statement says, "This person's name is Jack *or* this person's name is Jacqueline." In an OR statement, only one of the conditions needs to be true for the whole expression to be true.

Let's try using some NOT statements. Enter the following into your playground:

`let isAGirl = true`
❶ `!isAGirl && name == "Jack"`
`isAGirl && name == "Jacqueline"`
❷ `(!isAGirl && name == "Jack") || (isAGirl && name == "Jacqueline")`
	`true`
	`false`
	`true`
	`true`

The ! operator is used in the compound Boolean statement ❶, which you could read as "Our person is *not* a girl *and* our person is named Jack." That statement has two logical operators, ! and &&. You can combine as many logical operators as you want when you write compound Boolean expressions.

Sometimes it's a good idea to use parentheses to let the computer know what to evaluate first. Parentheses also make the code easier to read. This is similar to how you use parentheses when you use several math operations in one equation, as described in "Ordering Operations with Parentheses" on page 30. At ❷, we use parentheses to tell the computer to first check !isAGirl && name == "Jack" and then check isAGirl && name == "Jacqueline". After it has evaluated both parts, the computer can evaluate the OR part for the entire statement, which will be true because the second part is true. Again, in an OR statement, the whole expression is true if any of the conditions is true.

Table 3-3 shows the three logical operators and the compound expressions you can make with them, as well as their corresponding Boolean values.

Table 3-3: Compound Boolean Expressions with Logical Operators

Logical operator	Compound expression	Value
NOT (!)	!true	false
NOT (!)	!false	true
AND (&&)	true && true	true
AND (&&)	true && false	false
AND (&&)	false && true	false
AND (&&)	false && false	false
OR (||)	true || true	true
OR (||)	true || false	true
OR (||)	false || true	true
OR (||)	false || false	false

The first item of the table shows that something that is NOT true is false. Similarly, something that is NOT false is true.

With the AND operator, only something that is true && true is true. This means that the expressions on both sides of the && operator must be true for the && expression to be true. A compound expression that is true && false will evaluate to false. And a compound && expression in which both conditions are false will also evaluate to false.

When it comes to the OR operator, only one of the expressions on either side of the || operator must be true for the || expression to be true. Therefore, a true || true is true, and a true || false is also true. Only a compound OR expression in which both sides are false ends up being false.

CONDITIONAL STATEMENTS

Conditional statements fall into two categories: the if statement and the switch statement. These statements present the computer with a condition that the computer makes a choice based on.

IF STATEMENTS

An if statement starts with the keyword if followed by a *condition*, which is always a Boolean expression. The computer examines the condition and executes the code inside the if statement if the condition is true or skips over that code if the condition is false. Let's write some code that tests whether a kid is tall enough to ride a roller coaster. Enter the following code into your playground:

```
let heightToRideAlone = 48.0
var height = 49.5
❶ if height >= heightToRideAlone{
❷     print("You are tall enough to ride this roller coaster.")
   }
```

Here, we set 48 inches as the minimum height at which a kid can ride our roller coaster alone, and we set our rider's height to 49.5 inches. At ❶, we test whether the rider's height is greater than or equal to heightToRideAlone. If it is, the program says that they are tall enough to ride the roller coaster. To write our if statement, we put the keyword if in front of the condition height >= heightToRideAlone. Then we wrap the code that we want to execute when that condition is true in a set of braces ❷. Because our rider is tall enough, the computer will print "You are tall enough to ride this roller coaster." Hooray!

Let's see what happens if we change our rider's height. Change height to a number less than 48.0. This time, because the condition in the if statement evaluates to false, the program skips all of the code in the if statement and nothing happens.

else Statements

Often, you'll want to tell the computer to do one thing if a statement is true but something else if that statement is false. To do this, after the if statement and block of code, just type the keyword else followed by another block of code that you want to execute when the if condition isn't true. If the rider isn't tall enough to meet the condition, let's have the computer tell them they can't ride the roller coaster:

```
if height >= heightToRideAlone {
    print("You are tall enough to ride this roller coaster.")
❶ } else {
    print("Sorry. You cannot ride this roller coaster.")
}
```

Now if you change the rider's height to less than 48 inches, you'll see "Sorry. You cannot ride this roller coaster." That's because the else statement at ❶ tells the computer to print that message if the statement evaluates to false. In plain English, this is like saying, "If the rider is tall enough to ride the roller coaster, say they can ride it. Else, say they can't."

else if Statements

We could also test different conditions for the rider's height to create more rules for riding the roller coaster. We can do this by adding else if conditions. Let's add a new minimum height that requires the kid to ride with an adult:

```
let heightToRideAlone = 48.0
let heightToRideWithAdult = 36.0
var height = 47.5
```

```
    if height >= heightToRideAlone {
        print("You are tall enough to ride this roller coaster alone.")
❶ } else if height >= heightToRideWithAdult {
        print("You can ride this roller coaster with an adult.")
    } else {
        print("Sorry. You cannot ride this roller coaster.")
    }
```

The else if statement at ❶ checks whether the rider's height is greater than or equal to heightToRideWithAdult. If a rider is shorter than 48 inches but taller than 36 inches, then the line "You can ride this roller coaster with an adult." appears in the results pane. If they are too short to ride alone or with an adult, then the computer prints "Sorry. You cannot ride this roller coaster."

else if statements are neat because you can use them to test lots of different conditions, but it's very important that you pay attention to the order of these conditions. To show you what we mean, change the rider's height to 50.0 so that they are tall enough to ride alone. Then, change the order of the conditions in our if else statement by making height >= heightToRideWithAdult the first condition and height >= heightToRideAlone the second condition. What do you think will be printed? Take a look at Figure 3-1 to find out.

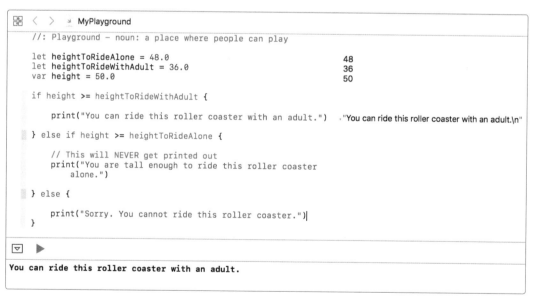

Figure 3-1: Be careful with your ordering of else if statements.

You can see that even though the rider is taller than heightToRideAlone, the program prints "You can ride this roller coaster with an adult." which is the expected output for a rider whose height is greater than heightToRideWithAdult but less than heightToRideAlone. We get this result because the rider's height matches the first condition, so the computer prints the first sentence and doesn't bother checking anything else.

Once any part of an if or else if statement is found to be true, the rest of the conditions won't be checked. In our example in Figure 3-1, the first condition is true, so the rest of the conditions are skipped. This can lead to unexpected results in your programs, so if you ever run into problems in your if or else if statements, check the order of the conditions!

When you're working with if, else, or else if statements, there are a few important rules. The first is that you can't have an else or an else if statement unless you write an if statement first. The second is that although you can have as many else ifs as you want after an if, you can have only one else—and that else must be last. The else is the catch-all case if none of the other things has happened.

CODE WITH STYLE

Pay close attention to the coding style that we use in this book. By *coding style*, we mean the way that the code is written, the number of spaces used, the indentation of certain lines, and what things go on a new line. Take a look at this code:

```
// The opening brace, {, of a block of code goes on
// the same line as the condition
if height >= heightToRideAlone {

    // Statements inside a block of code should be indented by 4 spaces
    print("You are tall enough to ride this roller coaster alone.")

// The closing brace, }, of a block of code goes at the start of a new line
} else if height >= heightToRideWithAdult {

    // Extra blank lines can be added between statements
    // to make the code look less crowded

    print("You can ride this roller coaster with an adult.")

} else {

    print("Sorry. You cannot ride this roller coaster.")
}
```

Notice that after the if condition we leave a space and then place the opening brace, {, on the same line. The block's closing brace, }, always goes at the start of the next new line. The statements contained within the braces are indented by four spaces. This is something that Xcode does automatically for you to make the code more readable. Feel free to add blank lines if it makes it easier for you to read. In general, you should always have at least one blank line before a chunk of code such as an if statement.

SWITCH STATEMENTS

Whereas an if statement is used only to evaluate a Boolean expression (something that must be true or false), a switch statement can evaluate and branch out on any number of conditions. You could use a switch to check the value of an integer and tell the computer to do one thing if the integer equals 1, something else if the integer equals 2, and so on. Or, you could create a string called dayOfTheWeek and write a switch statement that makes the computer do something different based on the value of dayOfTheWeek.

When the computer finds the first match, that block of code is executed. Take a look at the following code, which assigns student projects for different grade levels:

```
var studentGrade = 5
var studentProject = "To be determined"

❶ switch studentGrade {
❷ case 1:
        studentProject = "A country of the student's choice"
   case 2:
        studentProject = "The Iditarod"
   case 3:
        studentProject = "Native Americans"
   case 4:
        studentProject = "A state of the student's choice"
   case 5:
        studentProject = "Colonial times"
❸ case 6, 7, 8:
        studentProject = "Student's choice"
❹ default:
        studentProject = "N/A"
   }
```

The switch statement starts with the keyword switch followed by the *control expression.* In this example, the control expression is the variable studentGrade.

After the control expression, a set of braces begins at ❶, and the body of the switch statement is inside these braces.

The body of the switch statement is made up of one or more cases. In this example, there are six cases total. Each case starts with the keyword case followed by a value and a colon, as shown at ❷. If a case statement matches the control expression, the code just after the case will run. Each case must have at least one line of code, or you'll get an error. In this example, switch is used to change the string assigned to the variable studentProject from "To be determined" to the string in the case that matches the control expression.

Note that you can have multiple cases all do the same thing. You can see that students in grades 6, 7, and 8 all get to choose their own projects ❸. We specify this by writing the keyword case and then a comma-separated list of values.

Finally, a switch statement must account for every possible case or value of the control expression. In our example, because studentGrade is an Int, our switch statement needs to have a case for all possible Int values. But this would take a really long time to write since there are so many! For example, −7 is an Int, as is 1,000. Do you really want to write 1,000 cases?

Instead of writing a separate case for every value, you can use the keyword default as the last case, as we did at ❹. You simply type default followed by a colon (default:) and then whatever code you want to run if none of the other cases match. Notice that the default case doesn't have the word case in front of it. The default case is really helpful for taking care of values that you might not expect and lets you avoid writing so many case statements. In this example, we expect a value only of 1 through 8 for studentGrade, so we use the default case to cover all other possible values.

Try running this switch statement and see what you get. Then try changing the values to test for different conditions. Play around with it!

WHAT YOU LEARNED

In this chapter, you learned how to program the computer to make choices based on conditions using if and switch statements. You learned how to write Boolean expressions and compound expressions, and about the different comparison operators. Conditional statements are an essential programming tool and are seen in almost every useful program. In Chapter 4, we're going to tackle another important type of programming statement— the loop. Loops tell the computer to do something over and over again until it is time to stop the loop.

4

WRITING CODE THAT LOOPS

 You just learned that you use conditional statements to run different branches of code depending on which conditions are met. *Loops* are another way you can control the order of your programs. With a loop, you can tell the computer to execute a block of code as many times as you want. This lets you reuse chunks of code again and again so that you don't have to rewrite them!

In Swift, there are two main types of loops: for-in loops and while loops. The for-in loop tells the computer to run a loop a certain number of times, and it's useful when you know right off the bat how many times you want the code to repeat. The while loop tells the computer to keep running a loop over and over until a certain condition is met, which is great when you're more interested in repeating code based on events or conditions in your program. Let's dig into each type of loop and learn more about it!

OPEN THE DEBUG AREA

Before we get started writing loops, let's make sure your playground is set up to display the debug area. When you write for-in loops in the playground, the results sidebar on the right tells you only how many times a loop runs. To see the loop's output, you need to display the debug area of the playground by selecting **View ▸ Debug Area ▸ Show Debug Area** (⌘-SHIFT-Y). If this menu says Hide Debug Area, then it's already showing the debug area, and you don't need to do anything.

When you show the debug area, it appears at the bottom of your playground by default, and you can drag the divider line at the top of it to make it taller or shorter.

LOOPING THROUGH RANGES AND COLLECTIONS WITH FOR-IN

A for-in loop tells the computer to run the loop over a range of numbers or for each item in a collection. We'll talk more about collections in Chapter 6, but for now, think of a collection as a group of items—like a bag of marbles or a case of trophies. Let's see how we loop through a range of numbers first.

SAY HELLO!

You can use a for-in loop to tell the computer something like, "I want to run this bit of code 4 times." To do this, you write the for keyword, followed by a variable to count how many times the loop runs, then the in keyword, and finally the range of numbers that you want the loop to run through. Let's write a simple for-in loop that prints your name 4 times:

```
for ❶number in ❷1...4 {
    print("Hello, my name is Colin.") // Use your own name here!
}
```

The for-in loop begins with the keyword for, followed by a variable ❶ that will be used as a counter to go through the range of numbers. We named our counter variable number, but you can give this variable any name you want. After the counter variable comes the keyword in. This keyword tells the computer to expect a range of integers. After in, we provide the range that we want the for-in loop to use, 1...4 ❷. This is called a *closed range* from 1 to 4, and it indicates that the count starts at 1 and ends at 4. The three-dot symbol (...) is the *closed range operator*.

Let's add a line to our `for-in` loop so that we can see how `number` increases from 1 through 4. Add the following line right after the line that prints your name inside the loop:

```
print("And the value of number is now ❶\(number).❷\n")
```

Inside the `for-in` loop, we use `number` just as we would any other variable. This statement prints a string that contains the value of `number`. To embed variables and constants into strings, you type a backslash and then enter the variable or constant you want to print in parentheses, just like we did at ❶. This prints the variable's value with the rest of your string. Pretty cool!

To make the output prettier, at ❷ we also added an empty new line at the end of the sentence by writing the special character for a new line, `\n`. When that sentence is printed, the computer does not print `\n` but instead adds a new line, like when you press RETURN or ENTER on your keyboard.

Your screen should look like Figure 4-1. If you don't see the printed text, make sure the debug area is turned on by pressing ⌘-SHIFT-Y.

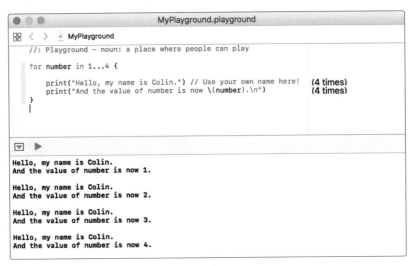

Figure 4-1: Debug area display of a for-in loop

The `for-in` loop will run 4 times. The first time the loop runs, `number` is equal to 1; the second time it runs, it's equal to 2; and so on until the final loop, when it's equal to 4. When `number` reaches the end of the range 1 through 4, the loop ends.

In a `for-in` loop, when the counter, `number`, cycles through the loop, increasing from 1 to 4, we say that the counter *iterates* over the range from 1 to 4. Each time the code inside a `for-in` loop is run, we call that an *iteration*.

You can change these numbers to set different ranges to loop through. Try it out and see what happens!

SAY GOOD MORNING!

In addition to looping through a range of numbers, the `for-in` loop is useful for looping through collections. Here, you'll use a collection called an *array*. We'll talk more about arrays in Chapter 6, but all you need to know right now is that an array is a list of items stored in a constant or variable. When you use a `for-in` loop to go through an array, you're telling your computer "for each item in the array, do something!" Let's write code that greets kids.

```
❶ let kidsInClass = ["Gretchen", "Kristina", "Jimmy", "Marcus", ↵
       "Helen", "Eric", "Alex"]

❷ for kidsName in kidsInClass {
❸     print("Good Morning \(kidsName)!")
   }
```

At ❶, we make our array called `kidsInClass`, which contains seven strings. The square brackets tell the computer that we're creating an array, and each string in our array is separated by a comma. (The arrow means that a long line has wrapped on the page—you don't need to enter the arrow.)

To print "Good Morning *kidsName*!" for each name in the `kidsInClass` array, at ❷ we write `for kidsName in kidsInClass`, followed by braces and our code. The code inside the braces will run once for each item in the array. These kinds of loops always follow the format `for constantName in collectionName`, where *constantName* is a name you choose to call each item from the collection inside the loop.

At ❸, inside the `for-in` loop, we write the code to print a greeting for each name. To do that, we use `kidsName` just like it's any other constant. `kidsName` exists only inside the braces of this loop, and it temporarily stores the current kid's name as the `for-in` loop loops through the array. This way, we can print each name on each cycle of the loop to wish everyone a good morning!

TESTING CONDITIONS WITH WHILE LOOPS

A `for-in` loop is great when you know how many times you want the computer to do something, but sometimes you might want the computer to do something over and over until a specific condition is met. For that, you should use a `while` loop.

There are two kinds of `while` loops: `while` and `repeat-while`. Both contain blocks of code that will be executed over and over again as long as a condition is true. The difference between the `while` loop and `repeat-while` loop is that the `while` loop checks the condition *before* it runs its block of code, and the `repeat-while` loop checks the condition *after* it runs its block of code. Let's look at some examples to see how each works!

GUESS MY NUMBER

The while loop keeps doing something until a certain condition is true. This works well for a guessing game, such as when you think of a number and make a friend guess what it is until they get it right. We can write a program that does this! You'll pick a number between 1 and 20, and the computer will try to guess what it is. Write the following code in a new playground:

```
❶ import Foundation

   let numberIAmThinkingOf = 7
❷ var currentGuess = -1

   print("Thinking of a number between 1 and 20. Guess what it is.")

❸ while ❹currentGuess != numberIAmThinkingOf {

       // Guessing a random number
❺      currentGuess = Int(arc4random_uniform(20)) + 1
       print("Hmmm... let me guess. Is it \(currentGuess)?")
   }

   // The right answer
   print("You guessed my number! The correct guess was \(currentGuess)!")
```

In this example, we use a special library, called the Foundation framework, that has the function we need to create a random number. To use this library, we write the line import Foundation ❶ at the top of our playground. (We'll discuss functions in more detail in Chapter 7.)

Next, we create a constant called numberIAmThinkingOf and set it to be any number between 1 and 20. Then, at ❷, we create a variable called currentGuess to represent the computer's guess and set it to -1. Setting the currentGuess variable to -1 is a good way to indicate that the computer hasn't guessed yet.

The while loop starts with the keyword while at ❸, followed by a condition at ❹. In this case, the condition checks whether currentGuess is not equal to numberIAmThinkingOf. If the condition is true, that means the computer still hasn't correctly guessed our secret number, and the statements inside the while loop run.

Because the while loop depends on a condition, it's really important that you include some way for the condition to change *inside* the while loop, or it will run forever and never get to the next part of your program! Unlike a for-in loop, a while loop doesn't have a counter that automatically increases or decreases. It's up to you to control it!

We do that at ❺ by having the computer guess a new number between 1 and 20 and then put that new number into currentGuess. Don't worry too much about completely understanding the line of code that does that; just know that Int(`arc4random_uniform(20)`) will create a random integer between 0 and 19, and we add a + 1 at the end of that line so we end up with a number between 1 and 20.

If you find that you've accidentally gotten yourself stuck in a loop that is running forever, the best thing to do is to comment out the `while` keyword by putting two slashes in front of it. That will stop the loop so you can figure out what went wrong.

When the computer finally guesses the correct number, the `while` loop ends and a nice message is printed to the console. The output should look something like Figure 4-2.

When you typed this program into a playground, how many times did your loop run? It's likely a different number of times than in Figure 4-2. This number-guessing program is an example of something you can do with a `while` loop that you couldn't do with a `for-in` loop. We have no way of knowing how many random guesses it will take until the computer gets the correct number, so we couldn't write a `for-in` loop to do this. A `while` loop lets the computer keep guessing as many times as it needs until it gets the right answer.

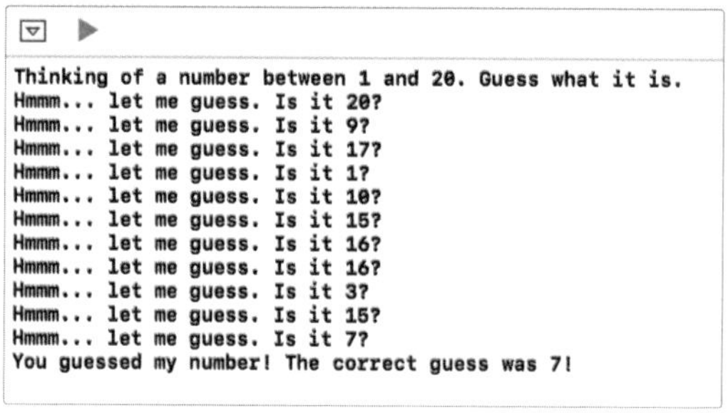

```
Thinking of a number between 1 and 20. Guess what it is.
Hmmm... let me guess. Is it 20?
Hmmm... let me guess. Is it 9?
Hmmm... let me guess. Is it 17?
Hmmm... let me guess. Is it 1?
Hmmm... let me guess. Is it 10?
Hmmm... let me guess. Is it 15?
Hmmm... let me guess. Is it 16?
Hmmm... let me guess. Is it 16?
Hmmm... let me guess. Is it 3?
Hmmm... let me guess. Is it 15?
Hmmm... let me guess. Is it 7?
You guessed my number! The correct guess was 7!
```

Figure 4-2: Output from the number-guessing program

SHRINK AWAY

The `repeat-while` loop is very similar to the `while` loop except it's written differently and the condition to end the loop is checked *after* the loop runs. We will test the `repeat-while` loop by deleting the letters in a sentence until it disappears.

Try out the following code:

```
import Foundation

var shrinking = "Help! I'm shrinking away!"

❶ repeat {
    print(shrinking)
    shrinking = ❷String(shrinking.characters.dropLast())
}

❸ while shrinking.characters.count > 0
```

In this example, we need to use a method that chops off the last character in a string. We need that same Foundation framework that we used in our guessing game, so enter `import Foundation` at the top of your playground. (We'll discuss methods in more detail in Chapter 8.)

When your computer sees a repeat-while loop, it runs the block of code after the repeat keyword ❶ and then checks whether the condition after the `while` keyword ❸ is true. In our example, we start by creating a variable string called `shrinking`. In our repeat block, we print our string, and then we cut off the last character. You don't have to memorize or understand the `dropLast()` method that does this; just know that the code at ❷ removes the last character from our string.

We are making a shorter string out of our shrinking string by taking off the last character and then saving that shorter string in the shrinking variable. This updates the value of `shrinking` to the new, shorter string. And in this case, we want to keep removing characters until we have no characters left. So the condition of our `while` loop is to repeat this process as long as the number of characters in shrinking is greater than 0. To determine the number of characters in a string, you enter `.characters.count` after the string name. Check out Figure 4-3 to see the incredible shrinking sentence!

```
Help! I'm shrinking away!
Help! I'm shrinking away
Help! I'm shrinking awa
Help! I'm shrinking aw
Help! I'm shrinking a
Help! I'm shrinking
Help! I'm shrinking
Help! I'm shrinkin
Help! I'm shrinki
Help! I'm shrink
Help! I'm shrin
Help! I'm shri
Help! I'm shr
Help! I'm sh
Help! I'm s
Help! I'm
Help! I'm
Help! I'
Help! I
Help!
Help!
Help
Hel
He
H
```

Figure 4-3: Help! I'm shrinking away!

WHICH LOOP TO USE?

As you can see, there are several ways to create a loop in your code. It's up to you, the programmer, to pick the one that's right for what you need to do. Keep in mind there is often no single right answer because the `for-in`, `while`, and `repeat-while` loops can do the same thing, depending on how they're written. You may find that you need a `while` or `repeat-while` loop when you don't know how many times a loop needs to run, but you can accomplish almost every `for-in` loop with a `while` loop. It's usually best to pick the one that you understand the best.

It's also perfectly fine to change your mind later and try a new technique if you think that a different type of loop will work better for a particular situation. The first code you write doesn't have to be perfect, and in fact (even for experienced programmers) it almost never will be! But the point of coding is to practice and problem-solve: write a little code, see how it works, and then go back and make it better.

NESTING AND SCOPE

So now you know how to write loops and conditional statements to make choices. You can also combine those elements in just about any way that you want. For example, you can put an if statement inside a for-in loop, a while loop inside an if block, or a for-in loop inside another for-in loop. When you combine loops and conditional statements, there are two important concepts you need to keep in mind: nesting and scope.

NESTING BLOCKS OF CODE

When you put one code block inside another block, it's called *nesting*. So if you write an if statement in a while loop, you would call that a *nested* if statement. Remember that when we say *code block*, we are referring to the code between opening and closing braces, {}. As an example, enter the following code, which outputs a triangle-shaped pattern of asterisks and dashes:

```
❶ for count in 1...10 {
       // NEST A
❷      if count % 2 == 0 {
           // NEST B
           var starString = ""
❸          for starCount in 1...count {
               // NEST C
               starString += "*"
           }
❹          print(starString)

❺      } else {
           // NEST D
           var dashString = ""
           for dashCount in 1...count {
               // NEST E
               dashString += "-"
           }
           print(dashString)
       }
   }
```

Take a look at Figure 4-4. We added some color to Xcode to help you see each nested block of code.

You can nest as many blocks of code as you want. In this example, we'll refer to each block of code as Nest A, Nest B, Nest C, and so on. As you can see in Figure 4-4, our program contains an outermost Nest A, which includes all of the code inside the for count in 1...10 statement. Nest A contains two nested blocks of code, Nest B and Nest D. And each of those nested blocks of code also contains a nest: Nest C is inside of Nest B, and Nest E is inside of Nest D.

```
//: Playground - noun: a place where people can play

for count in 1...10 {

    if count % 2 == 0 {                    Nest A

        var starString = ""              Nest B    (5 times)

        for starCount in 1...count {
                                    Nest C
            starString += "*"
        }

        print(starString)                           (5 times)

    } else {

        var dashString = ""              Nest D     (5 times)

        for dashCount in 1...count {
                                    Nest E
            dashString += "-"
        }

        print(dashString)                           (5 times)
    }
}
```

Figure 4-4: A nested `if-else` statement with nested `for-in` loops

Now let's dig into the code and see what's going on. At ❶, there's an outermost for-in loop, which we call Nest A, that will run 10 times as count increases from 1 to 10. Inside that for-in loop, there's a nested if-else statement at ❷ that will check whether count is even or odd. That if statement contains Nest B. To check if a number is even, we use the modulo operator (%), which tells us what the remainder will be when an integer is divided by another integer. If a number is divided by 2 and the remainder is 0, then it must be an even number. So to figure out if count is even, we check whether count % 2 == 0.

If count is even, we print a string of stars (*). We use count to determine how many stars to print. We do this by creating an empty starString and then using a nested for-in loop, Nest C, at ❸ to add a star each time starCount iterates from 1 to count. After the nested for-in loop is finished, at ❹ we print our starString, which now has count number of stars. We print a nested else statement ❺, which we're calling Nest D. When count is odd, we print out a string of dashes instead of stars, as instructed in Nest E.

CONSTANT AND VARIABLE SCOPE

In programming, a variable has *scope*, which refers to where the variable exists and where it can be used. When you declare a constant or variable inside a nested block of code, that constant or variable does not exist outside that nested block. That means its scope is limited to the block of code in which it was declared and to any nested code in that block. Figure 4-5 shows the scope of the variables of our nested code.

```
//: Playground — noun: a place where people can play

for count in 1...10 {
                                                    Nest A
    if count % 2 == 0 {                               count
                                            Nest B
        var starString = ""                   count                    (5 times)
                                            starString
        for starCount in 1...count {
                                        Nest C
            starString += "*"             count
                                        starString
        }                               starCount

        print(starString)                                              (5 times)
    } else {
                                            Nest D
        var dashString = ""                   count                    (5 times)
                                            dashString
        for dashCount in 1...count {
                                        Nest E
            dashString += "-"             count
                                        dashString
        }                               dashCount

        print(dashString)                                              (5 times)
    }
}
```

Figure 4-5: The scope of a variable or constant is limited to the nest in which it was declared, as well as any code nested in that nest.

There are five variables declared in our program: count, starString, starCount, dashString, and dashCount. The outermost nest, Nest A, can see only count. It doesn't have access to any variables or constants inside its nested blocks of code, which means you can't use variables or constants that are declared in Nests B or C. The variable starString is declared in Nest B. Nest B therefore has access to starString as well as anything created in Nest A, which includes count. Nest C has access to starCount, starString, and count. Similarly, in the else clause, Nest D has access to count and dashString, and Nest E has access to count, dashString, and dashCount. If you try to use a variable that a block of code can't access because it's outside its scope, you'll get an error. For example, you can't print dashString inside the outermost nest, Nest A.

Let's take a look at another example. We'll write code that creates a greeting. If it is morning, we want the greeting to be "Good Morning." Otherwise, we want the greeting to be "Good Afternoon." Enter the following code into your playground:

```
let isMorning = true

if isMorning {
    var greeting = "Good Morning"
} else {
    var greeting = "Good Afternoon"
}
print(greeting)
```

When you print greeting after this if-else statement, you get an error, as shown in Figure 4-6. The variable greeting is outside the scope of the if-else block, so the computer doesn't know what greeting is.

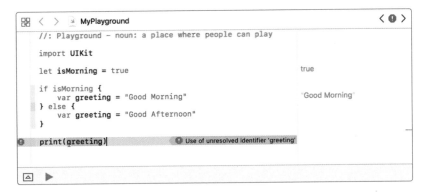

Figure 4-6: Trying to access greeting outside of its scope gives an error.

To solve this problem, you must declare greeting outside the if-else block. Rewrite the greeting code as follows to output the greeting:

```
  let isMorning = true
❶ var greeting = ""

  if isMorning {
      greeting = "Good Morning"
  } else {
      greeting = "Good Afternoon"
  }
❷ print(greeting)
```

This time, we declared greeting as an empty string before the if-else block, at ❶. Then, we set greeting to be either "Good Morning" or "Good Afternoon" depending on whether isMorning is true or false. Finally, we print the greeting at ❷, after the if-else block, because it was declared in the same scope as the print statement.

WHAT YOU LEARNED

In this chapter, you learned how to repeat code using loops. You learned that you can use either a for-in loop or a while loop to accomplish many of the same goals. A for-in loop is perfect for looping through a collection of items and doing one thing for each item, and a while loop is better suited when you do not know how many times a loop needs to run.

In Chapter 5, we'll introduce a new kind of variable in Swift—optionals. Optionals are variables that can either have a value or no value at all. They are useful when you need to create a variable, but you don't yet know its value.

5

KEEPING YOUR PROGRAMS SAFE WITH OPTIONALS

In this chapter, we'll cover a very cool feature in Swift: optionals. *Optionals* are variables that can either have a value or no value at all. Swift is different from many programming languages because normal constants and variables *must* have a value. This makes Swift a *safe* language because it prevents your code from failing when a variable is expected to have a value but one hasn't yet been set.

However, there will be times when you need to create a variable but don't have a value for it yet. In these cases, you can use an optional.

WHAT IS AN OPTIONAL?

You can think of an optional as a box that either contains something or is empty. For example, an optional String is just a box that either contains a String or is empty. When an optional is empty, it has the special value nil. In Swift, nil just means that there's no value.

When you declare a variable or constant, Swift expects it to hold a value. If you're not sure what value you want that variable or constant to hold, you can use an optional to avoid problems in your programs. Let's see how!

CREATING OPTIONALS

To create an optional, you declare a variable or a constant and add a ? after the data type. The ? lets Swift know that you want to make the variable or constant an optional. Like a variable or a constant, an optional can contain any data type.

Let's create an optional called futureTeacher as an example. Imagine that not all of the teachers at your school have been assigned to the next year's classes yet, so you don't know who your new teacher will be.

```
  var grade = 5                              5
❶ var futureTeacher: String?                nil
  // You can give an optional a value
❷ futureTeacher = "Ms. Gleason"             "Ms. Gleason"
  // Or you can set an optional to nil
❸ futureTeacher = nil                       nil
```

In this example, we create an optional variable, futureTeacher, that will store a String, by adding a ? after the data type. Unlike non-optional variables that we've used up until this point, an optional doesn't require an initial value. That part is—you guessed it—*optional*! At ❶, we didn't assign an initial value to futureTeacher, so its default value is the special value nil, which means it doesn't yet have a value.

Now that we've declared futureTeacher as an optional String, it can hold either nothing (nil) or a String. You change the value of an optional in the same way that you set the value for a regular variable, as shown at ❷. If you change your mind and want to set the optional to nil again, you can do so ❸. Note that you can't set a regular variable to nil! This is a special characteristic of optionals. In Figure 5-1, you can see that setting futureTeacher to nil is allowed, but setting grade to nil is not.

The reason you can't change grade to nil is because grade was not declared as an optional and is just a regular Int data type. Only optionals can hold either a value of the declared type or nil. Optionals are special like that.

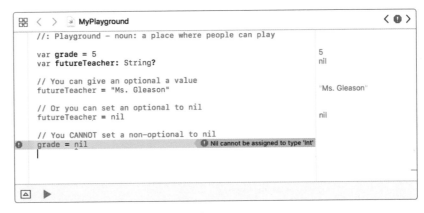

```
//: Playground - noun: a place where people can play

var grade = 5                                            5
var futureTeacher: String?                               nil

// You can give an optional a value
futureTeacher = "Ms. Gleason"                            "Ms. Gleason"

// Or you can set an optional to nil
futureTeacher = nil                                      nil

// You CANNOT set a non-optional to nil
grade = nil                    ⓘ Nil cannot be assigned to type 'Int'
```

Figure 5-1: You can't set a non-optional to nil.

UNWRAPPING OPTIONALS

Optionals make your code safer because they force you to plan for a situation in which they have no value. But this also means they require a little more work to use.

For example, you can't use an optional String the same way you would use a regular String. First, you need to check if there really is a String stored in your optional. If there is, then you can use it like any other String.

To check if your optional has a value that you can use, you need to *unwrap* it. Unwrapping an optional is like taking it out of a box. You wouldn't play with a birthday present without taking it out of the box, right? Well, you can't use an optional in your code without unwrapping it first, either. There are a few different ways to unwrap optionals. Let's see how they work!

Forced Unwrapping

One way to unwrap an optional is through *forced unwrapping*. Use forced unwrapping when you know that an optional has a value and you want the computer to access that value directly. You do this by entering an ! after the optional name. Enter this code into your playground:

```
   var futureTeacher: String?        nil
   futureTeacher = "Mr.Gale"         "Mr.Gale"
❶ print("Next year I think my teacher ↵    "Next year I think my teacher ↵
       will be \(futureTeacher).")            will be Optional("Mr.Gale").\n"
❷ print("Next year I know my teacher ↵    "Next year I know my teacher ↵
       will be \(futureTeacher!).")           will be Mr.Gale.\n"
```

In this example, we set futureTeacher to "Mr.Gale". If we try sticking the optional String variable futureTeacher into a print statement ❶, the value is printed as `Optional("Mr.Gale")`. That's not ideal! We just want the string `"Mr.Gale"`. To get that, you need to unwrap the optional. At ❷, we force-unwrap `futureTeacher` using `futureTeacher!`. Now the printed line `"Next year I know my teacher will be Mr.Gale.\n"` looks as expected.

When you use forced unwrapping, you must be sure that the optional has a value. If it's `nil`, you'll get an error. To see this for yourself, set `futureTeacher` to nil instead of `"Mr.Gale"`, as shown in Figure 5-2. If you force-unwrap an optional and it has a `nil` value, your program will crash.

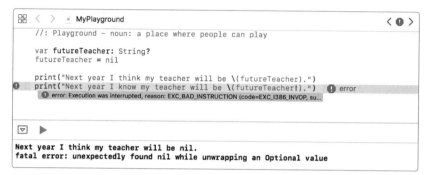

Figure 5-2: Force-unwrapping an optional with no value will cause an error.

Forced unwrapping should be used with caution and only when you can answer yes to the question, "Do I know this optional will always have a value at this point in the code?" You can make sure that an optional has a value by first checking whether it's equal to `nil` before trying to unwrap it. This is a safe way to force-unwrap an optional:

```
  var futureTeacher: String?
❶ if futureTeacher != nil {
❷     let knownTeacher = futureTeacher!
      print("Next year \(knownTeacher) will be ↵
          my teacher.")
❸ } else {
      print("I do not know who will be ↵          "I do not know who will be ↵
          my teacher next year.")                    my teacher next year.\n"
  }
```

At ❶, we check to make sure that `futureTeacher` has a value before we force-unwrap it. If `futureTeacher` is not equal to `nil`, we force-unwrap it and store its value in the constant `knownTeacher` ❷. If `futureTeacher` is `nil`, we print `"I do not know who will be my teacher next year."` using an else statement at ❸.

Optional Binding

Another way to unwrap an optional is to use *optional binding*. Optional binding works by temporarily binding the optional to a constant or variable and then providing a block of code that will run only when the optional does have a value. We do this using an `if-let` statement.

Add this code into your playground to see an if-let statement in action:

```
❶ if let knownTeacher = futureTeacher {
       print("Next year \(knownTeacher) will be ↵
           my teacher.")
❷ } else {
       print("I do not know who will be ↵
           my teacher next year.")
   }
```
```
"I do not know who will be ↵
    my teacher next year.\n"
```

The if-let statement checks whether the optional futureTeacher contains a value. If it does, the value will be assigned to the constant knownTeacher ❶, and the block of code in the braces that follows will be executed. In this case, the optional futureTeacher doesn't contain a value, so the block of code following the if-let statement isn't executed.

If you want something to happen when your optional has a nil value, then you can write an else block, like we did at ❷. In this example, we're telling the computer to look at futureTeacher and if it contains a value, the computer should call that value knownTeacher. If there's no value in futureTeacher, our program will output "I do not know who will be my teacher next year."

Did you notice the similarity between the block of code in the if-let statement and the block of code that you wrote checking whether futureTeacher is nil before force-unwrapping it and setting its value to knownTeacher? So, for example, this:

```
if let knownTeacher = futureTeacher {
    print("Next year \(knownTeacher) will be my teacher.")
}
```

is a better and more concise way of writing this:

```
if futureTeacher != nil {
    let knownTeacher = futureTeacher!
    print("Next year \(knownTeacher) will be my teacher.")
}
```

Try changing futureTeacher to a teacher's name and run this if-let statement again. You should see the sentence "Next year *teacher* will be my teacher." filled with the name you typed.

NOTE *Although this type of statement is called an if-let statement, you can also use if-var and temporarily assign the optional value to a variable instead of a constant.*

It's important to note that we're just temporarily assigning the value in futureTeacher to the constant knownTeacher. The constant knownTeacher only exists inside of the if-let statement's braces. If you want to access the value of futureTeacher later in the program, you'll have to make another if-let statement. That's what we mean when we say that using optionals requires a little more work on your part, because you'll have to unwrap the optional each time you want to use it.

Optional binding is a safe way to unwrap optionals when you're not sure if they contain a value. If the optional is nil, you won't get an error, and instead you can control what happens using an else statement.

You may be asking yourself, "How could you not know whether something has a value?" In our example, it's quite obvious that futureTeacher doesn't have a value because we set it to nil. But there are many times when you won't know whether an optional has a value. For example, suppose we asked the user to input a name for futureTeacher. The user may have typed a name or not. Users can be unpredictable. Maybe they were distracted and forgot to enter a name. There's no way to see what the user is doing until *runtime*—that is, when the program is actually running. If our program needs the user to set the value for futureTeacher, then it has to be ready to handle both possibilities (if the user typed a name or forgot) because at runtime either could be true.

Implicitly Unwrapped Optionals

As you have seen so far, optionals need to be unwrapped before your program can access the data they hold. Usually you will unwrap an optional every time you need to use it. But there are some rare cases where you will have a variable that has to be an optional and will always have a value. In these cases, rather than unwrap the optional every time you use it, you can declare it as an *implicitly unwrapped optional.* This tells the computer that the variable is an optional but will always have a value. An implicitly unwrapped optional, therefore, does *not* need to be unwrapped every time you use it; it's automatically unwrapped for you. Instead of creating the optional with a ? after the data type like a regular optional, you create an implicitly unwrapped optional by typing an ! after the data type.

You might be wondering when you would ever use these implicitly unwrapped optionals. A common use is when you write an app with a storyboard. When you want to connect variables in your code to objects in the storyboard, you make them implicitly unwrapped optionals. You'll see these come up in Chapter 10 while you're creating the Birthday Tracker app. These variables need to be optional (because the storyboard requires it), but they will always have a value (since they are connected to the storyboard, the storyboard will always give them a value before you use them).

Other than in this special case, you shouldn't be using implicitly unwrapped optionals very often. They aren't as safe as regular optionals and can cause your program to crash if used incorrectly. It's best to stick with regular optionals as much as possible.

A SPECIAL KIND OF OPERATOR: ??

There's a special kind of operator that's very useful when you're unwrapping optionals: the *nil coalescing operator*. It's impressive sounding, isn't it? It's actually quite easy to use, though, and can be a timesaver.

The nil coalescing operator is written as a pair of question marks between an optional and a default value, like *optionalThing* ?? *defaultThing*. When the optional has a value, the value will be used as usual, but when the optional is nil, the nil coalescing operator will use the default value instead.

Let's try an example with this operator:

```
    let defaultLunch = "pizza"                      "pizza"
❶   var specialLunch: String?                       nil
❷   var myLunch = specialLunch ?? defaultLunch      "pizza"
❸   print("On Monday I had \(myLunch) for ↵         "On Monday I had pizza for ↵
        lunch.")                                        lunch."
❹   specialLunch = "shepherd's pie"                 "shepherd's pie"
    myLunch = specialLunch ?? defaultLunch          "shepherd's pie"
❺   print("Today I had \(myLunch) for ↵             "Today I had shepherd's pie for ↵
        lunch.")                                        lunch."
```

At ❶, we create an optional String variable called specialLunch. Next, we set a variable called myLunch to either be the value of specialLunch if it contains a String or defaultLunch if it doesn't ❷. At ❸, when we print the value of myLunch, we can see that it's the default value of "pizza" because specialLunch is nil. When we set specialLunch to "shepherd's pie" ❹ and then use the nil coalescing operator again, the specialLunch value is unwrapped and put into myLunch ❺. As you can see, the nil coalescing operator is a quick way to either get an optional's value if it has one, or use some other value if it is nil.

WHAT YOU LEARNED

In this chapter, you learned about optionals, a great feature that makes Swift a safe language. Optionals force us to know which variables might not have a value so we can prevent any potential problems in our programs.

In Chapter 6, you'll learn about two collection data types: the array and the dictionary. Both are extremely useful for storing and managing collections of items. Items in an array are stored in an ordered list and can be accessed by an index number. Items in a dictionary are stored in unordered key/value pairs and can be accessed by the keys.

6

STORING COLLECTIONS IN DICTIONARIES AND ARRAYS

In previous chapters, you learned that you can store a single piece of information in a variable or constant. But what if you want to store a collection of things, like the names of all the places you've visited or all the books that you've read? In this chapter, we'll introduce you to arrays and dictionaries. They're both used to store collections of values. Using arrays and dictionaries, you can work with a lot of data at once and make your programs more powerful!

KEEPING THINGS IN ORDER WITH ARRAYS

An *array* is a list of items of the same data type stored in order, kind of like a numbered grocery list. Items in an array are stored by their *index*, a number based on where the item is positioned in the array.

When you write a grocery list, you usually start with the number 1, but in computer programming, an index starts at 0, not 1. So the first item in an array is always at index 0, the second item is at index 1, the third item is at index 2, and so on.

Let's create an array. If you already know what you're going to put into your array, you can create it and *initialize* it with those values. To initialize something in Swift is to give it some initial value so you can use it in your program. Let's say that you want to store a list of all of the national parks that you've visited. Enter the following into your playground:

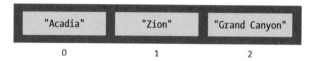

❶var nationalParks: ❷[String] = ["Acadia", ↵
    "Zion", "Grand Canyon"]

["Acadia", "Zion", ↵
    "Grand Canyon"]

This code creates an array variable called nationalParks and initializes it with the names of three national parks. Because we initialized this array to hold strings, you'll only be able to put strings in it.

Figure 6-1 shows how you can imagine your array. It's like a row of boxes containing the three names of national parks at indices 0, 1, and 2. Remember that the indices of an array always start at 0!

"Acadia"	"Zion"	"Grand Canyon"
0	1	2

Figure 6-1: The nationalParks array

USING MUTABLE AND IMMUTABLE ARRAYS

Our nationalParks array is a variable because we created it with the var keyword ❶. An array stored in a variable is called a *mutable* array. This means that you can change it by adding items, removing items, or swapping items in and out.

You can also create an *immutable* array. An immutable array is created with the keyword let instead of var. Similar to a constant, once an immutable array is created, nothing in it can be changed.

So when should you use a mutable array or an immutable array? It's best to use let if you know your collection will never change, like if you're storing the colors of the rainbow. You should use var if you need to change your collection, like if you're storing an array of your favorite T-shirts, which might change depending on what's in style!

USING TYPE INFERENCE

When we created our nationalParks array, we specified that we were creating an array of string values by adding a colon (:) and [String] ❷. This step is optional when you create an array and initialize it with one or more values because Swift will use type inference to determine the kind of data you want the array to hold. That means that you could just as easily have created the array by doing this:

var nationalParks = ❶["Acadia", "Zion", "Grand Canyon"]	["Acadia", "Zion", "Grand Canyon"]

Using type inference, Swift knows we initialized this array to hold strings, and it can hold only strings.

The list of parks that we created the array with is an example of an array *literal*. A literal is a value that is exactly what you see. It is not a variable or constant but rather just the value without a name. "Grand Canyon" is an example of a string literal, and 7 is an example of an integer literal. An array literal is a list of items contained between two square brackets and separated by commas, like ["Acadia", "Zion", "Grand Canyon"] ❶.

ACCESSING ITEMS IN AN ARRAY

Let's say you want to access an item in your array and use it in your program. Your friend asks you to tell them all about your travels, so you want to use the names of the national parks that you stored in the array. To access an item in your array, write the array name followed by the item's index inside square brackets:

print("The first park that I went to ↵
    was \(❶nationalParks[0]).")
print("The second park was ↵
    \(nationalParks[1]).")
	"The first park that I went to ↵
	    was Acadia.\n"
	"The second park was ↵
	    Zion.\n"

In this example, we are accessing the names of the national parks and then printing them to the screen using print. To get the first item in nationalParks, you use nationalParks[0] ❶. To access the second item in nationalParks, you use nationalParks[1].

WATCHING THE RANGE

One important point about arrays is that if you try to access an item at an index that's higher than the last index in the array, you'll get an error. In Figure 6-2, you can see that nationalParks[3] (which would be the fourth item in the array) gives you an error because there are only three national parks in the array, indexed from 0 to 2.

As you can see, you get an error message that says Index out of range. If you try to access an item that doesn't exist in your array, your app will crash!

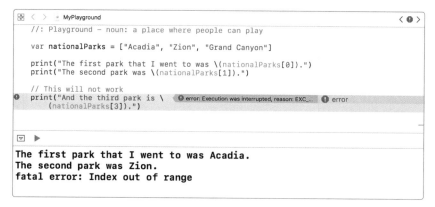

```
//: Playground – noun: a place where people can play

var nationalParks = ["Acadia", "Zion", "Grand Canyon"]

print("The first park that I went to was \(nationalParks[0]).")
print("The second park was \(nationalParks[1]).")

// This will not work
print("And the third park is \       error: Execution was interrupted, reason: EXC_...    error
    (nationalParks[3]).")
```

The first park that I went to was Acadia.
The second park was Zion.
fatal error: Index out of range

Figure 6-2: Trying to access an index in the array where nothing exists causes an error.

ADDING ITEMS TO AN ARRAY

One way to change an array is to add new items to it. There are a few different ways to do this, so let's take a look at each.

First, you can use an array's append(_:) method. *Append* means to add something. Using append(_:), you can add one new item to the end of your array. Say you go on another trip and visit the Badlands, and you want to add it to your list of national parks. To do that, add this code into your playground:

`nationalParks.append("Badlands")`	`["Acadia", "Zion", "Grand Canyon", "Badlands"]`

To use the append(_:) method, first write the name of your array followed by a period and then append. Then, put the item you want to add to your array inside the parentheses. In this case, you put "Badlands" inside the parentheses.

If you want to add something at a specific place in your array, use the array's insert(_:at:) method instead. This method takes two arguments: the item that you want to insert and the index of where it should go in the array. (We'll discuss arguments in more detail in Chapter 7.)

Let's say you totally forgot that you went to the Petrified Forest right after you visited the Grand Canyon, and you want to update your nationalParks array so it displays the parks in the order in which you visited them. To update your array, you could use the insert(_:at:) method to put the Petrified Forest in the right position:

`nationalParks.insert("Petrified Forest", at: 3)`	`["Acadia", "Zion", "Grand Canyon", ↵` `"Petrified Forest", "Badlands"]`

When you insert a new item at index 3, everything that was in the array at index 3 or higher gets scooted over to make room for the new item. That means the item that was at index 3 is now at index 4, the item that was at index 4 is now at index 5, and so on. After you add the Petrified Forest, `nationalParks` is now `["Acadia", "Zion", "Grand Canyon", "Petrified Forest", "Badlands"]`.

COMBINING ARRAYS

Not only can you add new items to an array, but you can also add two arrays together using the + and += operators. Let's say that you have the ingredients for a fruit smoothie in two arrays:

`let fruits = ["banana", "kiwi", "blueberries"]` `let liquids = ["honey", "yogurt"]`	`["banana", "kiwi", "blueberries"]` `["honey", "yogurt"]`

Now you can make a delicious smoothie by adding the `fruits` and `liquids` arrays.

`var smoothie = fruits + liquids`	`["banana", "kiwi", "blueberries", "honey", "yogurt"]`

The order of the ingredients in `smoothie` is the same as the order in `fruits` and `liquids`. If you created `smoothie` with `liquids + fruits`, then the liquids would come first.

You use the += operator to add an array to the end of your array. Add some whipped cream as follows for extra yumminess:

`smoothie += ["whipped cream"]`	`["banana", "kiwi", "blueberries", "honey", "yogurt", ↵` `"whipped cream"]`

Note that `["whipped cream"]` is an array even though it has a single item in it. When you're using += to append something to an array, you have to make sure you're only trying to add another array. If you were to just write the string `"whipped cream"` without the square brackets around it, you would get an error.

REMOVING ITEMS FROM AN ARRAY

There are several methods for removing items from an array. Let's start by looking at the array's `removeLast()` method. As you might have guessed from its name, `removeLast()` removes the last item from your array. Let's try it out with a `shoppingList` array:

`var shoppingList = ["milk", "bread", ↵`
`    "candy", "apples", "ham"]`
`let purchasedItem = shoppingList.removeLast()`
`// Check what is left in the shopping list`
`shoppingList`
	`["milk", "bread", ↵`
	`    "candy", "apples", "ham"]`
	`"ham"`
	
	`["milk", "bread", ↵`
	`    "candy", "apples"]`

Neat! Note that the `removeLast()` method returns the removed item, so you can store it in a new constant or variable if you want.

You can also remove an item from a specific index by using the `remove(at:)` method. Let's say that your mom doesn't want you buying any candy and takes that off the list:

`let notGoingToPurchase = shoppingList.remove(at: 2)` `shoppingList`	`"candy"` `["milk", "bread", "apples"]`

Just like when we added an item to the middle of our array and all the items scooted over to make room, if you remove an item from the middle of an array, the rest of the items will scoot back to fill in that empty space. The `"apples"` item that was at index 3 is now at index 2, where `"candy"` was.

You can also remove all items from an array with `removeAll()`. Try entering this into your playground:

`shoppingList.removeAll()`	`[]`

Note that trying to remove an item at an index that doesn't exist will give you an error:

`shoppingList.remove(at: 3)`	`error`

Our array doesn't have this many items (in fact, now it's empty!), so this throws an error. We'll also get an error if we use `removeLast()` on our empty array, because there's nothing in it—there's no last index at all! However, `removeAll()` is always safe to use, even on an empty array.

REPLACING ITEMS IN AN ARRAY

To replace an item in an array, you set the index of the array to the new value, as shown here:

`var favoriteAnimals = ["Lion", "Alligator", "Elephant"]`
`favoriteAnimals[2] = ❶"Unicorn"`
`favoriteAnimals[0] = ❷"Bearded dragon"`
`favoriteAnimals`
	`["Lion", "Alligator", "Elephant"]`
	`"Unicorn"`
	`"Bearded dragon"`
	`["Bearded dragon", "Alligator", ↵`
	`    "Unicorn"]`

At ❶, we replaced the item at index 2 (the third item) with `"Unicorn"` because magical animals count as favorite animals, too! At ❷, we replaced the item at index 0 (the first item) with `"Bearded dragon"`. No, that's not a real dragon—it's just a lizard!

Like any time you're working with array index numbers, you have to be sure an item exists in the array at that index before you change its value, or you will get an `Index out of range` error.

Figure 6-3 shows the error that occurs if you try to add "Standard poodle" using favoriteAnimals[3] = "Standard poodle". To add an item to the end of an array, you should use the append(_:) method or +=, as we covered in "Adding Items to an Array" on page 70.

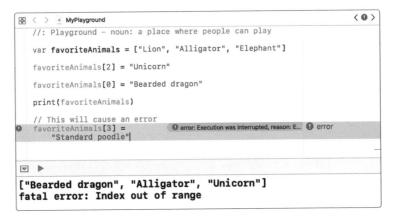

```
⊞ ‹ › ⬛ MyPlayground                                                    ‹ ❶ ›
     //: Playground - noun: a place where people can play

     var favoriteAnimals = ["Lion", "Alligator", "Elephant"]

     favoriteAnimals[2] = "Unicorn"

     favoriteAnimals[0] = "Bearded dragon"

     print(favoriteAnimals)

     // This will cause an error
 ❶ favoriteAnimals[3] =       ❶ error: Execution was interrupted, reason: E...  ❶ error
        "Standard poodle"


 ▼  ▶
["Bearded dragon", "Alligator", "Unicorn"]
fatal error: Index out of range
```

Figure 6-3: Don't try to replace a value at an index beyond the existing array.

Now you know how to change arrays however you might need to. You can add items, take items away, or replace items. Next, we'll look at how to use the properties of arrays to find out even more information about them.

USING ARRAY PROPERTIES

In addition to methods like append(_:) and removeLast(), arrays also have *properties*. An array's properties are variables or constants that contain some information about the array. Two really helpful properties that you might use are the Boolean property isEmpty and the integer property count.

The isEmpty property is true or false depending on whether the array is empty, and the count property will tell you how many items are in that array.

Check out how these two properties are used in the following if-else statement:

```
let mySiblings = ["Jackie", "Gretchen", "Jude"]          ["Jackie", "Gretchen", "Jude"]
❶ if mySiblings.isEmpty {
      print("I don't have any siblings.")
} else {
      print(❷"I have \(mySiblings.count) siblings.")      "I have 3 siblings.\n"
}
```

This if-else statement checks whether the array mySiblings is empty ❶. If it is, then "I don't have any siblings." is printed. But if there is something in the array, then the number of siblings that we have is printed: "I have 3 siblings." ❷.

LOOPING OVER AN ARRAY

Sometimes when you're working with arrays you might want to do something to every item in the array. You can use a for-in loop to do that! The following code will print every topping in a pizzaToppings array on a separate line:

```
let pizzaToppings = ["Cheese", "Tomato", "Pepperoni", ↵
    "Sausage", "Mushroom", "Onion", ↵
    "Ham", "Pineapple"]
for ❶topping in pizzaToppings {
    print(topping)
}
```
```
["Cheese", "Tomato", "Pepperoni", ↵
    "Sausage", "Mushroom", "Onion", ↵
    "Ham", "Pineapple"]

(8 times)
```

To write a for-in loop for the pizzaToppings array, we used the keyword for, followed by the constant topping, then the keyword in, and finally the name of our array, pizzaToppings. Then we put the statements that we want to run for each topping inside the braces of the for-in loop. The constant topping ❶ temporarily represents each pizza topping in the array as we loop through it. We could have chosen any name for this constant, but it's a good idea to pick something that makes sense. You can see the output of this for-in loop in Figure 6-4.

```
Cheese
Tomato
Pepperoni
Sausage
Mushroom
Onion
Ham
Pineapple
```

Figure 6-4: Output of the example for-in loop

Using for-in loops is great for printing every value in an array. If you're working with numbers, you can even use them to perform math operations on each item, which makes for some speedy calculations! The following code takes an array of numbers and calculates the square for each (the square of a number is that number multiplied by itself):

```
let myNumbers = [1, 4, 7, 10, 12, 15]
print("This is myNumbers array: ↵
    \(myNumbers)")
print("Here are the squares of all of ↵
    myNumbers:\n")
for number in myNumbers {
    print("\(number) squared is ↵
        \(number * number)")
}
```
```
[1, 4, 7, 10, 12, 15]
"This is myNumbers array: ↵
    [1, 4, 7, 10, 12, 15]\n"
"Here are the squares of all of ↵
    myNumbers:\n\n"

(6 times)
```

Figure 6-5 shows the results.

```
This is myNumbers array: [1, 4, 7, 10, 12, 15]
Here are the squares of all myNumbers:

1 squared is 1
4 squared is 16
7 squared is 49
10 squared is 100
12 squared is 144
15 squared is 225
```

Figure 6-5: Printing the squares for each number in the myNumbers array

DICTIONARIES ARE KEY!

A *dictionary* is also a collection of values, but instead of an ordered index, each value has its own *key*. Because there's no index, the values are not stored in any particular order. To access values in a dictionary, you look them up by their key.

A key must be unique. You can't have the same key more than once in the same dictionary. If there were two identical keys and you asked the computer to give you the value for one of them, the computer wouldn't know which one to choose!

Let's take a look at how to make a dictionary and write keys that will help you find all the information you need.

INITIALIZING A DICTIONARY

To create and initialize a dictionary, first write var and the name of your dictionary. Then write the keys and corresponding values inside a pair of square brackets, similar to an array. Let's create a dictionary to store the names of a few US states. The key for each state will be its two-letter abbreviation:

```
var usStates = [❶"MA": "Massachusetts", ↵      [❷"WA": "Washington", "MA": "Massachusetts", ↵
    "TX": "Texas", "WA": "Washington"]              "TX": "Texas"]
```

As you can see, there's a colon between each key and its value, and the key/value pairs are separated by commas.

Dictionaries are different from arrays in that they are *unordered*. Because of that, it's likely that the order of the states that you see in your results pane ❷ is different from the order in which you entered your states ❶. It might even be different than the order that's printed in this book!

As with arrays, you can use var to make a mutable dictionary or use let to make an immutable dictionary.

In Swift, all of the keys of a dictionary must be the same type, and all of the values of a dictionary must also be the same type, but the key type doesn't have to match the value type. For example, if you wanted to store a collection of fractions, you could use doubles for the keys and strings for the values:

`let fractions = [0.25: "1/4", ↵` `    0.5: "1/2", 0.75: "3/4"]`	`[0.75: "3/4", 0.25: "1/4", ↵` `    0.5: "1/2"]`

In this dictionary, all of the keys must be doubles, and all of the values must be strings. Again, you'll see that the order of the numbers in the results pane can be quite different from the order in which you wrote the fractions in your dictionary. This is fine because you don't need to know the order to access anything. You can find any item that you need by its key. Let's see how!

ACCESSING VALUES IN A DICTIONARY

Looking up a value in a dictionary is similar to how you access a value in an array except that you use a key inside the square brackets instead of an index, like this: `usStates["TX"]`.

There is a big difference, however, in how Swift returns the values from a dictionary. When you access a value at an index of an array, you are simply given the value. When you access a value with a key in a dictionary, you are given an optional.

In Chapter 5, you learned that optionals might contain a value or might be `nil`. The reason Swift returns optionals when you're looking up items in a dictionary is that the key you used might not exist in the dictionary, in which case there's no value to access. Trying to access a value that doesn't exist would give you a big fat error! To avoid that problem, Swift returns optionals. That means you need to unwrap any value you get out of a dictionary before you can do anything with it.

To unwrap an optional, first you check whether it exists using an `if-let` statement, just like we did in Chapter 5. The following code shows you how to get a value out of a dictionary:

```
if let loneStarState = ❶usStates["TX"] {
    print("I have \(loneStarState) in my ↵
        dictionary.")
} else {
    print("I don't have that state in my dictionary.")
}
if let sunshineState = ❷usStates["FL"] {
    print("I have \(sunshineState) in my dictionary.")
} else {
    print("I don't have that state ↵
        in my dictionary.")
}
```

```
"I have Texas in my ↵
    dictionary.\n"
```

```
"I don't have that state ↵
    in my dictionary.\n"
```

To retrieve "Texas" from the dictionary, we use `if let` to set a constant `loneStarState` to `usStates["TX"]` ❶. Because we have this state in our dictionary, the line `I have Texas in my dictionary.` is printed. Next we try to access a state that is not in our dictionary by using the key `usStates["FL"]` ❷. Thankfully, because we used an `if-let` statement, the program won't crash when the computer can't find this state. Instead, `I don't have that state in my dictionary.` is printed.

ADDING ITEMS TO A DICTIONARY

To add an item to a dictionary, first write the name of your dictionary and assign the new item to the key you want it to have in the dictionary. Let's add "Minnesota" to our `usStates` dictionary:

```
usStates["MN"] = "Minnesota"        "Minnesota"
usStates                            ["MN": "Minnesota", "WA": "Washington", ↵
                                        "MA": "Massachusetts", "TX": "Texas"]
```

Now when you look at `usStates`, you'll see that it's updated to `["MN": "Minnesota", "WA": "Washington", "MA": "Massachusetts", "TX": "Texas"]`. Remember, because you don't have to rely on indices, your new dictionary item might appear anywhere in the dictionary.

REMOVING ITEMS FROM A DICTIONARY

Removing an item from a dictionary is quite simple; you do so by setting the value to `nil`. Because the values in dictionaries are returned as optionals, you don't have to worry about `nil` causing any problems in your dictionary.

```
usStates["MA"] = nil        nil
usStates                    ["MN": "Minnesota", "WA": "Washington", "TX": "Texas"]
```

You can see that after you remove the value at the key "MA", `usStates` is updated to `["MN": "Minnesota", "WA": "Washington", "TX": "Texas"]`. Remember that `nil` is special and means that there's no value at all. That's why you don't see `"MA": nil` in our dictionary.

REPLACING ITEMS IN A DICTIONARY

Replacing an item in a dictionary is also easy. It works the same was as replacing an item in an array. You just set the item that you want to replace to something else. Say you create a dictionary of fruit colors:

```
var colorFruits = ["red": "apple", "yellow": "banana"]    ["yellow": "banana", "red": "apple"]
colorFruits["red"] = ❶"raspberry"                         "raspberry"
colorFruits                                               ["yellow": "banana", "red": "raspberry"]
```

At first we had the value "apple" for "red", but then we decided that "raspberry" is a better fruit to use since sometimes apples are green or yellow. To replace "apple" with "raspberry", we set colorFruits["red"] to its new value ❶.

You may remember that this is the same way we entered a new value into a dictionary. If the key already exists in the dictionary, then the value for that key is replaced. If the key doesn't already exist, then the new key/value pair will be added to the dictionary.

USING DICTIONARY PROPERTIES

Like an array, a dictionary also has an isEmpty property and a count property. For example, the following code shows how you can use the isEmpty property to check if a dictionary is empty, and if it isn't empty, the count property checks how many items you have. Imagine you have a basket of fruit for sale. You can use these properties to help you keep track of everything:

```
let fruitBasket = ["Apple": "$0.50", ↵        ["Apple": "$0.50", ↵
    "Banana": "$1.00", ↵                          "Banana": "$1.00", ↵
    "Orange": "$0.75"]                            "Orange": "$0.75"]
if fruitBasket.isEmpty {
    print("I do not have any fruit.")
} else {
    print("I have \(fruitBasket.count) ↵       "I have 3 pieces of fruit for ↵
        pieces of fruit for sale.")               sale.\n"
}
```

A dictionary also has two special properties: keys, which contains all of the dictionary's keys, and values, which contains all of its values. We'll use these two properties when we loop through the dictionary.

Let's write some code that loops through our fruit baskets and prints the price of each fruit.

LOOPING OVER A DICTIONARY

You can loop through a dictionary using a for-in loop. Because each item has a key and a value, you can do this in two different ways. This is how to loop through a dictionary using its keys:

```
for fruit in fruitBasket.❶keys {
    print("One \(❷fruit)costs \(❸fruitBasket[fruit]!)")      (3 times)
}
```

Here we use the dictionary's keys property ❶ to loop through fruitBasket and print its contents. We start by writing the keyword for, followed by a constant name fruit for the dictionary key, the keyword in, the dictionary name, a period, and keys.

Inside the braces of our for-in loop, we have access to both the key, which we call fruit ❷, and the value at that key when we force-unwrap its contents with fruitBasket[fruit]! ❸. That value will be the fruit's price.

In this case, it's safe to force-unwrap the value using an exclamation point because we know that the fruit key we're using is definitely inside the dictionary.

Any code we put inside the for-in loop will run once for every key in our dictionary. So you should see the print statement display three times.

We can also loop through the dictionary using its values property:

```
for price in fruitBasket.values {                               (3 times)
    print("I have a piece of fruit that costs \(price)")
}
```

We use the same style of for-in loop, but now we use a constant to refer to each value, which we call price, in the values property. When looping through values, we don't have access to the keys from inside the loop.

Another difference to note is that price is not an optional because it's accessed directly as a value in the fruitBasket dictionary. That means we don't have to unwrap it. You should still see the print statement printed three times. Figure 6-6 shows the output of both loops.

```
One Orange costs $0.75
One Apple costs $0.50
One Banana costs $1.00
I have a piece of fruit that costs $0.75
I have a piece of fruit that costs $0.50
I have a piece of fruit that costs $1.00
```

Figure 6-6: Looping through the keys and values
of a dictionary with a for-in loop

The order of your results might be slightly different from ours. That's because the items in a dictionary aren't in a numbered order like they are in an array! And because the order is not guaranteed, you might see a different order printed if you run the same code again.

WHAT YOU LEARNED

In this chapter, you learned how to store collections of items in an array and in a dictionary. To store items in an ordered list, you would use an array and look up each item by its index. If you wanted to store items by key instead, you would use a dictionary.

Knowing about arrays and dictionaries and how to use them is a powerful building block for almost any programming language. Next we will learn about functions, another very powerful tool. Functions are blocks of code that you create and name to perform a specific job. After you have written a function, you can use its name to call it from almost anywhere in your program.

7

FUNCTIONS ARE A PARTY, AND YOU'RE INVITED

One of the most useful tools found in every programming language is the function. A *function* is a block of code that you can use again and again to perform a specific task. You can write your own custom functions, but Swift comes with lots of built-in functions. You've already used a few, like the print(_:) function, which displays a string in the console.

IN WITH THE INPUT, OUT WITH THE OUTPUT

Functions can take *input* and return *output*, although they don't always have to. Input is information that you give to the function to perform its task, and output is something the function returns when it's finished performing that task.

The type of input that a function can take is defined in its *input parameters*. The values you pass in for those parameters are called *arguments*. For example, the string that you put between the parentheses of the print(_:) function is an argument. Sometimes an argument will have an *argument label* that describes it. The print(_:) function doesn't have an argument label, but we'll learn more about labels later in the chapter.

NOTE *In this book, when we refer to a function with one unlabeled input parameter, we put a (_:) after the function name. You'll see where that colon (:) comes into play soon!*

Let's look at an example in the playground:

```
print("Swift is awesome!")
```

In the debug area (press ⌘-SHIFT-Y), you'll see:

```
Swift is awesome!
```

The print(_:) function takes an input value but does not have a return value. In this case, the input value is the string "Swift is awesome!". The print(_:) function displays the string it's given in the debug console and then ends without returning anything. A function with no return value is sometimes called a *void function*. We'll see an example of a function with both input parameters and a return value in "Return Values" on page 91.

By writing functions that work with input and return output, you can create all kinds of applications!

WRITING A CUSTOM FUNCTION

Let's write a simple function that prints a *haiku*, which is a traditional Japanese poem composed of three lines, where the first and last lines have five syllables and the middle line has seven syllables. Enter this into your playground:

```
func❶ printAHaiku()❷ {
    print("Input and output,")
    print("This function needs neither one")
    print("To print a haiku")
}
```

First, you write the func keyword ❶, followed by your function's name. When you create a function, you must give it a name so you can call it when you want it to perform its task.

The rules for naming functions are the same as for naming variables: you start with a lowercase letter and capitalize each new word in the name using camel case. You should also give your function a name that describes what it does. Wouldn't you agree that printAHaiku() is a great name for a function that prints a simple Swift haiku?

After the function name, there's a pair of parentheses ❷. If your function has input parameters, you would include them inside these parentheses. In this example, you don't have any input parameters, so you just leave the parentheses empty.

The *body* of the function is enclosed in braces. This is where you'll write the function's code. You put the opening brace ({) on the same line as the function name and the closing brace (}) on its own line at the end of the function. In this example, the body of the function contains all the print statements that print the haiku.

To use a function, you simply write its name followed by the parentheses with any arguments inside them. This is a *function call*. In this case, because printAHaiku() has no input parameters, you don't need to pass in any arguments—just leave the parentheses empty.

To call printAHaiku(), add the following line to your playground after the closing brace of the function:

```
printAHaiku()
```

The console output is:

```
Input and output,
This function needs neither one
To print a haiku
```

Now that you've defined this function, you can call it any time you want, and the code inside the function will run. Make sure you have the debug area open (⌘-SHIFT-Y), as in Figure 7-1, so you can see the results.

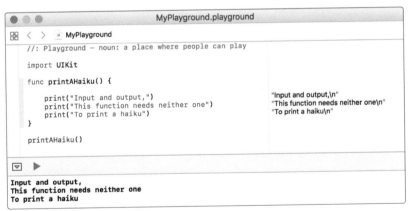

Figure 7-1: The function's output is displayed in the debug console.

Try calling the printAHaiku() function a bunch of times!

FUNCTIONS DO EVEN MORE WITH INPUT PARAMETERS

In our first example, you saw how functions can save you time and effort. When you write a function, you can call it wherever you want instead of having to repeat blocks of code in many places. This is certainly cool, but the real power of functions comes when you pass in one or more input values to produce different results.

MAKING PARTY INVITATIONS

Let's write a function called invite(guest:) that takes a person's name as input and creates a personalized invitation to a birthday party. Enter the following into your playground:

```
func invite(❶guest: String) {
    print("Dear \(❷guest),")
    print("I'd love for you to come to my birthday party!")
    print("It's going to be this Saturday at my house.")
    print("I hope that you can make it!")
    print("Love, Brenna\n")
}
```

If a function has an input parameter, you include it in the parentheses after the function's name ❶. You format an input parameter with its name first (in this example, guest), then a colon (:), and finally its data type (String in this case).

By default, the parameter name also acts as the argument label, so guest will be the argument label when you call this function. (You'll learn how to define separate parameter names and argument labels in "Argument Labels" on page 89.)

You write the data type of an input parameter after the colon, just like when declaring a variable. However, unlike with variable declarations, when defining function parameters, you must *always* declare the data type the function should expect; there's no type inference here.

To use the input parameter inside the function, you simply use its parameter name, just as you would any other constant ❷.

Of course, defining a function isn't enough. Now that the function is defined, let's call it in the playground to see what happens. You can call a function that has input parameters by entering the function name followed by, in parentheses, the argument label, a colon, and the argument, like this:

```
invite(guest: "Cathy")
```

When you call a function by writing its name, Xcode's autocomplete gives you a hint about what you're supposed to pass in to the function. In this case, when you start writing invite, you'll see a drop-down menu like in Figure 7-2.

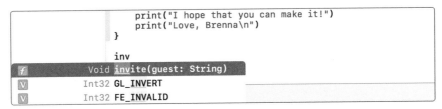

Figure 7-2: Xcode's autocomplete will show you a function's input parameters.

Press ENTER to autocomplete the function. Your cursor will move into the parentheses of the function (see Figure 7-3), where Xcode has automatically added some placeholder text telling you what type of input the function is expecting.

```
invite(guest: String)
```

Figure 7-3: Xcode is waiting for you to fill in the guest parameter.

NOTE *If you pass something that isn't a string to invite(guest:), such as invite(guest: 45), you'll get an error because the function is expecting a string.*

Simply type in "Cathy" or the name of another friend in place of String, and then press TAB to finish filling out the function call. It should look like Figure 7-4.

```
invite(guest: "Cathy")
```

Figure 7-4: An invite(guest:) function call

Now that you know how to fill out the function call, call invite(guest:) three times, using your own friends' names:

```
invite(guest: "Cathy")
invite(guest: "Meghan")
invite(guest: "Maddie")
```

The output looks like this:

```
Dear Cathy,
I'd love for you to come to my birthday party!
It's going to be this Saturday at my house.
I hope that you can make it!
Love, Brenna
```

```
Dear Meghan,
I'd love for you to come to my birthday party!
It's going to be this Saturday at my house.
I hope that you can make it!
Love, Brenna

Dear Maddie,
I'd love for you to come to my birthday party!
It's going to be this Saturday at my house.
I hope that you can make it!
Love, Brenna
```

With your invite(guest:) function, you're able to quickly print three party invitations, each addressed to a different friend!

INVITING ALL YOUR FRIENDS AT ONCE

You can also write a function that invites all of your friends at once by passing in an array of strings as arguments instead of a single string. In the same playground where you wrote invite(guest:), write the following invite(allGuests:) function to test this. Notice that the parameter name is now plural because we'll be inviting multiple guests at once.

```
func invite(allGuests: ❶[String]) {
}
```

In this example, when you declare the parameter of the function, you'll notice that [String] is in square brackets ❶. The square brackets declare the data type as an array and String indicates the data type of the values in the array. By using [String], we declare this function's input as an array of strings.

Inside the invite(allGuests:) function, we will want to use a for-in loop to go through our guests array and print an invitation for each guest. Remember how we just created a function that prints invitations? Let's use that here! Add the following to your invite(allGuests:) function (the gray text shows the existing lines):

```
func invite(allGuests: [String]) {
    for guest in allGuests {
        invite(guest: guest)
    }
}
```

In our for-in loop, we call the singular invite(guest:) function on each guest in the String array allGuests to invite each person to the birthday party. You might be wondering if invite(guest:) and invite(allGuests:) are the same function. After all, they're both called invite. Despite sharing a name, however, they're two different functions because they take different input parameters. This is a pattern that you'll see often in Swift.

To use the `invite(allGuests:)` function, we first create an array called friends, which we will then use in the function call.

```
❶ let friends = ["Cathy", "Meghan", "Maddie", "Julia", "Sophie", "Asher"]
❷ invite(allGuests: friends)
```

First, we create an array of six friends ❶. Then we call the function with our new array as the function's input ❷. This is the output you'll see in the debug console (the *--snip--* shows where we've omitted lines for space):

```
Dear Cathy,
I'd love for you to come to my birthday party!
It's going to be this Saturday at my house.
I hope that you can make it!
Love, Brenna

--snip--

Dear Asher,
I'd love for you to come to my birthday party!
It's going to be this Saturday at my house.
I hope that you can make it!
Love, Brenna
```

If you had to write out the invitation for each of these friends, it would take a lot of work. But with the power of functions, you've accomplished it with very few lines of code. Try creating your own array of friends; make it as long as you want! Then call the `invite(allGuests:)` function with your new array as input. What a piece of cake!

MESSAGING YOUR GUESTS

Imagine that the date of your party is fast approaching, and some of your guests haven't RSVPed yet. You want to get a final headcount and let the guests know to bring a bathing suit because it's going to be a slip-and-slide party. You can write a function that sends a custom message to each guest based on their RSVP status.

Your new function will take two input parameters: a `String` parameter for the guest's name and a `Bool` parameter for the RSVP status, which is either `true` or `false`. Enter the following code in your playground:

```
func sendMessage(guest: String,❶ rsvped: Bool) {
    print("Dear \(guest),")

❷   if rsvped {
        print("I'm so excited to see you this weekend!")
    } else {
        print("I hope that you can make it to my party.")
        print("Can you let me know by tomorrow?")
    }
```

```
    print("We will have a huge slip and slide, so bring your bathing suit!")
    print("Love, Brenna\n")
}
```

When a function takes more than one input parameter, you add a comma between each one ❶. Each parameter needs to have a parameter name, followed by a colon and the data type of the parameter. You can create a function that takes as many input parameters as you want, and they don't have to be the same type. In the sendMessage(guest:rsvped:) function, we're passing in a String for guest and a Bool for rsvped.

In the function body, we check the rsvped value to see if it's true ❷ and then print the corresponding message using an if-else statement. Notice, too, that the final print statements in the function definition will run whether the rsvped value is true or false because they're outside the braces of the if-else statement.

If your guest has RSVPed, they'll get this message:

```
Dear guest,
I'm so excited to see you this weekend!
We will have a huge slip and slide, so bring your bathing suit!
Love, Brenna
```

If not, they'll get a polite note asking them to respond:

```
Dear guest,
I hope that you can make it to my party.
Can you let me know by tomorrow?
We will have a huge slip and slide, so bring your bathing suit!
Love, Brenna
```

Let's call the function to see how it works. Try setting one guest's rsvped value to true and another guest's to false so you can see both messages in action.

```
sendMessage(guest: "Julia", rsvped: true)
sendMessage(guest: "Asher", rsvped: false)
```

As you can see, calling a function with more than one input parameter is similar to calling a function that has just one input parameter.

Xcode's autocomplete will help you fill out the input values by providing the argument labels for you. All you have to do is pass in the value you want to use. After filling out the guest name, press TAB, and Xcode will put the cursor right where you need it to fill out the next input value. (See Figure 7-5.)

```
sendMessage(guest: "Julia", rsvped: Bool )
```

Figure 7-5: Pressing TAB *after typing the guest's name will move your cursor over to the next input field.*

Xcode also tells you the data type of `rsvped`. Replace the placeholder text `Bool` with either `true` or `false`. If you try to pass in anything else, like a name or number, you'll get an error.

ARGUMENT LABELS

Did you notice that when you call `print(_:)`, you don't put an argument label in front of the input value? You write:

```
print("Swift is awesome!")
```

And if you try to include a label, you'll get an error:

```
print(inputString: "Swift is awesome!")
```

Some parameters have argument labels in function calls, and some don't. By default, when you write a function, every parameter will have an argument label, and it will be the same as the parameter name. However, if you write a function and don't feel like the argument label is necessary to make the code clear, then you can explicitly omit it in the function definition. In the `print(_:)` function, for example, it's obvious that the input you pass in is a string that will be printed. Having to include an argument label like `inputString` every time you call `print(_:)` would be annoying.

You can also create an argument label for each parameter that is different from the parameter name. You do this by entering the argument label, the parameter name, a colon, and finally the parameter's data type. You do all of this when you first declare the parameters inside the function parentheses after the `func` keyword. This is often done in Swift functions to make the function call look more like a sentence. Figure 7-6 illustrates the difference between an argument label and a parameter.

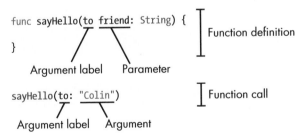

Figure 7-6: The sayHello() function has a custom argument label.

The input parameter of the `sayHello(to:)` function is `friend`, the argument label is `to`, and the passed-in argument in the function call is `"Colin"`. If you didn't have a separate argument label, when you called the function it would look like `sayHello(friend:)`, which sounds less like a full sentence.

In this section, we'll take a look at writing functions with custom argument labels. We'll also show you how to write a function in which you omit the argument labels altogether.

ADDING A CUSTOM ARGUMENT LABEL

Let's look at an example of how adding custom argument labels can make your code more readable. After your birthday party, you'll want to send thank you notes to all of your guests. Write the following function in your playground:

```
func sendThankYou(❶to guest: String, ❷for gift: String) {
    print("Dear \(❸guest),")
    print("Thanks for coming to my party and for the \(❹gift).")
    print("It was so great to see you!")
    print("Love, Brenna\n")
}
```

At ❶, we add a custom argument label, to, to the guest parameter that is passed in to the function. Similarly, at ❷, we add an argument label, for, to the gift parameter. The parameter names, guest ❸ and gift ❹, are used to refer to the parameters inside the function.

The argument labels, to and for, are used to label the arguments when the function is called, like this:

```
sendThankYou(to: "Meghan", for: "puzzle books")
```

Here you can see that to: is written in the function call before the first input value, and for: is written before the second input value. If a parameter has a custom argument label, you have to use it in your function call. Trying to use the parameter names instead will give you an error:

```
// This will not work
sendThankYou(guest: "Meghan", gift: "puzzle books")
```

Xcode's autocomplete will always fill in the argument labels for you, so you don't have to worry about calling a function incorrectly (see Figure 7-7).

```
sendThankYou(to: String, for: String)
```

Figure 7-7: Xcode autocompletes a function with the correct argument labels.

It's common for programmers to use prepositions like *to*, *from*, or *with* as argument labels. In this example, the function is used to send a thank you note *to* a guest *for* a gift. The code sendThankYou(to: "Meghan", for: "puzzle books") reads more like a sentence than sendThankYou(guest: "Meghan", gift: "puzzle books").

REMOVING AN ARGUMENT LABEL

If you don't want to use any argument labels in your function call, you can remove them by adding an underscore followed by a space in front of the parameter name. In the following example, we write a function for calculating volume that takes the three sides of a box as input. Because the function name makes it clear that you need to pass in three sides, you don't really need argument labels to make the code more readable.

```
func volumeOfBoxWithSides(❶_ side1: Int, ❷_ side2: Int, ❸_ side3: Int) {
    print("The volume of this box is \(side1 * side2 * side3).")
}
```

We remove the argument labels for the sides by placing an underscore in front of side1 at ❶, side2 at ❷, and side3 at ❸.

Now when you call the function, you just enter the parameter values without any labels.

```
volumeOfBoxWithSides(3, 4, 6)
```

This function will output "The volume of this box is 72.". Wouldn't it be useful if, instead of simply printing the volume of the box, you could store the result to use later in a variable or constant? Let's find out how to do that with return values!

RETURN VALUES

Let's try rewriting the volumeOfBoxWithSides(_:_:_:) function to return the volume instead of printing it to the console.

WHICH IS THE BIGGER BOX?

Say you have two differently shaped boxes and want to know which one will fit more stuff. First, write a volumeOfBox(_:_:_:) function that returns an Int for the box volume:

```
func volumeOfBox(_ side1: Int, _ side2: Int, _ side3: Int) ❶-> Int {
    let volume = side1 * side2 * side3
  ❷ return volume
}
```

To give a function a return value, use a dash and a greater-than sign to form an arrow (->) just after the input parameters of the function ❶ and then enter the data type of the return value. Note that you don't provide a name for the return value, just a data type. Inside the function body, you return the value by using the return keyword followed by the value that you want to return ❷. If you write a function that returns a value, then you *must* return that value inside the function, or you'll get an error. The function ends after you return the value. If you write any code inside the function after the return statement, it will be ignored, because return exits the function.

Call the function on two different boxes to see it in action:

```
❶ let volumeOfBox1 = volumeOfBox(6, 5, 3)       90
❷ let volumeOfBox2 = volumeOfBox(8, 4, 2)       64
```

At ❶, the volumeOfBox(_:_:_:) function calculates the volume of a box with side lengths of 6, 5, and 3, and the return value of 90 is stored in a constant called volumeOfBox1. At ❷, volumeOfBox2 with side lengths of 8, 4, and 2 is given the value of 64. Now let's print a message about which box is bigger:

```
if volumeOfBox1 > volumeOfBox2 {
    print("Box 1 is the bigger box.")

} else if volumeOfBox1 < volumeOfBox2 {
    print("Box 2 is the bigger box.")

} else {
    print("The boxes are the same size.")
}
```

You should see the string "Box 1 is the bigger box." output in your debug console.

CONDITIONAL RETURNS

You may want to return a different value depending on a condition. Let's write a function that takes an array of test scores and returns the average score. To get the average, you add the scores together and then divide by the total number of scores. Enter the following code in your playground:

```
func averageOf(_ scores:[Int]) -> Int {
❶   var sum = 0
❷   for score in scores {
        sum += score
    }

❸   if scores.count > 0 {
❹       return sum / scores.count
    } else {
❺       return 0
    }
}
```

First, we'll need to find the sum of all the values. At ❶, we define an Int variable called sum and sets it to an initial value of 0. The for-in loop at ❷ goes through each value in the scores array and adds it to the sum variable. When the loop is complete, the variable sum holds the sum of all of the scores. After we calculate the sum, all that's left is to divide it by the total number of scores, which is simply scores.count.

But what if the array is empty? You can't divide something by zero—in math class or in Swift. In Swift, trying to divide by zero will give you a division-by-zero error and crash your program. Therefore, when doing division, always make sure the number you're going to divide by is not zero, which is what we did by checking if `scores.count > 0` at ❸. At ❹, we return the average by dividing the sum of the scores by the number of scores in the array using `return sum / scores.count`. That's right! You can return any expression that evaluates to the correct data type, meaning we can skip the step of assigning the calculated average to a new variable and just return `sum / scores.count` because it evaluates to an `Int`.

In this function, we also need to return something when `scores.count` isn't greater than zero, or we'll get an error that the function is missing a return. We handle this by adding an `else` to our `if` statement that returns 0 ❺. You can test the code by calling the function on an array of scores and an empty array:

| ❶ `averageOf([84, 86, 78, 98, 80, 92, 84])` | 86 |
| ❷ `averageOf([])` | 0 |

When you pass a full array of test scores into the `averageOf()` function, as we do at ❶, the average value of the scores is returned and shown in the results pane. If you pass in an empty array, as we do at ❷, the return value is 0.

NOTE   *In this case, the `else` statement around `return 0` isn't really necessary. This is because if `scores.count > 0`, then the function will have ended already with `return sum / scores.count`. So if the computer has gotten past that `if` statement, then we know that `scores.count > 0` must not have been true, and we could just have a `return 0` without enclosing it in an `else`. However, the code is clearer and easier to understand if we leave the `else` statement in. Sometimes it's better to write a little extra code to make something clearer to others than it is to use a tricky shortcut.*

WHAT YOU LEARNED

You just added an important tool to your Swift tool belt—creating and calling your own functions! Functions are used extensively in programming to do all sorts of amazing things!

In Chapter 8, we'll show you how to create custom objects by writing a class definition. This will let you make constants and variables with types other than the ones already included in Swift, which will come in handy when you create apps!

8

CUSTOM CLASSES AND STRUCTS

Up to this point, the variables and constants you've been using were simple `Int`, `Double`, and `String` data types. You've also learned how to work with collections of data like arrays and dictionaries. In this chapter, you'll learn how to create your own type of data by writing a custom class that can be anything you want!

A *class* is a package that contains different types of data and functions that use that data. A custom class is a new data type that you can use to create *objects*. In the real world, an object is something that can be seen and touched, like a backpack, a cat, or a car. In Swift, objects can either represent these real-world objects, or they can be objects that don't exist outside your application, such as a view controller object that controls what is shown on an iPhone. An object in programming is defined as something in a program that can have state and behavior. The *state* describes the current condition of the object. If we made an object in our code to represent a backpack, its state could be its size, color, or whether it is full of books. The *behavior* is what the object does or can do. If we made a cat object, its behaviors could be to chase mice, purr, or scratch a tree.

The class is like a blueprint for creating objects. For example, say you have an `Airplane` class that represents different planes. The class is a structure to make a new `Airplane` object, but it isn't an object itself. An individual object that you create with a class is called an *instance* of that class. For example, we could use the `Airplane` class to create a specific `boeing787` airplane that flies from Boston to San Francisco and holds a certain amount of jet fuel and a specific number of passengers. In this case, `boeing787` would be an instance of the data type `Airplane`.

The `Airplane` class could include data like a `Double` specifying the amount of `jetFuel` that is left in the tank and an `Int` for the `numberOfPassengers`. In Swift, the data inside a class are the class's *properties*. Properties make up the object's state. The properties of a class (like `jetFuel` and `numberOfPassengers`) are variables and constants, just like the ones that you've seen before. Likewise, the functions in a class are called the class's *methods,* and they are exactly like the functions you've already learned about. The `Airplane` class could have a method called `fly(from:to:)` that is used to make the airplane fly from one airport to another.

MAKING A CLASS

Let's create a `BirthdayCake` class. This class will have properties for the size of the cake and the lucky birthday person's name and age. There will be a method in the `BirthdayCake` class to display a greeting on the top of the cake. Before we add these things, though, we need to write the class definition.

WRITING A CLASS DEFINITION

First let's open a new playground and call it *BirthdayCakes*. In Xcode, you can create a new playground using the Xcode menu by selecting **File ▸ New ▸ Playground**. Choose the **Blank** iOS template and then save your playground with the name *BirthdayCakes*. Type the following into your new playground to make your `BirthdayCake` class:

```
class BirthdayCake {
}
```

You start by writing the keyword `class` followed by your class's name. Your class name should always start with an uppercase letter and then be in camel case after that. This is different from constant, variable, and function names, which always start with a lowercase letter. This is because we're creating a new Swift data type, BirthdayCake, and data types always start with an uppercase letter (like Double or String).

After the class name, you type an opening brace, {, and then, at the end of the class, you type a closing brace, }. All the properties and methods of this class will be written inside those two braces. That way Swift knows that they belong to that class.

The class definition for BirthdayCake is like a blueprint to make birthday cakes. Once we create that blueprint by writing the BirthdayCake class, we can use it to make as many instances of cakes as we want with the same or different properties.

STORING INFORMATION IN PROPERTIES

Now let's add some properties to our BirthdayCake definition. A property of a class can either be a constant or a variable and is created with the keywords let or var, just like regular constants or variables. Add these three property definitions inside the braces of the BirthdayCake class:

```
class BirthdayCake {
❶ let birthdayAge = 8
❷ let birthdayName = "Jude"
❸ var feeds = 20
}
```

Here we created constants for the birthdayAge ❶ and the birthdayName ❷ of the birthday person as well as a variable for the number of people that the cake feeds ❸.

When you create a property, you can assign it a *default property value*, which is the value that you give to the property in its definition. In our case, we've given birthdayAge the default value of 8, birthdayName the default value of "Jude", and feeds the default value of 20.

When we create instances of a class (which we'll do next), all the properties inside the instance *must* be set to some initial value. In other words, the properties need to be *initialized*. That's why we're setting default property values here, but we can also initialize the values by using a custom initializer. We'll get to custom initializers in "Customizing Each Cake with Initializers" on page 100.

NOTE   *If you won't know the value of a class property until after the class is created, or if that class property won't always exist, then you should make that class property an optional. You learned about optionals in Chapter 5.*

CREATING AN INSTANCE OF A CLASS

After you've written a class definition, you can create an instance of that class with let or var, same as with any other data type. Create a BirthdayCake instance and store it in a constant called myCake by adding the following line of code in your playground:

```class BirthdayCake {``` `--snip--` ```}``` `let myCake = BirthdayCake()` ❶	`BirthdayCake`

You use the keyword let and then declare the constant by writing its name. To create a BirthdayCake instance, you need to use an *initializer*. An initializer is a special method that's called to create a new instance of a class and to set the instance's properties. In this case, we're creating the cake using the default initializer, which is the pair of empty parentheses at ❶. This means that the new myCake instance's properties will use the default properties we initialized it to earlier in the class definition.

We just made a cake! Great! Now let's see who this cake is for and how many candles the cake will need by accessing the values of its properties.

ACCESSING THE PROPERTIES OF A CLASS

After you create an instance of your class, you can access its properties using *dot notation*, which just means that you write the instance name, followed by a dot, followed by the property name. The dot tells Swift that the property we want to access is inside the instance. Use dot notation to print some output about myCake by adding the following code in your playground:

`let myCake = BirthdayCake()` ❶ `let age = myCake.birthdayAge` `print("My cake is going to need \(age) ↵` `    candles.")` ❷ `print("The cake will say Happy ↵` `    Birthday \(myCake.birthdayName)!")`	`8` `"My cake is going to need 8 ↵` `    candles.\n"` `"The cake will say Happy ↵` `    Birthday Jude!\n"`

After creating myCake, we can use the properties of the BirthdayCake class to find out whom the cake is for and how old that person is. To print the number of candles we need on the cake, we store myCake.birthdayAge in an Int constant called age ❶. Then we use age in a string that we output to the console.

You can also use an object's properties directly in print() instead of storing them in a constant, just as you would any variable. We put myCake.birthdayName ❷ right into the string that is output to the console. If a property of a class is a variable like our BirthdayCake property feeds, then you can change its value by setting it to something else as long as the new value is the same data type as the old value. Say that your friends can really eat a lot and you cut extra-large slices of cake. Changing the number of people that the cake can feed is easy! Add this code to the playground:

`print("The cake will say Happy ↵`
`    Birthday \(myCake.birthdayName)!")`
`print("They say this cake feeds ↵`
`    \(myCake.feeds).")`
	`"They say this cake feeds ↵`
	`    20.\n"`

❶ `myCake.feeds = 10`
`print("But really it only feeds ↵`
`    \(myCake.feeds).")`
	`"But really it only feeds ↵`
	`    10.\n"`

You change the value of the `feeds` property of `myCake` simply by setting it to a new value of the same data type ❶. Just remember that you can only do this if the property of your class is a variable and not a constant. Only variables can change, and trying to change a constant like `birthdayAge` or `birthdayName` will give you an error. For example, if you try to change `birthdayName` from `"Jude"` to `"Kevin"`, you'll get an error like the one in Figure 8-1.

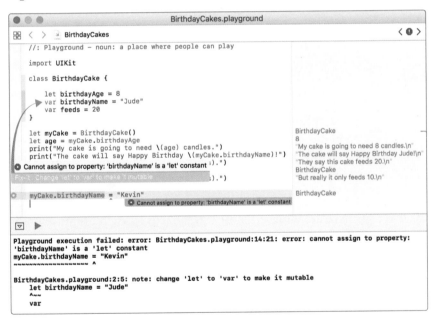

Figure 8-1: You can't change a constant property like `birthdayName`, so Xcode will suggest a Fix-it like changing `let` to `var`.

When this happens, you can click the red circle next to the error to get a pop-up with more information. Xcode will often try to help you by making a Fix-it suggestion, which in this case is to change `let` to `var`.

Xcode has also shown us where it wants us to make that change by putting a light gray `var` in front of the `birthdayName` property inside the `BirthdayCake` class. If you wanted to accept the change, you could double-click the Fix-it line and have Xcode automatically make the change for you. In this case, we don't want to change the birthdayName to a var, so just click outside of the Fix-it pop-up to make it go away. Also, if you added the line of code that caused the error, myCake.birthdayName = "Kevin", remove it before continuing.

You may be wondering why we're using constants for the birthdayAge and the birthdayName. Shouldn't we be able to make lots of cakes and use different names and ages? The answer is yes! When you make a birthday cake, you know whom it's for and how old they are, and those facts won't change for that cake. That's why those two properties are constants. But other cakes will be for other people with different ages. Right now, our birthday cake instances will always be for someone named Jude who is eight years old.

If we want to make customized cakes for lots of people, we need to add some code that lets you create an instance of a new BirthdayCake with any birthday person's name and age. We can do that by writing a custom initializer for our BirthdayCake class.

CUSTOMIZING EACH CAKE WITH INITIALIZERS

As we covered earlier, an initializer is a special method inside the class definition whose job is to create an instance of a class. By default, classes always have a hidden initializer that creates an instance of the class with the default properties, if there are any. This is the initializer that we used when we created myCake using BirthdayCake(). The pair of empty parentheses represents the default initialize. The properties in myCake were set to the default values when we created it.

If you want to initialize an instance of a class to custom values, you can do this in the default initializer in your class definition. Since the initializer is a method, you can add code to the initializer and it will execute that code when the instance is created. Before, if we wanted a BirthdayCake instance, it always had to start out as a cake with the default properties. The birthdayName and birthdayAge would always start out as "Jude" and 8. But with a custom initializer, we'll be able to set each instance to whatever value we want. Let's add some functionality to this initializer in BirthdayCake.

Setting Property Values Using an Initializer

The simplest initializer takes no input parameters and is written with the keyword init followed by a set of parentheses. Let's add this initializer to BirthdayCake and use it to set the values of birthdayAge and birthdayName, and then output a statement when the instance is created saying that the cake is ready. Change the code inside your BirthdayCake class so that it looks like this:

```
class BirthdayCake {
❶ let birthdayAge: Int
❷ let birthdayName: String
   var feeds = 20
```

```
❸ init() {
    ❹ birthdayAge = 6
    ❺ birthdayName = "Dagmar"
    ❻ print("\(birthdayName)'s cake is ready!")
    }
}
```

At ❶ and ❷, we change our property declarations of birthdayAge and birthdayName to no longer include a default value. We're going to set the values of these two property constants inside our initializer instead. This is required because all the properties must have a value when an instance of the class is created. If you create a property without giving it a value, you need to specify the data type of the property by putting a colon after its name followed by the type. In this case, we say that birthdayAge is an Int and birthdayName is a String.

At ❸, we add our initializer, a special type of function whose name is always just the init keyword. It can contain any number of input parameters, but it never has a return value. You don't write the func keyword before an initializer because it's special. Inside the init(), we set birthdayAge to 6 ❹ and birthdayName to "Dagmar" ❺. Even though we declared that our birthdayAge and birthdayName are constants created with let, we're allowed to assign a value to them one time (and one time only) in an initializer because we haven't assigned them values yet. If you had assigned a value to birthdayAge before assigning it inside the initializer, you would get an error. Finally, we output a statement that the cake is ready ❻.

Insert the following lines of code to test out creating a cake using this new initializer:

```
class BirthdayCake {
    --snip--
}

❶ let newCake = BirthdayCake()                    BirthdayCake
  newCake.birthdayAge                             6❷
  newCake.birthdayName                            "Dagmar"❸
```

As soon as you create the new cake ❶, you should see "Dagmar's cake is ready!" displayed in the debug console. And when you access the birthdayAge and birthdayName properties, you can see their new values in the results panel of the playground at ❷ and ❸.

Creating an Initializer with Input Parameters

We can also write our own custom initializers to create cakes with different values for the birthdayAge and birthdayName properties. Let's add a second initializer that takes two input parameters, one for birthdayAge and one for `birthdayName`. Add the following code to your `BirthdayCake` class so it looks like this:

```
init() {
    --snip--
}

❶ init(age: Int, name: String) {
❷     birthdayAge = age
❸     birthdayName = name
      print("\(birthdayName)'s cake is ready!")
   }
}
```

Now we can make a birthday cake for anyone! At ❶, we create a second initializer to take two input parameters just as though we were creating a regular function. We place the input parameters in the parentheses after the function name, which is just the keyword `init`. We give each input parameter a name, followed by a colon (:) and the parameter's data type. If there is more than one parameter, they are separated with commas. Notice that it's fine to have multiple `init` functions, but they have to take different input parameters. Otherwise, Swift wouldn't know which one you were trying to use!

Inside the second initializer, we set the `BirthdayCake` class properties to the parameters by simply assigning them. At ❷, we assign `birthdayAge` to the `age` parameter that is passed in to the initializer, and at ❸ we assign `birthdayName` to the `name` parameter.

Now that we have our new initializer, let's use it to make a birthday cake!

Calling an Initializer with Input Parameters

To create an instance with a custom initializer, pass input values between its parentheses with their labels. Add the following code after the `BirthdayCake` class definition:

```
class BirthdayCake {
    --snip--
}
let twinsCake = BirthdayCake(age: 11, name: "Colin and Brenna")
```

Did you notice that Xcode helped you with autocomplete? When you type in the first parenthesis after `BirthdayCake`, Xcode offers you the template seen in Figure 8-2.

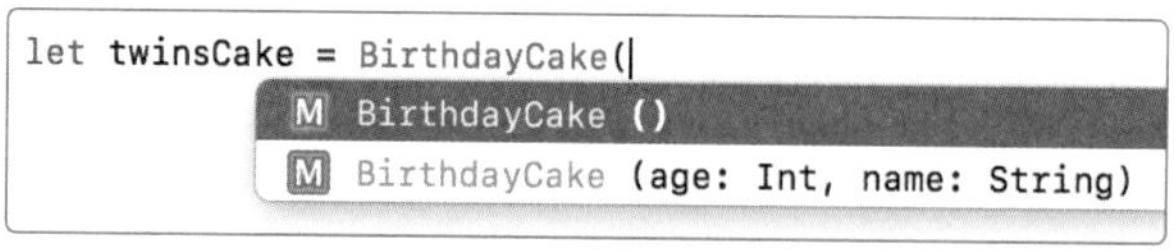

Figure 8-2: The drop-down autocomplete template for an initializer

Once autocomplete pops up, press the down arrow and then RETURN (or double-click the second initializer suggestion with the new parameters), and Xcode should write the argument labels for you, leaving you to fill in each value (see Figure 8-3).

```
let twinsCake = BirthdayCake(age: Int , name: String )
```

Figure 8-3: Hit RETURN on the second suggestion, and Xcode will write the argument labels with placeholders showing each argument's data type.

Autocomplete is a huge help when you're writing code. If you want to create a BirthdayCake but don't remember the initializer's parameters, you don't have to look at the BirthdayCake class definition. Just start typing BirthdayCake, and Xcode will show you all the initializers and their parameters.

Next, you'll learn how to write a method so you can do things to your birthday cakes!

ADDING A BIRTHDAY GREETING METHOD

Let's add a method to our BirthdayCake class that will write a customized message on a cake. We'll call this method message(shouldIncludeAge:), and it will take one input parameter to decide whether the person's age should be displayed in the greeting. The method will return a greeting as a string. Write the following code *inside* your BirthdayCake class definition after the second initializer:

```
    init(age: Int, name: String) {
        --snip--
    }

❶ func message(❷ shouldIncludeAge: Bool) -> ❸ String {
        if shouldIncludeAge {
            return "Happy \(birthdayAge) Birthday \(birthdayName)!"
        }
        return "Happy Birthday \(birthdayName)!"
    }
}
```

As you can see, writing a method is exactly like writing any other function except that it's nested inside a class. The keyword func comes before the function name ❶, followed by a pair of parentheses that contain the input parameters ❷. If the function has a return value, then an arrow (->) is added, followed by the return value data type ❸. In this case, we're going to return a string.

A method written inside a class body has access to the properties of that class. This is because both the method and the properties are contained inside the class and therefore have the same scope (which we covered in "Constant and Variable Scope" on page 55). This is why you can use `birthdayAge` and `birthdayName` inside `message(shouldIncludeAge:)` without having to pass them in as parameters.

Now that we've written this method, let's use it! Enter the following code *outside* of your `BirthdayCake` class.

```
class BirthdayCake {
    --snip--
}
❶ let brownieCake = BirthdayCake(age: 11, ↵
    name: "Gretchen")
❷ brownieCake.message(shouldIncludeAge: true)
```

```
"Happy 11 Birthday ↵
    Gretchen!"
```

After creating `brownieCake` ❶, we call the method using dot notation ❷. We pass in `true` to print the age on the cake. The `message(shouldIncludeAge:)` method is an *instance method* because it will work only when it's called on a `BirthdayCake` instance. If you tried to use this method outside of the `BirthdayCake` class without calling it on a `BirthdayCake` instance using dot notation, you would get an error. Try writing this outside of `BirthdayCake`:

```
class BirthdayCake {
    --snip--
}
message(shouldIncludeAge: false)
```

As you can see, this doesn't work. You should get an error message like `"Use of unresolved identifier 'message'"`. What's more, you should notice that autocomplete isn't helping you out by finding the method like it usually does when you start typing. Swift recognizes `message(shouldIncludeAge:)` only when it's called on a `BirthdayCake` instance.

WRITING A HELPER METHOD

It's great having a method that will display a nice message, but `"Happy 11 Birthday"` isn't quite right. We need to output the age as an ordinal number, as in `"Happy 11th Birthday"`. This will be a little tricky. Since we also have to account for birthday numbers that don't end in *th*, like 1st, 2nd, and 3rd, we can't just add a *th* to the birthday age.

To solve this problem, let's write a helper method called `ordinalAge()`. A *helper method* is just a method that is used inside of a class. We'll create the method `ordinalAge()` and have it turn the `birthdayAge` into the correct ordinal number to display as a string. This method will be used inside `message(shouldIncludeAge:)` to display the perfect birthday message.

Since most of our birthday ages will end in *th*, we can set up a suffix variable to hold that string and stick it onto the end of the `birthdayAge`. We'll need to handle some special cases, though, since numbers that end with a 1, 2, or 3 don't have a *th* suffix. On top of that, there are other special cases, like the ages 11, 12, and 13, which all end in 1, 2, or 3 but use the *th* suffix like other numbers. We'll need to figure out a good way to handle all of these.

Add the following code *inside* the BirthdayCake class, right *after* the message(shouldIncludeAge:) method:

```
func message(shouldIncludeAge: Bool) -> String {
    --snip--
}

func ordinalAge() -> String {
❶   var suffix = "th"
❷   let remainder = birthdayAge % 10
❸   switch remainder {
    case 1:
        if birthdayAge != 11 {
            suffix = "st"
        }
    case 2:
        if birthdayAge != 12 {
            suffix = "nd"
        }
    case 3:
        if birthdayAge != 13 {
            suffix = "rd"
        }
❹       default:
        break
    }
❺   return "\(birthdayAge)" + suffix
}
```

Our new method ordinalAge() takes birthdayAge and returns an ordinal number with the correct suffix as a string. To set this up, we create a variable suffix and set it to "th" ❶. Next, we use the modulo operator to find out what the remainder would be after dividing birthdayAge by 10 ❷. That will tell us if the birthdayAge ends with a 1, 2, or 3, since the remainder will be the same as the last digit in birthdayAge. We'll use this information to figure out what the suffix after birthdayAge should be. At ❸, we use a switch statement and set suffix to "st", "nd", or "rd", depending on the remainder. If remainder is 1, then suffix is "st"; if remainder is 2, then suffix is "nd"; and if remainder is 3, then suffix is "rd".

Since the birthday ages 11, 12, and 13 all end with remainders 1, 2, and 3 but use the "th" suffix, they're exceptions to the case statements we set up. In order to handle these, we've included if statements in each case. If remainder is something other than 1, 2, or 3, the default case of the switch statement will be called ❹.

In Swift, a switch statement must be *exhaustive* and include all possible cases, so this default case is required even though we don't want to do anything for these values of remainder because suffix should keep its value of "th". You must write at least one line of code for each case in a switch statement, or you'll get an error. When you don't want to do anything for a case, you can just use the break keyword, which skips the program to the next block of code. Forcing you to fill out every case and to explicitly call break when you don't want to execute code in a switch is one of the ways in which Swift is a safe language. It gives you less room for error.

After we figure out what value suffix should be, we create a string out of the birthdayAge at ❺ and return this with the correct suffix added to it.

To use this new method inside of message(shouldIncludeAge:), change the way the age is displayed like this:

```
func message(shouldIncludeAge: Bool) -> String {
    if shouldIncludeAge {
        return "Happy \(ordinalAge()) Birthday \(birthdayName)!"
    }
    return "Happy Birthday \(birthdayName)!"
}
```

Because we're calling ordinalAge() from *inside* the BirthdayCake class, we can call it without using dot notation.

Now when you look at the code that displays the brownieCake message, you should see a perfectly formatted age!

brownieCake.message(shouldIncludeAge: true)	"Happy 11th Birthday Gretchen!"

You call message(shouldIncludeAge:) in the exact same way as you did before, but the return value has changed because the age is now being displayed as an ordinal number.

A SPECIAL PROPERTY CALLED SELF

Every class instance comes with a special property called self, which refers to the class itself. You can think of it as an instance's way of saying this is *my* property or method. You really don't need to write self very often, but there are some occasions where it's necessary so that Xcode knows exactly what you're referring to.

For example, you may need to use self inside initializers or other methods in a class that take parameters. If those parameters have the same names as properties in your class, then you need to use the self keyword to tell Swift you want to use the property in your class and not the parameter that you passed in with the same name. Let's look at a simple RocketShip class as an example.

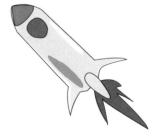

Enter the following into your playground:

```
class RocketShip {
❶  var destination: String
❷  init(destination: String) {
❸      self.destination = destination
    }
}
let myRocketShip = RocketShip(destination: "Moon")
myRocketShip.destination
```

RocketShip
"Moon"

At ❶, we create a Rocketship class with a destination property. At ❷, we make an initializer that takes a parameter with the same name, destination. The initializer creates an instance of RocketShip with that destination parameter value.

At ❸, we set the destination property of our RocketShip instance to the value of the destination parameter that we are passing into init() at ❷. We do this by putting the self keyword and a period in front of the destination property inside the initializer. This tells Swift that self.destination is the destination we defined at ❶ since it's the RocketShip class's property. When there is no self in front of destination, Swift knows that it is the parameter that has been passed to init() at ❷. When a property has the same name as a local variable or parameter, Swift will always assume that you are referring to the local variable or parameter that was passed in unless you add the self keyword. In the last two lines of code, we create a rocket ship called myRocketShip that is destined for the moon.

You only need to use the self keyword if your parameter name is the same as your property name. You can avoid writing self by writing initializers that have different parameter names, like this:

```
class RocketShip {
    var destination: String

    init(❶someDestination: String) {
        destination = someDestination
    }
}
```

In this case, we call the destination parameter of the init function someDestination ❶. Now, in the init() method, there can be no confusion between the property destination and the passed-in parameter someDestination, so the self keyword isn't necessary anymore. However, you can still write self.destination without getting an error.

CLASS INHERITANCE

One neat thing that a class can do is inherit from another class. Class *inheritance* means that you can create a new class using an existing class as a starting block. The class that other classes inherit from is called a *superclass*, and the classes that inherit from the superclass are its *subclasses*.

When a subclass inherits from a superclass, it gets all of that superclass's properties and methods, which you can tweak to suit your needs. The subclass can also have its own properties and methods that didn't come from the superclass. Every subclass can have only one superclass, but there's no limit to the number of subclasses that a superclass can have.

CREATING A SUPERCLASS

Let's make a superclass called FarmAnimal as an example. We can give our FarmAnimal class two properties: a String for a name, and an Int for the number of legs. We'll also give the FarmAnimal class two methods—one called sayHello(), which will return a greeting, and one called description(), which will output a simple description of the animal. First let's open a new playground to work in and call it *FarmAnimals*. Do you remember how to do that using the Xcode menu? If you need a refresher, flip back to "Writing a Class Definition" on page 96. After you've opened a new playground, enter the following code into it:

```
class FarmAnimal {
    var name = "farm animal"
    var numberOfLegs = 4
    func sayHello() -> String {
   ❶ return "Hello I'm a farm animal!"
    }
    func description() {
   ❷ print("I'm a \(name) and I have \(numberOfLegs) legs.")
    }
}
```

The FarmAnimal class is intended to be used as a superclass, which is why at ❶ it returns "Hello I'm a farm animal!" from its sayHello() method even though we know farm animals wouldn't actually say this. They'd say "oink oink" if they're a pig or "moo" if they're a cow or "neigh" if they're a horse. The line at ❷ in the description() method will display a string stating the farm animal's name and how many legs it has.

CREATING A SUBCLASS

Now that we have a FarmAnimal superclass, let's make a Sheep subclass. Write the following code underneath your FarmAnimal class to create this subclass:

```
class FarmAnimal {
    --snip--
}

❶ class Sheep: FarmAnimal {

  ❷ override init() {
      ❸ super.init()
      ❹ name = "sheep"
    }

  ❺ override func sayHello() -> String {
        return "Baa Baa"
    }
    override func description() {
      ❻ super.description()
      ❼ print("I provide wool to make blankets.")
    }
}
```

To create a subclass from another class, add a colon after the subclass name, followed by a space and the name of the superclass that you want your class to inherit from, just like we did at ❶. You can make a subclass from any class that exists in Swift, even from a built-in class.

In our Sheep subclass, we want to set the name property inherited from the FarmAnimal superclass to "sheep" instead of "farm animal". To do this, we need to *override* the default initializer of the FarmAnimal superclass, which the Sheep subclass has inherited. In Swift, when a subclass overrides a method it inherits, it means that the subclass uses its own definition of a method that also exists in a superclass.

If you take a look at the FarmAnimal class, you won't see any init() method. Remember, if you don't create your own init(), there's always a hidden init() that's added by default.

In our Sheep class, we override this hidden init() method by writing the keyword override before init() at ❷. When we override the init() method, we first need to call the init() method of the FarmAnimal class because it sets up the properties and methods that the Sheep class needs to inherit. We do this at ❸ by using the keyword super, followed by dot notation and init(). The keyword super refers to the superclass of the instance in the same way that self refers to the instance itself. After super.init(), at ❹, we can set the name property that is inherited from the FarmAnimal superclass from "farm animal" to "sheep".

The Sheep class also overrides the two methods provided in the FarmAnimal superclass, sayHello() and description(). We want the sayHello() method of a Sheep to return "Baa Baa", so we override sayHello() to do just that. You override an instance method the same way that you override an initializer: you just write the keyword override before the func keyword, as we did at ❺. Then we tell the function to return the string "Baa Baa".

Next, we'll override the description() method so it says something about sheep. We want the Sheep class's description() method to do what the FarmAnimal class's description() method does and then print something extra. To do this, we call super.description() ❻, which displays "I'm a sheep and I have 4 legs." in the debug console. Then we have our Sheep description ❼, which prints the extra sentence "I provide wool to make blankets." when description() is called on a Sheep object.

Test out your new subclass by creating a Sheep and then calling its sayHello() and description() methods to see what it can do:

```
class Sheep: FarmAnimal {
    --snip--
}
let aSheep = Sheep()                    Sheep
aSheep.sayHello()                       "Baa Baa"
aSheep.description()                    Sheep
```

If you did everything correctly, you should see this output in your debug console:

```
I'm a sheep and I have 4 legs.
I provide wool to make blankets.
```

As an exercise, create another subclass of FarmAnimal to create a pig that will output a custom greeting in sayHello() and print an appropriate description of itself!

DETECTING THE DATA TYPE BY TYPECASTING

There may be times when you know only the superclass data type of an instance but you also want to know what subclass it is. To find out, you'll need to use *typecasting*. Typecasting lets you see what data type an instance is, and it also lets you *downcast* an instance from its superclass into one of its subclasses.

For example, say that Farmer John has an array of FarmAnimal objects that consists of a few sheep, chicken, and pig objects. When he steps through his array, he wants to know what kind of animal each FarmAnimal is, and, if it's a Chicken, he wants to collect its eggs.

There are two operators used in typecasting: is and as. The is keyword is used to check if an instance is a particular data type, and the as keyword is used to downcast an instance to one of its subclasses.

Let's begin by creating a Chicken class for Farmer John. Enter the following into your *FarmAnimals* playground after your Sheep class:

```
class Sheep: FarmAnimal {
    --snip--
}

class Chicken: FarmAnimal {

❶  var numberOfEggs = 0

    override init() {
        super.init()
        name = "chicken"
    ❷  numberOfLegs = 2
    }

    override func sayHello() -> String {
        return "Bok Bok"
    }
    override func description() {
        super.description()
        print("I lay eggs.")
        if numberOfEggs == 1 {
            print("I have one egg for you now.")
        } else if numberOfEggs > 0 {
            print("I have \(numberOfEggs) eggs for you now.")
        }
    }

❸  func layAnEgg() {
        numberOfEggs += 1
    }
❹  func giveUpEggs() -> Int {
        let eggs = numberOfEggs
        numberOfEggs = 0
        return eggs
    }
}
```

The Chicken class is similar to the Sheep class, but at ❶, we add an extra property to keep track of the Chicken's eggs: numberOfEggs. We also change the Chicken's numberOfLegs to 2 at ❷ in the initializer, because who's ever heard of a chicken with four legs?!

At ❸ and ❹, we add two new methods: layAnEgg(), which increases the chicken's egg count, and giveUpEggs(), which returns the number of the Chicken's eggs and resets numberOfEggs to 0. Notice that we don't put the keyword override in front of these two functions. You only put override in front of a function that you are overriding from the superclass.

Create two `Chicken` objects and have them lay some eggs by entering the following into your playground:

```
class Chicken: FarmAnimal {
    --snip--
}
let chicken1 = Chicken()
chicken1.layAnEgg()
let chicken2 = Chicken()
chicken2.layAnEgg()
chicken2.layAnEgg()
```

Now you're ready to make Farmer John's animals array. We'll put three `Sheep` objects, three `Chicken` objects (including the two with eggs that we just created), and a `Pig` object into animals. If you didn't create a `Pig` class in the previous section, then feel free to leave the pig out!

```
let chicken2 = Chicken()
chicken2.layAnEgg()
chicken2.layAnEgg()
let animals = [Sheep(), chicken1, chicken2, Sheep(), Chicken(), ↵
    Sheep(), Pig()]
```

Remember that in Swift, an array can only contain items of the same data type. We didn't specify the type of the animals array, so Swift will use its type checker to discover that each item is a subclass of `FarmAnimal`, and it will make the array type `[FarmAnimal]`.

Now, when Farmer John goes around his farm to check on his animals, he can use the keyword is to find out which type of `FarmAnimal` each one is. Let's help him do this by looping through the animals array and printing various strings depending on what type of `FarmAnimal` each animal is:

```
let animals = [Sheep(), chicken1, chicken2, Sheep(), Chicken(), ↵
    Sheep(), Pig()]
for animal in animals {
❶  if animal is Sheep {
        print("This is what my sheep says: \(animal.sayHello())")
❷  } else if animal is Chicken {
        print("My chickens say: \(animal.sayHello())")
❸  } else if animal is Pig {
        print("And here is my pig: \(animal.sayHello())")
    }
}
```

For each animal in the animals array, we check whether it matches a data type using the keyword is followed by the specific data type. For instance, at ❶, we check whether the animal is of the `Sheep` class with if animal is `Sheep`. This condition will evaluate to true if the animal is a `Sheep` and false if it isn't.

In the else-if block at ❷, we check whether animal is of the Chicken class and, if it is, we print "My chickens say: Bok Bok". Lastly, if the animal isn't a Sheep or a Chicken, then it's a Pig ❸. If you didn't write a Pig subclass, don't worry—you can still make this code work by removing the final if-else clause that checks if animal is Pig and the braces and print statement that go along with it.

When the playground is done running (be patient—it might take a minute or two!), you should see something like this in your debug console:

```
This is what my sheep says: Baa Baa
My chickens say: Bok Bok
My chickens say: Bok Bok
This is what my sheep says: Baa Baa
My chickens say: Bok Bok
This is what my sheep says: Baa Baa
And here is my pig: Oink
```

Now Farmer John can tell which subclass his animals are!

REFINING THE DATA TYPE BY DOWNCASTING

Now we know the subclass of each animal in the animals array. Next, we want to have Farmer John collect eggs from his chickens, but we'll need to do a bit more work to get Swift to let him do that. First, we'll need to have the chickens lay some eggs.

Let's try to get our chickens in the for-in loop to lay some eggs. Add this line of code to the for-in section for a Chicken and see what happens:

```
} else if animal is Chicken {
    print("My chickens say: \(animal.sayHello())")
    animal.layAnEgg() // error FarmAnimal has no member layAnEgg
} else if animal is Pig {
```

In our for loop, even if we know a specific animal is of type Chicken, Swift still treats it as a FarmAnimal class and not as a Chicken class. That means if we try to get this animal to lay an egg here, we'll get an error because it's a FarmAnimal and FarmAnimal doesn't have a layAnEgg() method.

To get this animal to lay eggs, we first have to downcast the animal from the FarmAnimal class to the Chicken subclass. We do this by using the as keyword. Change the code for a Chicken to the following:

```
} else if animal is Chicken {
    print("My chickens say: \(animal.sayHello())")
❶  let chicken = animal as! Chicken
    chicken.layAnEgg()
    chicken.description()
} else if animal is Pig {
```

In this for-in loop, when we find out that the animal is a Chicken data type, we downcast it into a chicken constant using the as keyword ❶. Swift also makes us include a ! after as to force-downcast the animal into a Chicken class. This is similar to using a ! to force-unwrap an optional, which you learned about in Chapter 5. In this case, it's safe to force the FarmAnimal into a Chicken because we know that the animal is a Chicken class after our check if animal is Chicken.

If you are unsure whether the animal is a Chicken, then you should put a ? after the as keyword. For example, when Farmer John goes around his farm to collect the eggs, he only wants to get them from his Chicken objects. Here is a good way for him to do it without bothering to check for Sheep or Pig objects:

```
  let animals = [Sheep(), chicken1, chicken2, Sheep(), Chicken(), ↵
      Sheep(), Pig()]
❶ var gatheredEggs = 0
  for animal in animals {
    ❷ if let chicken = animal as? Chicken {
          chicken.layAnEgg()
          print("Picking up \(chicken.numberOfEggs) eggs.")
        ❸ gatheredEggs += chicken.giveUpEggs()
      }
  }
❹ print("I gathered \(gatheredEggs) eggs today!")
```

At ❶, Farmer John starts with 0 gatheredEggs. This time, when Farmer John steps through his animals array, he first wants to know if he can downcast animal into a chicken so that he can gather its eggs. If he can't downcast animal, then the animal isn't a chicken, so Farmer John doesn't need to gather any eggs. This happens with the if-let statement at ❷. Only animals that are Chicken objects can be cast into a chicken using as? Chicken. If the animal is a sheep or a pig, then the if-let statement is skipped.

In this case, we must use as? to downcast instead of as! because when we're stepping through the animals array, we don't know if the animal can be turned into a chicken or not. If you tried to force-downcast a Sheep into a Chicken with as!, you would get an error. Downcasting using as? will also give you an optional value, so that's why we use an if-let statement to unwrap animal as? Chicken into chicken.

Once Farmer John has his chicken, he takes its eggs by using the Chicken class's giveUpEggs() method, and he adds those eggs to his gatheredEggs at ❸. Finally, after the for loop is finished at ❹, he prints the number of eggs that he has gathered from his animals.

VALUE TYPES AND REFERENCE TYPES

Classes let you create your own data types in Swift, and they can be used much like any other data type (such as an Int, Bool, Double, String, or Array). There is, however, one *big* difference between a class and these other types of data: all of the data types that you have worked with until now are *value types*. But classes are *reference types*. That means the way that you store them in variables is a little different. Let's see how.

If you create a variable that holds an `Int` value type and then assign it to a new variable, the value is copied into the new variable behind the scenes. This means that if you change the value of the new variable, the original variable *doesn't* change. To get a better understanding of this, open another new playground, call it *KidsAndCouches*, and enter the following:

``
  var myAge = 14
❶ var yourAge = myAge
  print("My age is \(myAge) and your ↵
      age is \(yourAge)")
❷ yourAge = 15
  print("Now my age is \(myAge) and ↵
      your age is \(yourAge)")
``
	``
	14
	14
	"My age is 14 and your ↵
	    age is 14\n"
	
	"Now my age is 14 and ↵
	    your age is 15"❸
	``

We first set a variable `myAge` to 14. Next, we create a new variable called `yourAge` and assign `myAge` at ❶. When you print the values of both variables, they are both 14.

After that, we change the value of `yourAge` to 15 ❷. This time, when you print the values of both variables, you can see in the output at ❸ that `yourAge` is 15, but `myAge` is still its original value of 14. This is because when we assigned `myAge` to `yourAge` at ❶, just the *value* of `myAge` was copied and put into `yourAge`. This is what happens when you assign a variable or constant of one value type to another variable or constant.

Classes behave differently because they are reference types. This means that when you create a variable instance of a class, an object is created and stored in a location within the computer's memory. So, if you create another new variable instance and assign it to the first variable, what you are really doing is making the new instance point to the same location in the computer's memory as the first instance, so the variables are both *referring* to the same object. If you change one variable, the other one will change, too, since they both refer to the same object. To see this in action, add this to your *KidsAndCouches* playground:

``
  print("Now my age is \(myAge) and ↵
      your age is \(yourAge).")
  class Kid {
      var age: Int
      init(age: Int) {
          self.age = age
      }
  }
❶ var finn = Kid(age: 9)
❷ var nathan = finn
  print("Nathan is \(nathan.age) and ↵
      Finn is \(finn.age)")
``
	``
	
	Kid
	Kid
	"Nathan is 9 and ↵
	    Finn is 9\n"
	``

To see what happens when we assign one instance of a class to another instance, we create a Kid class with one property, age. Next, we create a Kid named finn with an age of 9 ❶. Then we create a Kid named nathan and assign finn to nathan ❷. Because we're dealing with classes, this means we're doing more than just assigning the value of finn to nathan. The variables finn and nathan point to the exact same Kid object (see Figure 8-4).

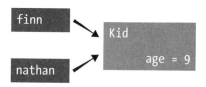

When you write nathan = finn, you've just told Swift nathan and finn are the *same* object. We can see this if we change Nathan's age to 10. Enter the following code.

Figure 8-4: The variables finn and nathan point to the same Kid, age 9.

```
  print("Nathan is \(nathan.age) and ↵
      Finn is \(finn.age)")
❶ nathan.age = 10
  print("Now Nathan is \(nathan.age) and ↵
      Finn is also \(finn.age)")
```

```
Kid
"Now Nathan is 10 and ↵
    Finn is also 10\n"❷
```

We set Nathan's age to 10 ❶. When you print the age of both Nathan and Finn, you can see that changing Nathan's age also changed Finn's age ❷. This is because nathan and finn are just two names for the same object.

It's often useful to have different variables referring to the same object, but in this case, these are two different people. So, rather than assigning nathan equal to finn, it would make more sense to create a new Kid instance for nathan, like this:

```
var finn = Kid(age: 9)
var nathan = Kid(age: 10)
print("Nathan is \(nathan.age) and 8
    Finn is \(finn.age)")
```

```
Kid
"Nathan is 10 and ↵
    Finn is 9\n"
```

Now we have a new, separate instance of a Kid class, nathan, that can be changed without affecting the other instance, finn. Figure 8-5 shows that finn and nathan now each refer to a separate Kid object.

That's something to keep in mind when you're working with variables and classes! If you need multiple objects, make sure that you initialize them as new objects.

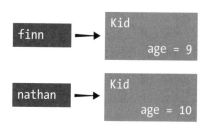

Figure 8-5: The finn and nathan variables now refer to two separate objects that can have their ages changed without affecting each other.

USING STRUCTS

A *struct* looks a lot like a class and is used in many of the same ways. Structs have properties and methods, just like a class. However, there are two key differences between a struct and a class. First of all, structs don't have inheritance. You can't make a substruct from a superstruct like you can make a subclass from a superclass. Second, a struct is a value type, not a reference type like a class.

Let's take a look at an example of a simple struct that has one property and one method. Write the following code in your playground:

```
❶ struct Couch {
      var numberOfCushions = 3
      func description() -> String {
          return "This couch has \(numberOfCushions) cushions."
      }
  }
```

Creating a struct is just like creating a class, except you use the `struct` keyword in front of the name instead of the `class` keyword, as we did at ❶. We've created a `Couch` struct with a variable property for the `numberOfCushions`. We have also added a description method to our `Couch` struct that will tell us how many cushions it has. Now let's create two `Couch` instances with the following code:

```
  struct Couch {
      --snip--
  }
❶ var myFirstCouch = Couch()                    Couch
❷ var mySecondCouch = myFirstCouch              Couch
❸ myFirstCouch.description()                    "This couch has 3 cushions."
❹ mySecondCouch.description()                   "This couch has 3 cushions."
```

We create `myFirstCouch` as an instance of the `Couch` struct ❶. This instance has the default value of 3 for `numberOfCushions`. Next, we create `mySecondCouch` by assigning it to `myFirstCouch` ❷. Since we're dealing with a struct, `mySecondCouch` now contains a copy of the value in `myFirstCouch`. At ❸ and ❹, we look at the description of each couch and see that they both have 3 cushions as expected. Let's change the number of cushions on `mySecondCouch`:

```
  var mySecondCouch = myFirstCouch
  myFirstCouch.description()
  mySecondCouch.description()
❶ mySecondCouch.numberOfCushions = 4            Couch
❷ myFirstCouch.description()                    "This couch has 3 cushions."
❸ mySecondCouch.description()                   "This couch has 4 cushions."
```

Now we set a new number of cushions on `mySecondCouch` at ❶ and then take another look at the description of each `Couch` at ❷ and ❸. This is the interesting part. The first Couch still has 3 cushions, but mySecondCouch has 4 cushions. So the two Couch instances are *not* the same thing, as they would be if we were dealing with classes. The second Couch is just a copy of the first Couch, so when we change the second Couch, the first one doesn't change.

If we define Couch as a class instead of a struct, the output would change to show that modifying one Couch instance modifies both Couch instances, because they're the same object, not a copy of each other. Test this out by changing the word in front of Couch from struct to class.

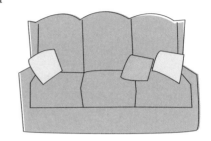

```
class Couch {
    var numberOfCushions = 3
    --snip--
}
```

After you make that change, you should see that changing the numberOfCushions value of mySecondCouch also changes the numberOfCushions value of myFirstCouch.

	Couch
mySecondCouch.numberOfCushions = 4	
myFirstCouch.description()	"This couch has 4 cushions."
mySecondCouch.description()	"This couch has 4 cushions."

When should you use a struct instead of a class? Apple recommends using structs when you need to store a group of related values that are okay to pass around by value (copying) instead of by reference. For example, you'll see that when we start building our Schoolhouse Skateboarder app in Chapter 14 and need to deal with x- and y-coordinates, we use a CGPoint, which is a simple struct that holds an x value and a y value.

WHAT YOU LEARNED

Congratulations! Now you know how to create your own data types using classes! You learned how to create a class with its own properties, initializers, and methods. You also learned how to create a subclass of a superclass and how to override the superclass methods.

Now you're ready to start working on your first app. The next few chapters will focus on creating BirthdayTracker, an iPhone app that lets you input your friends' birthdays and notifies you when to wish them a happy birthday.

PART 2
BIRTHDAY TRACKER

9

CREATING BUTTONS AND SCREENS ON THE STORYBOARD

The BirthdayTracker app helps you keep track of your friends' birthdays by letting you save birthdays into a list and pinging you with reminders. We will be building this app over the next five chapters. In this chapter, we'll show you how to set up the parts of the app that the user sees.

We'll make two screens: one that displays the list of birthdays and one that lets you add a person's name and birthday to the list. Then, in Chapters 10 to 13, we'll show you how to take user input, display birthdays onscreen, save the birthdays, and ping the user with a notification when it's someone's birthday.

Are you ready to make an app? Let's go!

AN OUTLINE OF YOUR APP

By the end of this chapter, we'll have two screens for the BirthdayTracker. We'll call these the "Birthdays" and "Add a Birthday" screens, as shown in Figure 9-1.

Figure 9-1: A look at the finished app we'll build over the next few chapters

The Birthdays screen shows you a list of birthdays that you've added, and the Add a Birthday screen is where you can add new birthday entries.

In Xcode, a screen includes a *view* and a *view controller*. The view is what you see on the screen, and the view controller contains all your Swift code to control the view. You can see in Figure 9-1 that the Birthdays view has an Add button in the top-right corner that looks like a plus sign (+).

The Add button will bring up the Add a Birthday view, where the user can input the birthday details of a new friend. Let's get started by creating a new Xcode project for our BirthdayTracker.

CREATING A NEW XCODE PROJECT

So far, you've been writing most of your code in the playground. The playground is a great place to learn to code, but to write an app that runs on an iPad or iPhone, you'll need to create an Xcode project, like you did for the Hello World app in Chapter 1.

In the Xcode menu, go to **File ▸ New ▸ Project**. Select **iOS** at the top of the dialog and **Single View App** for your project template and then click **Next**.

In the dialog that appears, Xcode will ask you to set a few options for your new app. Since this is just an example, you don't need to take this part *too* seriously. Setting these values is much more important when you're writing an app that you plan to sell or distribute on the App Store. Name your app **BirthdayTracker**, make sure that the Language is **Swift**, and check the box for **Use Core Data**. Your Organization Name and Organization Identifier should be prefilled with the values that you entered when you created the Hello World app in Chapter 1.

Click **Next**. In the dialog that opens, choose where you want to save your project and click **Create**. Your Xcode project should open automatically. Take a moment to make sure that you have a file called *BirthdayTracker.xcdatamodeld* listed in your Project navigator (see Figure 9-2).

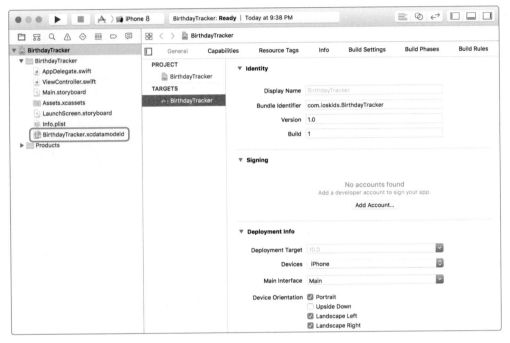

Figure 9-2: Make sure that you have a BirthdayTracker.xcdatamodeld file in your new project.

You need *BirthdayTracker.xcdatamodeld* to save birthdays on the iPhone. If it's missing, that means you didn't check the Use Core Data box when you created the Xcode project. Don't worry—that's really easy to fix.

If your *BirthdayTracker.xcdatamodeld* is missing, close your project (File ▸ Close Project) and start over again by creating a new Xcode project with the Use Core Data box checked. When you're asked if you want to replace the BirthdayTracker project, just click **Replace** and you'll be all set!

Your new BirthdayTracker Xcode project will open. If you haven't added your Apple account to Xcode, you'll see a message that says "No accounts found" in the Signing section of the General app settings. You don't need to add an account unless you want to run the app on a real device. (Remember that you can also run your apps on Xcode's simulator.) To add your Apple account to Xcode, click the **Add Account** button. (For more detailed instructions about adding your Apple account, see "Your First App!" on page 5.)

This General settings screen is also where you set the type of device and the device orientations you want your app to run in. Select **iPhone** from the drop-down menu next to Devices. We want the BirthdayTracker app to run only in *portrait* mode. Portrait mode is the regular orientation of the phone, with the home button on the bottom. *Landscape* mode is when you turn the phone sideways and the screen rotates as well, so that the width of the screen is now the phone's height and the height of the screen is the phone's width. The BirthdayTracker app won't look that great in landscape mode, so we won't have the screen change when the user turns their phone sideways. The app would look fine upside down, but it can be disorienting for the user if the screen flips when they turn their phone around with the home button at the top, so we won't support upside down either. In the Deployment Info section, next to Device Orientation, uncheck the boxes next to **Landscape Left** and **Landscape Right** and make sure that **Portrait** is the only box that's checked.

Let's take a look around Xcode. Select *ViewController.swift* in the left Navigator pane and you should see something like Figure 9-3.

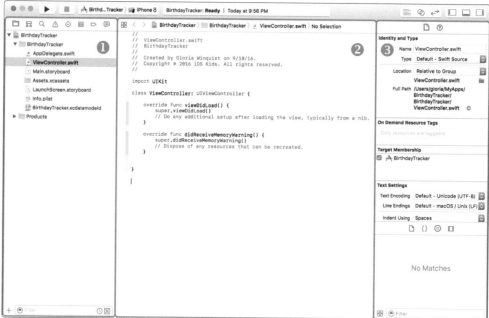

Figure 9-3: Anatomy of an Xcode project window

On the left is the Navigator pane ❶, which you can hide or show by going to **View ▸ Navigators ▸ Hide/Show Navigator** or by pressing ⌘-0. You'll use the Navigator to select and view the files in your project.

The Editor pane is in the center of the window ❷. This is where you will write your code! This is also where you can change your app's settings and lay out the items that will be displayed in the app using the storyboard, which you saw in Chapter 1. We'll talk more about the storyboard soon.

On the right is the Utilities pane ❸, which you can hide or show by selecting **View ▸ Utilities ▸ Hide/Show Utilities** or by pressing ⌘-OPTION-0. When the storyboard is open, the Utilities pane will let you configure the size and placement of objects in your app.

ADDING THE APP ICON

Most apps come with some sort of icon that displays on the home screen of the user's device. We'll start our BirthdayTracker app by adding an app icon. You can download the two images we'll use for the icon from *https:// www.nostarch.com/iphoneappsforkids/*. Download the ZIP file, and you'll have a folder named *ch9-images* inside your *Downloads* folder with the image files you need. Once you have these, select *Assets.xcassets* from the Project navigator. This opens the *asset catalog* of the app, which is where you put any *assets* (images, sounds, and so on) that your app is going to use, including the app icon. In fact, the asset catalog already comes with a placeholder where you can add your icon. Select **AppIcon** from the menu on the left of the catalog, and you should see several placeholders for images.

To add an app icon that will display on the iPhone's home screen, you need to provide the 2x and 3x images for the icon set labeled *iPhone App*. The 2x size works for the smaller iPhones, such as the iPhone 5, 6, 7, and 8. The larger iPhones, such as the iPhone 6 Plus, 6s Plus, 7 Plus, 8 Plus, and iPhone X use the 3x size images. You'll learn more about sizing images for different screen resolutions in Chapter 14.

Adding the icons to the asset catalog is easy! After you download the provided images, open your *Downloads* folder in Finder. Then simply drag the image *cake@2x.png* to the iPhone App 2x box and *cake@3x.png* to the 3x box. When you are finished, your asset catalog should look like Figure 9-4.

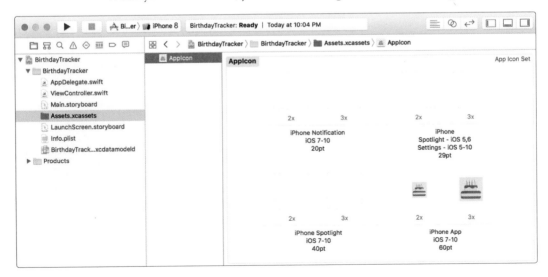

Figure 9-4: We now have an app icon!

In addition to an app icon, apps also have a display name that is shown under the icon on the home page. By default, this is just the app name, BirthdayTracker. However, that name is a bit too long to fit under the app icon, so let's change it to a shorter name: Birthdays. To do this, go back to the settings page by selecting the BirthdayTracker project in the Project navigator. At the top in the Identity section, you can change the display name of the app. Simply enter **Birthdays** in the Display Name text field. This will just change the name that's displayed under your app icon. The name of your project will still be BirthdayTracker.

Now that we have set our app icon and display name, let's create the app screens!

DISPLAYING YOUR FRIENDS' BIRTHDAYS

Select *Main.storyboard* from the Project navigator to bring up the storyboard. This is where we'll design the *user interface* of the application. The user interface is just a fancy name for the things the user will see and use to interact with the app—the images, text, buttons, and so on. The *storyboard* lets you visually organize your app's screens. We'll use the storyboard to see all of the screens that are used and the connections between them.

Once you've selected *Main.storyboard*, hide the navigation pane by pressing ⌘-0 so that you have more screen room. Your storyboard should already contain one view controller.

Now take a look at the top of the Utilities pane. You should see a menu with six buttons. These buttons are used to toggle between six *inspectors*, which are tools that help you look more closely at elements in your storyboard and allow you to change the settings of those elements. When you select one of the inspectors, it will appear in the Utilities pane.

INSPECTING STORYBOARD ITEMS

Figure 9-5 shows a close-up view of the inspector selection bar that appears in the Utilities pane when the storyboard is open.

Figure 9-5: There are six inspectors that you can use in the Utilities pane of the storyboard.

Let's go through the inspectors from left to right. The page icon opens the File Inspector. This is where you can change settings for the storyboard file. In this book and in most of your applications, you won't use this inspector.

The next inspector, indicated by a question mark icon, is the Quick Help Inspector. This inspector will give you detailed class information about the item you have currently selected in the storyboard.

The third inspector, with the ID card icon, is the Identity Inspector. This is where you can set a custom class for a storyboard item.

The next two inspectors are the two that you'll use most often when you work in the storyboard, and we'll refer to them frequently in the text. The Attributes Inspector has an icon that looks like a shield. This inspector is used to set various attributes of the selected item in the storyboard. It can be used to set the text of a label, the color of a button, or the type of box displayed around a text input field, for instance. The Size Inspector, with the ruler icon, is used to set the size and screen placement of each storyboard item.

Finally, there is the Connections Inspector, which has an icon that looks like an arrow in a circle. This can be used to connect items in your storyboard to pieces of code that you write in your classes. We'll show you how to do this in Chapter 10.

ADDING THE TABLE VIEW CONTROLLER

Our first view controller will be the Birthdays view controller. This will be a special class of view controller that displays a list, which in Xcode is called a *table view controller*. In our app, the table view controller will display a list of your friends' birthdays! For now it'll just look like an empty screen, and you'll learn to display the birthday data in "Creating the Birthdays Table View Controller" on page 156.

Let's add a table view controller to the storyboard. This step is easier if you first zoom out from the storyboard so that you can see the view controllers better. Double-click the whitespace outside of the view controller in the storyboard to do this. Now your screen should be zoomed out.

At the bottom of the Utilities pane is a section with four buttons at the top. Select the third button, which looks like a square inside a circle. This is the Object Library, where you'll find items to add to your storyboard. Scroll through the Object Library list until you find the Table View Controller, or use the filter bar at the bottom of the pane to search for "table view controller." Then click and drag that object onto your storyboard. Drop it right next to the view controller that is already there. Your storyboard should look like the one in Figure 9-6.

Notice that after you add the table view controller, a Table View Controller Scene entry appears in the outline view on the left, with a Table View Controller inside of it. A scene in your storyboard represents an onscreen area in your app. For an iPhone app, there is usually only one scene on the screen at a time, and that scene fills the entire screen. An iPad app can have two or more scenes on the screen at the same time.

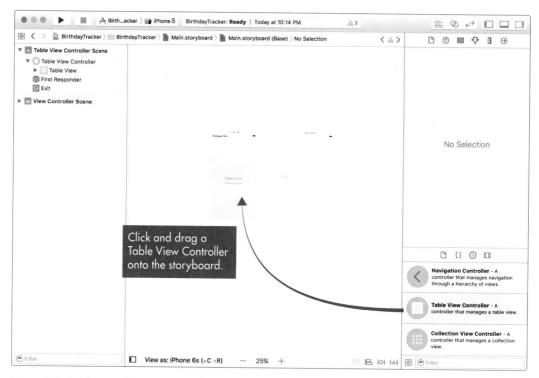

Figure 9-6: Adding a table view controller to the storyboard for the Birthdays screen

The next step is to make this new view controller the first screen that appears when you run the app, since we want the list of birthdays to appear when the user opens the app. The steps to do this are shown in Figure 9-7.

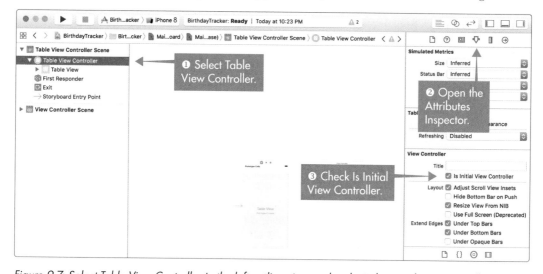

Figure 9-7: Select Table View Controller in the left outline view and make it the initial view controller.

First, select **Table View Controller** in the outline view ❶. Then bring up the Attributes Inspector in your Utilities pane ❷. There, check the box for **Is Initial View Controller** ❸. Once you do this, an arrow should appear to the left of your table view controller in the storyboard. The arrow means that the app will show this view controller when it first starts up.

ADDING THE NAVIGATION CONTROLLER

Now we'll add a title to the view controller that says "Birthdays" and an Add button that will bring up the Add a Birthday view controller. To do this, we'll first put the table view controller into a *navigation controller*. A navigation controller manages one or more view controllers. It comes with a *navigation bar*, which sits at the top of the view controller. The navigation bar can display a title for the view controller along with buttons to the right and left sides that navigate to other screens in the app. You see this bar at the top of the screen in several iOS apps, such as the Settings app and Messages app.

Select **Table View Controller** in the outline view. Once you've selected it, you'll need to embed the table view controller into a navigation controller using the Xcode menu. Go to **Editor ▸ Embed In ▸ Navigation Controller**.

After the table view controller is embedded into a navigation controller, your storyboard should look like the one in Figure 9-8. The navigation controller will show up as a screen in the storyboard.

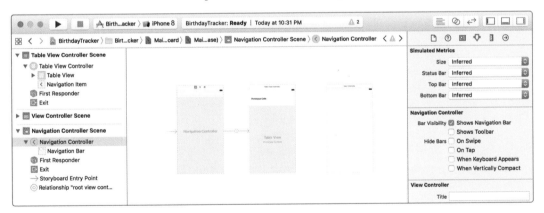

Figure 9-8: The navigation controller

Each view controller in a storyboard represents one screen of your app that the user will see, but a navigation controller is a bit different. Even though it looks like a separate screen in the storyboard, a navigation controller is really just a container that holds the other view controllers that user moves between in your app. Embedding a view controller inside a navigation controller means your app can navigate from one view to another and back again.

You should see gray navigation bars at the top of the navigation controller and the table view controller. When the app is run, the navigation bars tell the user the title of the screen they are on and may also contain buttons and arrows they can use to go to other screens. In order to use the navigation bar to tell the user what screen they are on, we'll need to title our screens. Now is a good time to zoom back in on the storyboard. Double-click in the whitespace of the storyboard to zoom in, and then scroll the view so that you can see the table view controller. To add a title to the table view controller, click **Navigation Item** under **Table View Controller Scene** in the outline view on the left.

When this is selected, you can enter a title for the screen in the Attributes Inspector on the right. We want the navigation bar to display "Birthdays" for the title, so enter **Birthdays** in the Title field on the right. You should see that after you complete this step and press RETURN, the Table View Controller Scene entry in the outline view automatically updates to Birthdays Scene.

Next, we'll make an Add button so you can add birthdays!

ADDING A BUTTON

We want users to be able to open the app, look at their list of birthdays, and add a birthday to that list. Let's make a button that lets them do that!

We need to add a button to the navigation bar that leads to the Add a Birthday scene so that the user can input a birthday. Find the Bar Button Item in the Object Library and then drag and drop it onto the right side of the table view controller's navigation bar, as shown in Figure 9-9.

Now we want to turn this button into an Add button. Lucky for us, Xcode has a built-in Add button we can use. In the Attributes Inspector, change the System Item of the bar button item to **Add**. You should see the button turn into a plus sign (+).

Next, we need to tell the button what to do when it is tapped. We want it to open up the Add a Birthday view controller, so we need to connect the Add button to that view controller. First, double-click the storyboard to zoom out, just to make sure that you can see both the Birthdays table view controller and the plain view controller that will eventually become your Add a Birthday view controller. Hold down CONTROL and drag from the + button to the middle of the empty view controller on the right side of your storyboard. Let go of the mouse when the view controller is highlighted. That will bring up a connection dialog like the one in Figure 9-10.

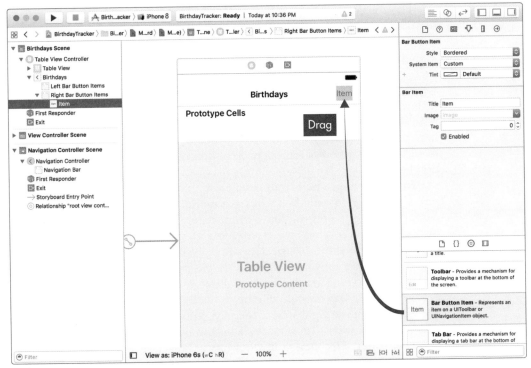

Figure 9-9: Drag a Bar Button Item onto the navigation bar of the Birthdays view controller.

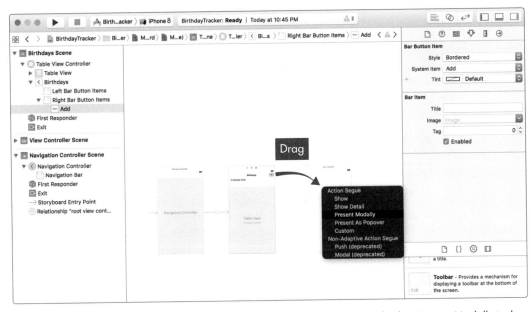

Figure 9-10: Drag from the Add button to the neighboring view controller and select Present Modally in the dialog that appears.

The connection dialog gives you several options for the kind of *segue*—the transition from one screen to the next—you want to make between the two view controllers. Click the **Present Modally** option in the connection dialog. This will make the view controller come onto the screen as a *modal* view controller. On the iPhone, a modal view controller comes onto the screen from the bottom of the phone, and it does not automatically come with a back button to return to the previous screen. Instead, a modal can have other buttons, like Cancel or Save. There are other types of segues, like the Show segue, in which a view controller is pushed onto the screen from the right and which has a back button on the left side of the navigation bar.

In an iOS app, when you present a screen for getting and saving user input, the screen should be shown as a modal with a Cancel button. Otherwise, if you use something like a Show segue with a back button, you could have a situation in which the user enters all of their input and then taps the back button without saving anything! With a Cancel button, the user has to tap deliberately to cancel out of the screen.

To see a good example of a modal input view controller, take a look at the Calendar app on your iPhone or iPad. When you open it up, there is a + button on the right side of the navigation bar that you can tap on to add a calendar event. Tapping the + button brings up a modal New Event view controller. This view controller has a Cancel button on the left to cancel out of the screen without saving and an Add button on the right to create the new event before dismissing the modal. You should see that the New Event modal comes onto the screen from the bottom and then goes back down when it is dismissed. We want the user to save birthdays, so we'll also use a modal.

Now let's try running our app to see what we've done so far! To run the app, first choose a device simulator by clicking the device listed next to BirthdayTracker in the upper-left corner of Xcode (see Figure 9-11).

Figure 9-11: Set the device that the simulator will run in the top left of the Xcode window next to your app's name. Here, the device is set to iPhone 8.

This will bring up a list of device options for running your app. We're going with the iPhone 8. After you have chosen your simulator, click the play button in the upper-left corner or use the keyboard shortcut ⌘-R.

When the simulator opens to run your app, you can adjust its size if it's too large to fit on your computer screen. Click the simulator to select it and then go to **Window ▶ Scale** and select a smaller scale in the simulator menu. You can also adjust the size by pointing your mouse in the bottom-right corner of the simulator and then clicking and dragging to the desired size.

So far, not too much happens when you run the app. You should see your first Birthdays screen with a + button, as shown earlier in Figure 9-1.

Obviously, at this point, your Birthdays screen will be empty. Tapping the + button will bring up a second empty screen. Once you've finished looking at your app, close it by clicking the stop button in Xcode, which is next to the play button you pressed earlier. When you stop the app, you should now see your app icon on the home screen of the simulator! (See Figure 9-12.)

That's it! We now need to configure that second screen so that it can be used to add a birthday!

SETTING UP CONTROL INPUTS AND LABELS

Let's start designing the Add a Birthday view controller by adding its title. To do this, you'll need to embed it in a navigation controller of its own. When a view controller is a modal, it doesn't inherit the navigation bar from the navigation controller already on our storyboard. The navigation controller is what provides a navigation bar, so we

Figure 9-12: The BirthdayTracker app icon has been added to the home screen.

need to embed the modal view controller in its own navigation controller. Select the plain view controller by clicking it in the storyboard. Then go to **Editor ▸ Embed in ▸ Navigation Controller**. Now you should see that a navigation item has been added to the outline view under View Controller Scene. Click this new navigation item and then add the title **Add a Birthday** in the Attributes Inspector. These are the same steps that you followed when adding the title "Birthdays" to your table view controller.

Now when the Add a Birthday view controller appears in the app, it will be labeled with its title at the top.

ADDING YOUR FRIENDS' NAMES AND BIRTHDAYS

When you enter your friends' birthdays in Chapter 10, each entry in your app will have a first name, a last name, and a birthdate. Let's add some *input controls* to the Add a Birthday view controller so that the user can enter all of that information for each person. Input controls are things like text fields or drop-down menus that let users enter data into your apps. We'll get started by adding the input control labels for all the information users can add.

Adding and Positioning Labels

Let's make a label that says "First Name" for your Add a Birthday view controller. This label will be next to a text field where you'll input your friends' first names. Find and drag a label object from the Object Library onto the Add a Birthday view controller (see Figure 9-13).

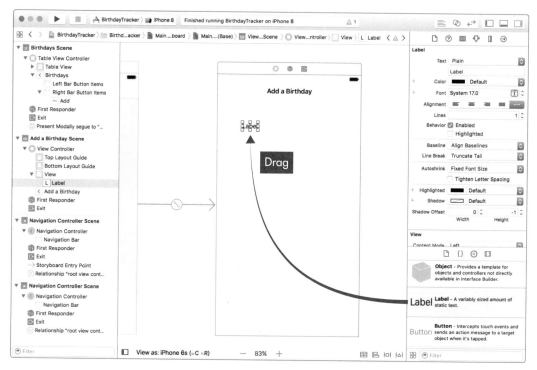

Figure 9-13: Add a label to the Add a Birthday view controller.

Next, change the display text for the label. In the Attributes Inspector, click the Label text box and enter **First Name** as the display text, as shown in Figure 9-14.

Now we want to set the size and position of the label using the Size Inspector. In the Xcode storyboard, width and height are measured in *points*. Note that 1 point is not 1 pixel. Depending on what type of device your app is running on, 1 point will translate into either 1 pixel, a 2×2 pixel square, or a 3×3 pixel square. These three scale factors are referred to as @1x, @2x, and @3x (the same sizes we talked about when we set up our app icon). Devices also don't all have the same point resolution and can range from 320 to 1,024 points wide and 568 to 1,366 points tall.

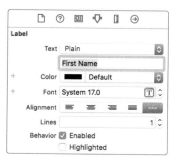

Figure 9-14: Making the label display First Name

Only the oldest models of iPhones and iPods use a @1x scale factor, and you won't be able to run your app on those models (BirthdayTracker will support only iOS 10+). Chances are your phone or iPod uses a @2x scale factor unless it is an iPhone 6 Plus, 6s Plus, 7 Plus, 8 Plus, or iPhone X, which use a @3x scale factor.

An object's position on the screen is also based on points. The x-position of the object is the distance in points from the left side of the screen to the left side of the object. The y-position is the distance from the top of the screen to the top of the object. (See Figure 9-15.) We'll set the x-position and y-position of every library object we add to the view controller.

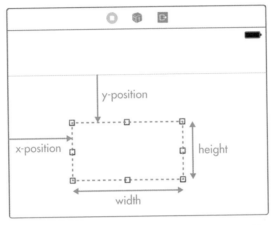

Figure 9-15: Showing the x-position, y-position, width, and height of an object on the screen

We want to position our first label so that it's not on the edge of the screen but still leaves enough room for its text input field and the other labels and inputs. In the View section of the Size Inspector, set the x-position to **20**, the y-position to **100**, and the width to **100**. Leave the height as **21**.

After you've done this, repeat these steps to add two more labels to the Add a Birthday view controller: a Last Name label and a Birthdate label. We'll need to position our other labels and inputs so that they don't overlap. In some cases, this might get tricky and could take some time. For this app, we've calculated places for you to put your objects in an iPhone 8 screen. Later, we'll explain how to make your app work with other devices. Table 9-1 lists the sizes and positions that you should give to each label.

Table 9-1: Settings for Input Labels in the View Controller

Display text	X-position	Y-position	Width	Height
First Name	20	100	100	21
Last Name	20	170	100	21
Birthdate	20	250	100	21

You can see that all of the labels have the same x-position so that they line up vertically, but they each have a different y-position. Each label has a height of 21, so the y-positions need to be at least 21 points greater than the next closest label. Since we're adding our input controls underneath each label, too, we've made the y-positions larger to accommodate both the height of the label and the height of the input controls.

Great! Now your storyboard should look like the one in Figure 9-16.

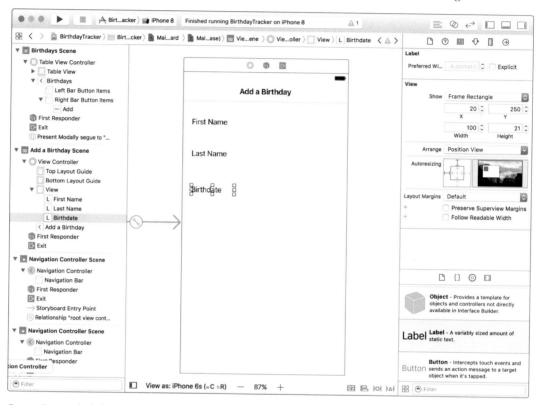

Figure 9-16: Labels for inputs have been added to the view controller.

Next you'll add two *text fields*, which will let you enter first and last names. A text field is a UI element of the UITextField class, which is used to display an editable text area on your screen. When the user taps in a text field, the keyboard will automatically come up, and they will be able to enter a line of text into the field.

Adding Text Fields

Drag two text field objects from the Object Library onto your view controller. One will be used to enter first names, and the other will be used to enter last names. Give the two text fields the sizes and positions seen in Table 9-2. You do this using the Size Inspector, just as you did for the labels.

Table 9-2: Text Fields for Inputs in the View Controller

Text field	X-position	Y-position	Width	Height
First Name	20	130	335	30
Last Name	20	200	335	30

The last thing you need to add is a wheel called a *date picker*. This will let you easily input birthdates.

Adding the Date Picker

The date picker is the standard tool used in iOS apps to allow a user to select a date or a time. It can contain both a date and a time, like the date picker used in the Calendar app (see Figure 9-17).

The date picker can also show just the time, like the date picker used for adding an alarm in the Clock app, or just the date, which is what we will use in BirthdayTracker.

Scroll through the Object Library until you find a date picker and then click and drag it onto the view controller under the Birthdate label. Using the Size Inspector, make the x-position **0** and the y-position **280**.

Figure 9-17: The date picker is used for date selection when adding an event in the Calendar app.

You'll want to tweak a couple of the date picker's properties. Click the date picker to select it. Then, in the Attributes Inspector, set the Mode of the date picker to display **Date** instead of Date and Time (see Figure 9-18).

The date picker is set to display the current date by default. Let's change this date to be your birthdate instead! Change the Date field from Current Date to **Custom**. When you do this, a new box will appear. Change this date to your birthdate.

Figure 9-18: Change the date picker's settings.

Let's test how the app works so far by running it! The sizes that we have used for our input controls fit well on an iPhone 8 screen. So select the iPhone 8 simulator and hit the play button in the top-left corner. This time, when you hit the + button on the Birthdays view controller, the Add a Birthday screen should display, as shown in Figure 9-19.

Figure 9-19: The text fields and date picker fit perfectly on the iPhone 8 screen.

This looks great on the iPhone 8, but what about other devices? Choose a smaller simulator to run the app on, like the iPhone 5s, and run the app again. You'll see that things don't look quite right.

All the elements that you added to the storyboard appear, but the text fields are running off the edge of the screen. Now that you have all of your elements on the screen, the next step is to make them fit correctly on any screen size. We'll do this with a tool called *auto layout*.

MAKING YOUR APP LOOK PERFECT ON EVERY DEVICE WITH AUTO LAYOUT

The iPhone alone comes in three different screen sizes, and it's possible that more sizes will be coming in the future. You'll want to design your apps so that they look good on any device. This means that you'll want your app to adjust the positions and sizes of everything in the app to suit the device that your app is running on. Auto layout uses something called *layout constraints* to place the elements on the screen. You'll need to add these constraints in the storyboard.

First, select **View Controller** in the outline view in the left panel. Next, take a look at the four icons in the bottom-right corner of the Editor pane (see Figure 9-20).

At the bottom of the screen's storyboard pane is a ribbon with icons, and the rightmost icon before the Utilities pane is a triangle between two vertical lines. Hover your mouse cursor over that icon, and it should show a label that says Resolve Auto Layout Issues. Click this icon to bring up a menu of suggestions. Click **Add Missing Constraints**.* When you do this, you'll see that a whole bunch of layout constraints were added to the Add a Birthday scene.

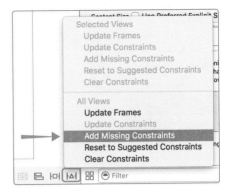

Figure 9-20: To add auto layout constraints, bring up the auto layout menu by clicking the fourth icon at the bottom of the Editor.

These auto layout constraints make sure that each element is sized correctly to fit onto the screen. For example, auto layout makes it so that the date picker is sized to fit the width of the screen and does not run off its edge. Auto layout will also make sure that there are 20 points before and after each text field so that they are centered nicely on the screen.

Now run the app again on the iPhone 5s simulator. This time, the Add a Birthday screen should look perfect.

ADDING SAVE AND CANCEL BUTTONS

To finish things up, we'll show you how to make Cancel and Save buttons for the Add a Birthday view controller's navigation bar. The buttons won't do anything just yet. We're just going to set them up. In Chapter 10, we'll add some code so that they cancel out of the Add a Birthday screen and save a birthday to the app.

To add the Save button, drag a Bar Button Item from the Object Library and place it on the *right* side of the navigation bar. We're going to change this button into a Save button, just like we did with the Add button. Select the button item, and then use the Attributes Inspector to turn it into a Save button.

Finally, let's add the Cancel button. Drag another Bar Button Item from the Object Library, and this time place it on the *left* side of the navigation bar. Use the Attributes Inspector to turn it into a Cancel button, just like you did with the Save button. Your view controller should look like the one shown in Figure 9-21.

---

* In some versions of Xcode, the Add Missing Constraints option is disabled. This is an Apple bug. In that case, choose the option **Reset to Missing Constraints** to add the missing constraints.

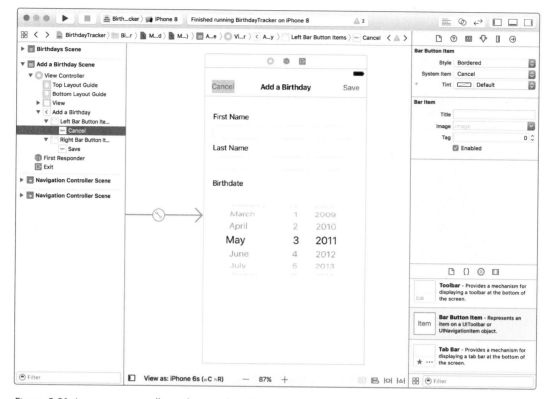

Figure 9-21: Input view controller with Cancel and Save buttons

Now run your app again to see the new buttons!

Tapping the + button on the Birthdays table view controller should bring you to the Add a Birthday view controller, where you can enter a person's name and birthdate. Tapping on the Cancel and Save buttons doesn't do anything just yet—we'll implement both of those in Chapter 10!

WHAT YOU LEARNED

In this chapter, you started making a BirthdayTracker app by creating the basic user interface for the Birthdays and Add a Birthday screens. You also created the Birthdays screen using a table view controller and made it so that users can navigate between screens using an Add button and a navigation controller.

Now that you have the basic skeleton of your app working, you'll spend Chapter 10 programming the Cancel and Save buttons so you can add and save birthdays in the app!

10

ADDING A BIRTHDAY CLASS AND HANDLING USER INPUT

In Chapter 9, you set up the visual interface for your app by creating view controllers, buttons to navigate between them, and the screen that takes user input. Now it's time to dig into the programming! In this chapter, we'll show you how to code your app and connect it to your storyboard. You'll write `Birthday` and `AddBirthdayViewController` classes so you can add birthdays using the input controls that you created in the previous chapter.

THE BIRTHDAY CLASS

In this section, you'll write a temporary Birthday class that will store your birthdays but won't permanently save the birthday data on the device. We'll replace it later with a better solution, but this approach will let us test our input controls.

> **NOTE** *Sometimes when you're programming, you'll need to write apps with many parts that will work together. You may write one part of the app first, like we did with the input controls, but to test that part, you might need some other code you haven't written yet. When that happens, you can quickly write some temporary test code that you'll rework after you've finished making the rest of your app work. That's what we're doing with the Birthday class—we'll replace it in Chapter 12.*

If you don't already have it open, open your BirthdayTracker app in Xcode. Make sure you can see the Project navigator (⌘-0).

CREATING A NEW FILE

First, you'll create a file where you'll write the Birthday class. A file in Xcode is just like any other computer file—it's a type of document. When you write an app in Swift, you'll write your classes and functions in Swift files. Just like how Word files have the extension *.doc* or *.docx* and PDF files end with *.pdf*, a Swift file has the extension *.swift* after its name.

If you want to add a new class to your application, create a new Swift file to write that class. You can write as many classes as you want in the same file, but it's easier to organize your project if you keep classes in separate files with filenames that match each class's name. CONTROL-click the *BirthdayTracker* folder in the Project navigator and choose the **New File...** option from the menu, as shown in Figure 10-1.

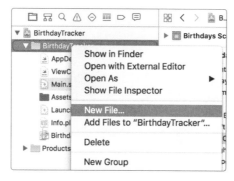

Figure 10-1: Creating a new file in Xcode

This brings up a dialog like the one in Figure 10-2. Here you're asked to select the kind of file you want to create, which is a generic, empty Swift file. Select **iOS** at the top of the dialog, select **Swift File**, and then click **Next**.

*Figure 10-2: Choose **Swift File** for the template.*

Finally, name the file *Birthday* and click **Create**. You should see *Birthday.swift* listed in the *BirthdayTracker* folder of the Project navigator. Click it and you should see an empty *Birthday.swift* file, as shown in Figure 10-3.

Figure 10-3: The Birthday.swift *file*

Notice that at the top of the file, Xcode has automatically written some copyright information in code comments. The name that comes after "Created by" is pulled from your Contact Card in your computer's Contacts application. After the copyright year, you should see the Organization Name that you used in Chapter 1 when you created your first Xcode project. Every time you create a new file in Xcode, this commented header is automatically included.

Now that you have your *Birthday.swift* file, you can create the Birthday class to store your birthdays.

WRITING THE BIRTHDAY CLASS

Your Birthday class will have three constant properties: firstName, lastName, and birthdate. The properties firstName and lastName should be of type String, but birthdate will be a special class built into Swift called Date, which is specifically made to handle dates and times. We'll use the Date class's functionality to alert the user about birthdays. Enter the following into *Birthday.swift* under the import Foundation statement.

Birthday.swift

```
class Birthday {

    let firstName: String
    let lastName: String
❶   let birthdate: Date

❷   init(firstName: String, lastName: String, birthdate: Date) {

❸       self.firstName = firstName
        self.lastName = lastName
        self.birthdate = birthdate
    }
}
```

You can see the new Date data type at ❶. A Date is declared just like any other variable.

At ❷, you add an initializer to the Birthday class that takes a firstName, lastName, and birthdate as input parameters. Then, using the self property, you set them to the class properties ❸. This will let you pass names and dates to the Birthday class to store a birthday.

NOTE   *We'll be building each code file for the projects step-by-step. The final versions are available from* https://www.nostarch.com/iphoneappsforkids/.

PROGRAMMING USER INPUT

At this point, you have a Birthday class that can hold a friend's name and birthdate, and you have input fields in the storyboard that you set up in Chapter 9. But the Birthday class and the input fields aren't connected, so the user's input isn't stored as a Birthday. It's time to write code to make the interface add birthdays. To do that, you'll create a new AddBirthdayViewController class to manage the input fields in the Add a Birthday Scene in the storyboard. (Remember that a view is controlled by a view controller, which is what you'll make next.)

CREATING THE ADD BIRTHDAY VIEW CONTROLLER

When you make an app and start with a Single View App template, Xcode automatically creates a file called *ViewController.swift*, which contains a ViewController class that represents and controls a view with code. The view controller in the storyboard is managed with this ViewController class, which we'll rename AddBirthdayViewController so that the class's name describes what it will be doing.

To change the name of the file *ViewController.swift*, select it and click inside its name in the Project navigator so that it's highlighted (see Figure 10-4). Then type the new filename, *AddBirthdayViewController*.

Next, you need to change the name of the ViewController class to AddBirthdayViewController. You do this inside the file by changing the line:

Figure 10-4: Changing the file-name of ViewController.swift

```
class ViewController: UIViewController
```

to the line:

```
class AddBirthdayViewController: UIViewController
```

You won't need the built-in method didReceiveMemoryWarning(), so you can clean up your code by deleting that method. Now your class should look like this:

AddBirthdayViewController.swift

```
class AddBirthdayViewController: UIViewController {

    override func viewDidLoad() {
        super.viewDidLoad()
        // Do any additional setup after loading the view,
        // typically from a nib
    }
}
```

UIViewController is a class that comes with built-in methods for managing views that appear onscreen when you run your app. AddBirthdayViewController is a *subclass* of UIViewController, which lets us control the view controller in the storyboard by implementing our own versions of some of UIViewController's built-in methods.

The UIViewController class has four useful built-in callback methods that will be called when the view controller is created and appears on or disappears from the screen. These callback methods are:

viewDidLoad() This method is called as soon as the view controller has been created but before its view appears on the screen. This is a great place to do any initial setup of the view that you want to do only once.

viewWillAppear(_:) This method is called after `viewDidLoad()` and before each time the view controller's view appears on the screen.

viewDidAppear(_:) This method is similar to `viewWillAppear(_:)` except it is called after a view controller's view appears on the screen.

viewWillDisappear(_:) This method is called when the view controller's view is about to leave the screen.

You can override any of these methods in your subclass `UIViewController`. The first of these, `viewDidLoad()`, is very useful. Swift expects anyone who subclasses `UIViewController` to use this method, so it automatically adds a placeholder to the template for `viewDidLoad()` when you subclass `UIViewController`.

Swift doesn't give you placeholder code for the other three methods. If you decide to use one, you can start typing it and autocomplete will fill in the details.

It's important to note that although `viewDidLoad()` is called only one time—when the view controller is first created—`viewWillAppear(_:)` is called every time the view controller's view is about to appear onscreen. So, if another screen is put on top of a view controller's screen and then removed so that the view controller's screen reappears, `viewWillAppear(_:)` will be called again but `viewDidLoad()` will not, because the view controller was already sitting there loaded behind another screen. If you want the view to be refreshed with new information every time it appears, you can override `viewWillAppear(_:)`.

In Chapter 12, we'll be using the `viewWillAppear(_:)` method to refresh our birthday list. Also, in "Setting a Maximum Birthdate" on page 149, we'll override `viewDidLoad()` in `AddBirthdayViewController`. For right now, however, we can leave these methods alone and connect our code to the inputs we set up in Chapter 9.

CONNECTING CODE TO THE INPUT CONTROLS

In the storyboard, our Add a Birthday view controller has a First Name text field, a Last Name text field, and a Birthdate date picker. To use these input controls, we need to refer to them in the code, which we do by assigning variables to the input controls that are connected to the screen elements with IBOutlets. Add the following three properties to the top of the `AddBirthdayViewController` class before the `viewDidLoad()` method (the gray lines indicate some of the existing code, for placement):

AddBirthdayViewController.swift

```
class AddBirthdayViewController: UIViewController {

❶ @IBOutlet var firstNameTextField: ❷UITextField!
   @IBOutlet var lastNameTextField: UITextField!
   @IBOutlet var birthdatePicker: UIDatePicker!

   override func viewDidLoad() {
```

`@IBOutlet` ❶ is a special keyword that is put in front of properties that can be hooked up in the storyboard. IB stands for *interface builder*, which is the part of Xcode where we work on our storyboard. When you put the keyword `@IBOutlet` in front of a property, a little circle appears in the margin next to it, as shown in Figure 10-5. This indicates that you can connect the property to an element in the storyboard. When the circle isn't filled in, it means the property hasn't been connected yet.

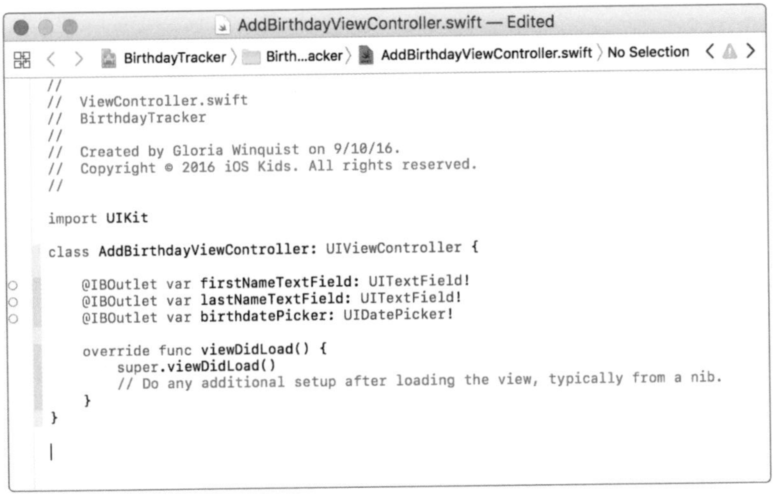

```
● ● ●                    AddBirthdayViewController.swift — Edited

⊞ < >   BirthdayTracker ⟩  Birth...acker ⟩  AddBirthdayViewController.swift ⟩ No Selection  < ⚠ >

    //
    //  ViewController.swift
    //  BirthdayTracker
    //
    //  Created by Gloria Winquist on 9/10/16.
    //  Copyright © 2016 iOS Kids. All rights reserved.
    //

    import UIKit

    class AddBirthdayViewController: UIViewController {

        @IBOutlet var firstNameTextField: UITextField!
        @IBOutlet var lastNameTextField: UITextField!
        @IBOutlet var birthdatePicker: UIDatePicker!

        override func viewDidLoad() {
            super.viewDidLoad()
            // Do any additional setup after loading the view, typically from a nib.
        }
    }
```

Figure 10-5: `AddBirthdayViewController` with IBOutlet properties for the input controls

The data type of the `firstNameTextField` property, `UITextField!` ❷, is an implicitly unwrapped optional because when the view controller is first created, IBOutlets have `nil` values. As soon as the view is loaded, however, IBOutlets are given the value of what they are connected to in the storyboard.

CONNECTING YOUR CODE TO THE STORYBOARD

Now that you've created `AddBirthdayViewController` and the properties for the input controls, it's time to hook up the First Name and Last Name text fields and the Birthdate date picker.

First, change the class of the Add a Birthday view controller in the storyboard to `AddBirthdayViewController` so you can use that class to manage the view controller. Select *Main.Storyboard* in the Project navigator. Next, select **Add a Birthday Scene** in the left outline view and open the Identity Inspector in the right pane. You should see a Custom Class section at the top. Change the class to **AddBirthdayViewController**, as shown in Figure 10-6.

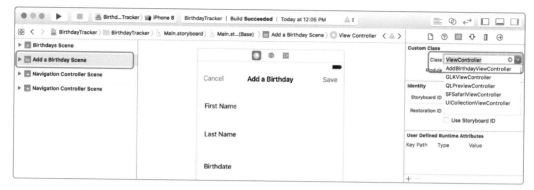

Figure 10-6: Change the class of the view controller to **AddBirthdayViewController**.

Now connect the AddBirthdayViewController's IBOutlet properties to the text fields and date picker in Add a Birthday Scene. Click the triangle next to Add a Birthday Scene in the left outline view to expand the menu of items in that scene. Then, CONTROL-click **Add a Birthday** next to the yellow view controller icon to open a connection dialog.

In the connection dialog, under Outlets, you can see the birthdatePicker, firstNameTextField, and lastNameTextField. Connect the birthdatePicker by clicking the empty circle next to it and dragging to the date picker in the storyboard. When the date picker object is highlighted in blue, you can let go (see Figure 10-7).

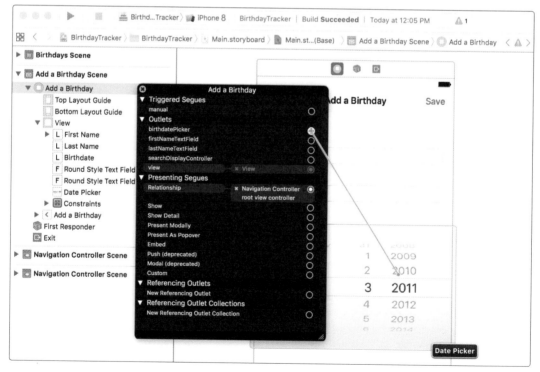

Figure 10-7: Connecting the date picker to the birthdatePicker outlet

You'll know that the connection was successful if you see Birthdate Picker listed next to `birthdatePicker` in the connection box with the connection circle filled (see Figure 10-8). You can only connect the `birthdatePicker` outlet to a date picker. If you try to connect it to a label or another type of view, nothing will happen. Xcode knows that the `birthdatePicker` has to be connected to a `UIDatePicker` class because that's the data type we gave it in `AddBirthdayViewController` when we created the property.

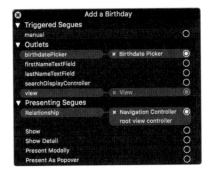

Figure 10-8: The birthdatePicker outlet has been successfully connected.

Next, connect the `firstNameTextField` by clicking and dragging from its circle to the text field underneath the First Name label. Finally, connect the `lastNameTextField` to the text field underneath the Last Name label.

You're done with the storyboard for the time being. Let's go back to *AddBirthdayViewController.swift* to set a maximum birthdate in code.

SETTING A MAXIMUM BIRTHDATE

It wouldn't make sense for a person to have a birthdate in the future, so let's write some code to prevent `birthdatePicker` from selecting future dates. We can do this kind of setup by modifying the `viewDidLoad()` method in the `AddBirthdayViewController`. We talked about the `viewDidLoad()` method in "Creating the Add Birthday View Controller" on page 145. It's automatically added to our view controllers, so find this method in the `AddBirthdayViewController` and add the following line of code to it:

AddBirthdayViewController.swift

```
override func viewDidLoad() {
    super.viewDidLoad()

❶   birthdatePicker.maximumDate = Date()
}
```

`viewDidLoad()` is already a method of the `UIViewController` class, so we need to override it using the `override` keyword, like so: `override func viewDidLoad()`. Note that it's important to leave the line `super.viewDidLoad()` in the method. When you create a subclass, like `AddBirthdayViewController`, and override a method from the original superclass, you want to make sure that you also call the method on the superclass. Apple could have some special code that runs in the `UIViewController` `viewDidLoad()` that we don't know about, so not calling this superclass method could lead to unexpected errors.

To set the `maximumDate` of the `birthdatePicker`, all you have to do is enter `birthdatePicker.maximumDate = Date()` at ❶. The `Date()` method creates a new date that is the current date and time. Try running the app now. It should be impossible to select any date in the future!

Next, you'll write some code so that you can save a `Birthday` and cancel adding a `Birthday` from this view controller using the buttons you made in Chapter 9.

SAVING A BIRTHDAY

Now to implement the Save button! When the user taps Save, the app should create a `Birthday` from the information that was entered and then save the user input.

HOOKING UP THE SAVE BUTTON

Let's start by making a `saveTapped(_:)` method that is called every time the user taps the Save button. Add the following code to `AddBirthdayViewController` right after the `viewDidLoad()` method:

AddBirthdayViewController.swift

```
override func viewDidLoad() {
    --snip--
}

❶ @IBAction func saveTapped(❷_ sender: ❸UIBarButtonItem) {
    ❹ print("The save button was tapped.")
}
```

`@IBAction` at ❶ is a keyword that connects a function directly to an element in a view controller and allows us to specify code that should run when the user takes an action on that element. In this case, we're going to add a function that will run when the user taps Save. When you write an IBAction method, you should always include a parameter for the UI element that triggered the method. Typically, an underscore is used to hide the argument label and the parameter name is sender ❷, but you can call this parameter whatever you want. In this case, we want the `saveTapped(_:)` method to be called whenever the user taps Save, which is a `UIBarButtonItem`. So we specify that the type of sender is `UIBarButtonItem` ❸. The `print(_:)` method at ❹ helps us see when the Save button has been tapped as we're testing the code.

Hooking up `saveTapped(_:)` to the Save button is like hooking up an IBOutlet to a storyboard element. Go back to your *Main.storyboard* file. CONTROL-click the Add a Birthday line to open a connection dialog. At the bottom of the connection dialog is a section called Received Actions, as shown in Figure 10-9. In that section, click and drag from the circle next to saveTapped: to the Save button in the Add a Birthday view controller to connect them.

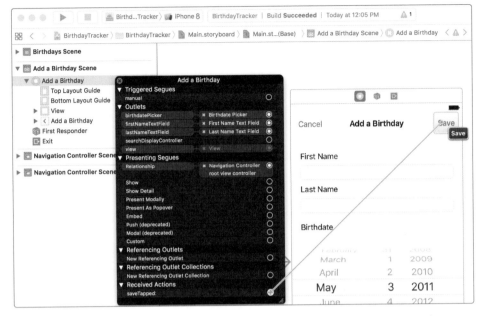

Figure 10-9: IBActions are listed at the bottom of the connection dialog under Received Actions.

Try running your app again. When you tap the Save button, the message "The save button was tapped." should be displayed in your debug console.

READING TEXT FROM A TEXT FIELD

Let's add code to the saveTapped(_:) method that will get the first and last names out of firstNameTextField and lastNameTextField after the user enters them.

The UITextField class has an optional String property called text. This text property has a value of whatever has been typed into the text field, so you can use it to get the user's input in saveTapped(_:) with the following code:

AddBirthdayViewController.swift

```
@IBAction func saveTapped(_ sender: UIBarButtonItem) {
    print("The save button was tapped.")

❶  let firstName = firstNameTextField.text ?? ""
❷  let lastName = lastNameTextField.text ?? ""
    print("My name is \(firstName) \(lastName).")
}
```

At ❶, you create a constant firstName and set its value to firstNameTextField .text if it exists (that is, if the user entered a value) or to the empty string "". You can do this using the nil coalescing operator (??) that you learned about in Chapter 5. We're using constants and not variables here because we won't change the value of the first and last names the user enters.

Then do the same thing with `lastName` at ❷. After you retrieve values for `firstName` and `lastName`, print them to the console so you can see them when you run your app.

Run your app to see what happens. Try tapping the Save button without entering anything in the text fields and then try again after entering a first and last name. You should see output similar to this:

```
The save button was tapped.
My name is  .
The save button was tapped.
My name is Dagmar Hedlund.
```

Cool! Now you can put a name into your app and see the computer output it in your debug console. Let's focus on getting a date output next.

GETTING A DATE FROM A DATE PICKER

Getting a date from the `birthdatePicker` is just as easy as getting the text out of `firstNameTextField` or `lastNameTextField`. The `UIDatePicker` class has a date property, which is the date currently being displayed by the picker. For the `birthdatePicker`, this is `birthdatePicker.date`. When a user changes the `UIDatePicker`, the date property also changes, so you can use `birthdayPicker.date` to access a birthday the user inputs.

Add the following lines to your `saveTapped(_:)` method:

AddBirthdayViewController.swift

```
@IBAction func saveTapped( _ sender: UIBarButtonItem) {
    --snip--
    print("My name is \(firstName) \(lastName).")
    let birthdate = birthdatePicker.date
    print("My birthday is \(birthdate).")
}
```

Run the app now and see what happens. You should see something similar to the following output:

```
The save button was tapped.
My name is Dagmar Hedlund.
My birthday is 2011-05-03 04:00:00 +0000
```

At this point, we have a `firstName`, a `lastName`, and a `birthdate`—the three pieces of data that we need to create a `Birthday`! You'll notice that the date displayed in the debug console is in a strange format, which also includes a time and +0000 for a time zone offset. Don't worry too much about this for now. We'll discuss date formats and how to display a date without a time in Chapter 11.

CREATING A BIRTHDAY

Now that your code can access the firstName, lastName, and birthdate input that the user provided, you can use this information to create a Birthday using the Birthday class initializer.

First, delete the print statements from the saveTapped(_:) method since we'll replace them with print statements that test out the newBirthday instance instead. Then add the following lines to the saveTapped(_:) method.

AddBirthdayViewController.swift

```
@IBAction func saveTapped(_ sender: UIBarButtonItem) {
    --snip--
    let birthdate = birthdatePicker.date
❶  let newBirthday = Birthday(firstName: firstName, lastName: ↵
        lastName, birthdate: birthdate)

    print("Created a Birthday!")
❷  print("First name: \(newBirthday.firstName)")
    print("Last name: \(newBirthday.lastName)")
    print("Birthdate: \(newBirthday.birthdate)")
}
```

At ❶, you create a newBirthday instance using the Birthday class initializer and pass in constants for firstName, lastName, and birthdate. After you create newBirthday, at ❷, you output its properties into the debug console using dot notation. The printed output will be the same as with the earlier print statements, but this time you're getting the values from the newBirthday instance. Run the app, enter a birthday, and tap Save to see what happens. You should see output in your debug console similar to the following:

```
Created a Birthday!
First name: Dagmar
Last name: Hedlund
Birthdate: 2011-05-03 04:00:00 +0000
```

For now, tapping the Save button only creates a Birthday. You'll learn how to display this Birthday in the Birthdays view controller in Chapter 11.

ADDING THE CANCEL BUTTON

When the user taps Cancel, it means they no longer want to add a Birthday, and the Add a Birthday screen should go away. Let's implement this behavior by adding a cancelTapped(_:) method to our class, which will call a built-in UIViewController method called dismiss(animated:completion:). This method does just what it says it does—it dismisses the currently displayed view controller. Add the following method right after the `saveTapped(_:)` method in your `AddBirthdayViewController` class:

AddBirthdayViewController.swift

```
@IBAction func saveTapped(_ sender: UIBarButtonItem) {
    --snip--
        print("Birthdate: \(newBirthday.birthdate)")
}

@IBAction func cancelTapped(_ sender: UIBarButtonItem) {
  ❶ dismiss(animated: true, completion: nil)
}
```

The function `dismiss(animated:completion:)` ❶ takes two parameters. The `animated` parameter is used to animate the closing screen. Pass in true so users can see the Add a Birthday screen slide down off the screen. It'll look just like a professional app! The second parameter is an optional closure called `completion`. A *closure* is a block of code that can be passed in to the function. The `completion` closure can be used if there is any code that you want to run after the view controller is dismissed. Because you don't need anything to happen here, you can just pass in `nil`.

The final step is to hook up `cancelTapped(_:)` to the Cancel button. You do this exactly the same way that you hooked up the `saveTapped(_:)` method to the Save button. Go to *Main.storyboard* and bring up the connections dialog for the Add Birthday view controller. Click and drag from the `cancelTapped(_:)` method listing to the Cancel button.

After you've done that, run the app, tap + to get to the Add a Birthday screen, and tap **Cancel**. You should see Add a Birthday slide down the screen and disappear.

WHAT YOU LEARNED

In this chapter, you learned how to hook up written code to your app's visual interface. You also learned how to use the input text fields and date picker to create a `Birthday` object with `firstName`, `lastName`, and `birthdate` properties. Right now you can save `Birthdays`, but you can't see them after you saved them. In Chapter 11, we'll show you how to display a list of your birthdays in a Birthdays table view controller.

11

DISPLAYING BIRTHDAYS

Time to show off those birthdays! In Chapter 10, you created the Add Birthday view controller so that you could add new `Birthday` objects into your app with the `Birthday` class. In this chapter, you'll create a Birthdays table view controller that can display your added birthdays in a *table view*, which shows a list of items the user can scroll through and select. Then you'll learn how to make the Add Birthday view controller tell the Birthdays table view controller when a `Birthday` object is added so that the new birthday can be shown in the table view.

MAKING THE BIRTHDAY LIST

It's one thing to be able to add birthdays, but you'll also want to display a list of birthdays. For that you need to create another class, `BirthdaysTableViewController`, which will subclass `UITableViewController`, a special kind of view controller with a table view. `UITableViewController` contains several built-in methods that allow you to code things like how many rows the table view should have and what should be displayed in each row. We'll want to have as many rows as we have birthdays and to display one birthday in each row.

CREATING THE BIRTHDAYS TABLE VIEW CONTROLLER

CONTROL-click the *BirthdayTracker* folder in the Project navigator and choose **New File...** from the menu. In Chapter 10, we created the Swift file *Birthday.swift*, which Xcode prepared for us with nearly nothing in it. To create a new file this time, we'll tell Xcode we want to subclass an existing iOS class. Depending on the base class, Xcode will create a file containing some code that you'll customize to your needs. To create the file, select **iOS** at the top of the window and then select the **Cocoa Touch Class** template, which will automatically format the new class file (see Figure 11-1).

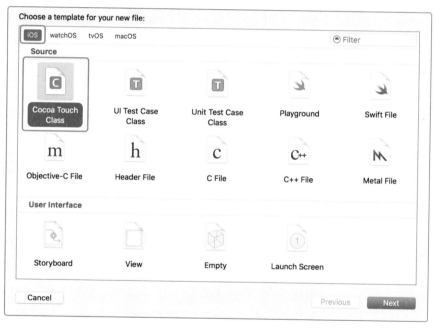

Figure 11-1: To subclass an existing class, choose **iOS** *and then* **Cocoa Touch Class**.

When you choose this option, you'll see a second dialog where you can name your new class and specify which class you'll subclass. First, in the Subclass field (the second field in the dialog), type `UITableViewController`. This will automatically fill in the class field with the subclass name. Once that happens, type `Birthdays` in front of `TableViewController` so that the whole class name is `BirthdaysTableViewController`. This is a shortcut so you don't have to type as much. Make sure to choose **Swift** in the Language drop-down menu as well, and then click **Next**. Then select **Create** in the final dialog to create your new file.

In *BirthdaysTableViewController.swift*, Xcode has provided a template with several commented-out methods. You can clean up the code by getting rid of methods we won't use. Delete just the comments in viewDidLoad(), and then delete the entire didReceiveMemoryWarning() method and the methods tableView(_:moveRowAt:to:) and tableView(_:canMoveRowAt:), which have to do with moving rows in the table view. When you're finished, the contents of BirthdaysTableViewController should look like Figure 11-2. There are still several commented-out methods, but we're keeping those to use later!

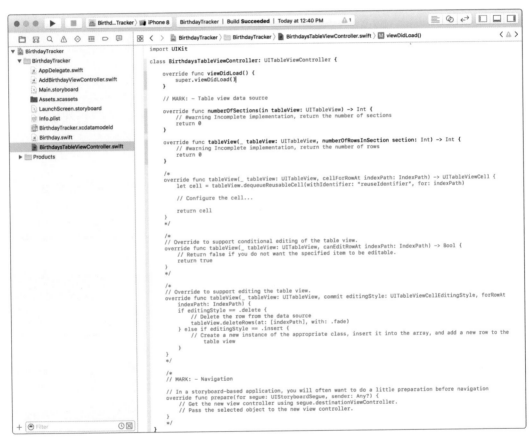

Figure 11-2: The BirthdaysTableViewController cleaned up!

Next, you need to make the Birthdays table view controller the BirthdaysTableViewController class. To do this, go to *Main.storyboard* and select the **Birthdays** scene. Using the Identity Inspector in the right pane, change the class from UITableViewController to BirthdaysTableViewController, as shown in Figure 11-3.

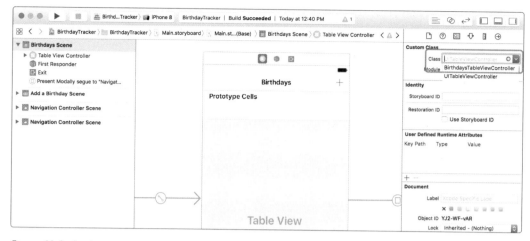

Figure 11-3: Setting `BirthdaysTableViewController` as the class of the Birthdays scene

Now that you have the Birthdays table view controller set up in the storyboard, the next step is to make cells in your table that will display each birthday.

ADDING CELLS TO THE TABLE VIEW

Each birthday will be displayed in a `UITableViewCell` in the Birthdays table view controller. A table has boxes organized into rows and columns that contain information. These boxes are called *cells*. Similarly, a table view also has cells that are all instances of, or a subclass of, the `UITableViewCell` class. We'll put each birthday into its own cell in our table view.

We'll start by creating those cells in the story-board, and then we'll fill them with our `Birthday` objects later. In the left outline menu, click the triangle by Birthdays and then click the triangle by Table View to open those sections. Then select **Table View Cell ❶**, as shown in Figure 11-4.

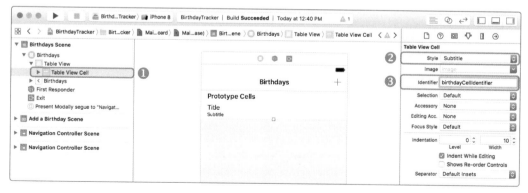

Figure 11-4: Creating a Subtitle style table view cell and setting its identifier

Next, open the Attributes Inspector. Using the drop-down menu under **Style**, set the cell's style to **Subtitle** ❷ so that the cell now has a Title label and a Subtitle label. You'll display each person's name in the Title and birthday in the Subtitle.

Finally, enter `birthdayCellIdentifier` in the Identifier field ❸. You'll use this identifier later when you fill in the cell contents.

That's it! You've finished your work in the storyboard.

You may be wondering why we have just one cell in our table view in the storyboard when we'll have more than one birthday to show in the list. If you look at Figure 11-4 again, you'll notice that the cell is labeled *Prototype Cells*. This means that the cell you just customized is a *template* for all the cells you want to appear in your table view. The identifier you gave the cell is how your code will tell the table view to produce each cell for you to put birthdays in. You'll see how this works soon.

WORKING WITH DATES

Swift has a special data type called Date that is used for storing date values. A Date object is actually a date and a time. Open your playground and enter the following:

`let today = Date()` `print(today)`	`"Nov 21, 2017, 6:45 AM"` `"2017-11-21 10:45:31 +0000"`

We've just assigned the current date and time the code was run to the variable today. When you print today, it's in the format `"2017-11-21 10:45:31 +0000\n"`. What if you wanted it to display as Tuesday, November 21, 2017, instead? Or just 11/21/17? To display a date in a particular way, you use a *date formatter*, which is a DateFormatter object that you create and give a date format style. DateFormatter is a helper object that is used to create a display string from any date, and a *date format style* is a property of DateFormatter that tells the formatter what style to use. You can create your own date format styles manually, but there are also styles that are included in Swift and ready to use. Add the following to your playground:

❶ `let formatter = DateFormatter()` ❷ `formatter.dateStyle = ↵` `    DateFormatter.Style.full` ❸ `formatter.string(from: today)`	`"Tuesday, November 21, 2017"`

At ❶ you create a formatter. Then at ❷, you set the style of the formatter to Style.full, which will print the day of the week as well as the full month name, date, and year. Finally, you create a string from the date using the string(from:) method of the DateFormatter class ❸. You can see that you now have turned the

(continued)

date into the nicely formatted string "Tuesday, November 21, 2017". Table 11-1 shows the different strings that are created from the five `DateFormatter.Style` options available in Swift.

Table 11-1: Date Formatter Styles and Their Date Strings

DateFormatter.Style	Date string
none	""
short	"11/21/17"
medium	"Nov 21, 2017"
long	"November 21, 2017"
full	"Tuesday, November 21, 2017"

You can also specify your own custom way of displaying a date using the `dateFormat` property of the `DateFormatter`. Perhaps you only want the month and day. Or maybe you want a four-digit year displayed in the short style. Doing either is really easy, and you don't even have to create a new `DateFormatter`—you can just change the `dateFormat` on `formatter` and then ask it for a new string. Add the following code to your playground to display dates with a specific format:

```
❶ dateFormatter.dateFormat = "MM/dd"
   dateFormatter.string(from: today)          "11/21"

❷ dateFormatter.dateFormat = "MM/dd/yyyy"
   dateFormatter.string(from: today)          "11/21/2017"
```

At ❶, you specify that you only want the month and the date in an `MM/dd` format—that is, a two-digit month followed by a two-digit date. If you want to display the month as three letters, then use `MMM`. To display the full name of the month, use `MMMM`. At ❷, we change the date format to use a four-digit year. A two-digit year would be `yy`. Here are a few other ways to use a `dateFormat` to display a custom date string.

```
❶ formatter.dateFormat = "MM.dd.yy"
   formatter.string(from: today)              "11.21.17"

   formatter.dateFormat = "dd-MMM-yyyy"
   formatter.string(from: today)              "21-Nov-2017"

❷ formatter.dateFormat = "EEE MMM dd"
   formatter.string(from: today)              "Tue Nov 21"

❸ formatter.dateFormat = ↵
       "EEEE -*- MMMM dd -*- yyyy"
   formatter.string(from: today)              "Tuesday -*- November 21 ↵
                                                 -*- 2017"
```

If you want to include separators, you add them to your dateFormat string. For example, if you want periods as separators, then you can create a dateFormat like "MM.dd.yy" ❶. To display an abbreviated day of the week, use EEE ❷. For the full day, use EEEE ❸. These are only a few examples. By using combinations of M, d, y, and E, you have an endless number of ways to display a date!

SETTING UP THE BIRTHDAYS TABLE VIEW CONTROLLER

The Birthdays table view controller will display a list of all the birthdays stored in the app. Do you remember what you use to store a list of items? That's right—an array! You'll create an array in the BirthdaysTableViewController to store all the birthdays. To do this, give the BirthdaysTableViewController a birthdays property that is an array of Birthday objects. At the top of the class, right above the viewDidLoad() method, insert this line to add a variable array property called birthdays:

BirthdaysTableViewController.swift

```
class BirthdaysTableViewController: UITableViewController {

    var birthdays = [Birthday]()

    override func viewDidLoad() {
```

This line creates an empty array of Birthday instances. It needs to be a variable and not a constant because you'll want to add a saved Birthday to this array every time the user adds a Birthday with the Add Birthday view controller. You'll see how to do that in "Making the Birthdays Table View Controller Conform to Protocol" on page 168.

NOTE   *Remember that the final versions of the project files are available from* https://www .nostarch.com/iphoneappsforkids/.

The BirthdaysTableViewController will also need a dateFormatter property to display the birthdate as a nicely formatted string. Add a dateFormatter right underneath the birthdays array:

```
    var birthdays = [Birthday]()

    let dateFormatter = DateFormatter()

    override func viewDidLoad() {
```

Note that the dateFormatter is a constant that is created with let. Even though you'll change the dateFormatter's properties, like the dateStyle and timeStyle, you'll never change the dateFormatter itself.

You'll also need to set up the `dateFormatter` so that it will display the birthdates as fully formatted strings like `"Tuesday, December 17, 2008"`. As you saw in Chapter 10, a good place to do this is the `viewDidLoad()` method, which is called when the Birthdays table view controller is loading its view. This is the perfect place to do any setup that is needed for this class.

```
override func viewDidLoad() {
    super.viewDidLoad()

❶  dateFormatter.dateStyle = .full
❷  dateFormatter.timeStyle = .none
}
```

At ❶, you set the `dateStyle` of the `dateFormatter` so that it will display a formatted date string for each `Birthday`. Did you notice how we just wrote `.full` instead of `DateFormatter.Style.full`? Swift knows what type to expect for the `dateStyle` of a `DateFormatter`, so it lets us take this little shortcut. At ❷, you set the `timeStyle` of the `dateFormatter` to `.none` so that the time won't be shown.

DISPLAYING BIRTHDAYS IN A TABLE VIEW

The `BirthdaysTableViewController` class has a table view that is used to display a list of items in a single column. The table view has one or more sections containing rows, and each row contains a cell. A section in a table view is a grouping of rows that can be displayed with or without a header. An example of an app that shows a table view with several sections is the Settings app, as shown in Figure 11-5. It displays a list of rows that have been broken up into different sections.

Each section and row of a table view is identified with an index number. These numbers start at 0 and then increase by 1 as you go down the table view. For example, the Privacy line in the Settings app is found at section 0, row 1. The News setting is at section 1, row 3.

In the middle of the `BirthdaysTableViewController` class, there is a section called *Table view data source* with three methods. The table view controller uses these methods to determine what's going to be displayed inside its table view.

`numberOfSections(in:)`   Tells the table view how many sections it should have

`tableView(_:numberOfRowsInSection:)`   Tells the table view how many rows will be displayed in each section

`tableView(_:cellForRowAt:)`   Sets up each cell that's going to be displayed in each row of the table view

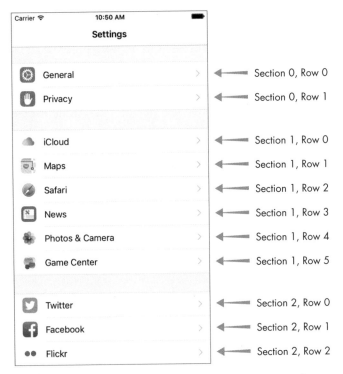

Carrier 🛜　10:50 AM　▬

Settings

⚙️ General	>	⟵ Section 0, Row 0
✋ Privacy	>	⟵ Section 0, Row 1
☁️ iCloud	>	⟵ Section 1, Row 0
🗺️ Maps	>	⟵ Section 1, Row 1
🧭 Safari	>	⟵ Section 1, Row 2
📰 News	>	⟵ Section 1, Row 3
🌸 Photos & Camera	>	⟵ Section 1, Row 4
🎮 Game Center	>	⟵ Section 1, Row 5
🐦 Twitter	>	⟵ Section 2, Row 0
Ⓕ Facebook	>	⟵ Section 2, Row 1
•• Flickr	>	⟵ Section 2, Row 2

Figure 11-5: The Settings app uses sections to group rows of different device settings.

The table view data source methods are called by the table view controller every time the table view is reloaded. Xcode automatically gives you these method templates when you make a subclass of a UITableViewController. You need to implement all three methods for the app to work, even though you'll never call them directly in your code. The UITableViewController class implements the UITableViewDataSource protocol, which comes with these data source methods, to determine what will be displayed inside the table view. We'll discuss protocols in "Delegation" on page 166. For now, you just need to know that a UITableViewController uses these methods to display its content, and it automatically calls these methods so you don't need to call them.

Let's start with the method numberOfSections(in:). The Birthdays table view controller is a list that just displays Birthday instances, so it doesn't need multiple sections. To set the number of sections in the table view, we just need to return 1.

BirthdaysTableViewController.swift

```
override func numberOfSections(in tableView: UITableView) -> Int {
    return 1
}
```

This method takes a `UITableView` called `tableView` as a parameter, which is the table view that uses this class as its data source. We don't need to worry about making this connection because the `UITableViewController` comes with a built-in table view that is automatically hooked up to these methods. Each birthday will be displayed in its own row. So in `tableView(_:numberOfRowsInSection:)`, in order to have the right number of rows for all of your birthdays, you need to return the number of `Birthday` instances that you have in your `birthdays` array. Do you remember the `count` property of an array? It's an integer that tells you how many items are in that array, and it's perfect for this situation! Change this method to the following:

```
override func tableView(_ tableView: UITableView, ↵
    numberOfRowsInSection section: Int) -> Int {
    return birthdays.count
}
```

In addition to the `tableView` parameter, `tableView(_:numberOfRowsInSection:)` also takes an `Int` called `section`. When the table view is loading itself, this method is called for each section in the table view. In our case, we have only one section, so we don't need to bother checking which section of the table view is being displayed here. We know it's section 0, and we want it to have as many rows as there are birthdays, so we write `return birthdays.count`.

Finally, you need to implement `tableView(_:cellForRowAt:)` so that the table view will know what to put inside each cell. Since this method is commented out, you need to uncomment it by deleting the `/*` and `*/` that surround it. (Be careful not to accidentally uncomment the other methods after it!) After you've done that, change it to the following code:

```
override func tableView(_ tableView: UITableView, cellForRowAt ↵
    indexPath: IndexPath) -> UITableViewCell {

❶  let cell = tableView.dequeueReusableCell(withIdentifier: ↵
        "birthdayCellIdentifier", for: indexPath)

❷  let birthday = birthdays[indexPath.row]

❸  cell.textLabel?.text = birthday.firstName + " " + ↵
        birthday.lastName

❹  cell.detailTextLabel?.text = dateFormatter.string(from: ↵
        birthday.birthdate)

❺  return cell
}
```

You don't call the method `tableView(_:cellForRowAt:)`. It's called when the table view is loaded onto the screen. It's called for each cell on the screen and takes two parameters, `tableView` and `indexPath`. You already know what the `tableView` parameter is for. An `IndexPath` is a Swift struct that's used to represent a row's position in a table view. An `IndexPath` instance has a `section` property and a `row` property. Since this method will be called many times (once for every row in the table), we need the `indexPath` to know which section and row we're currently configuring. The `indexPath.section` property gives the section number, and the `indexPath.row` gives the row of the table view cell. The five lines of code inside `tableView(_:cellForRowAt:)` will do the following:

- Create a `UITableViewCell`
- Figure out which `Birthday` in the `birthdays` array will be displayed inside the cell
- Make two labels to display the birthday person's name and birthdate in the cell
- Return the cell ready for display in the table view

Let's go through this code line by line.

First, create the `UITableViewCell`. The code at ❶ does this using the method `dequeueReusableCell(withIdentifier:for:)`. Before you can start using this method on a cell, though, you need to tell the method which cell you want to use from the storyboard. Earlier, when you were in the storyboard, you gave your cell the identifier `birthdayCellIdentifier` (see Figure 11-4). This identifier links your code to the cell and tells your method that it's using the right cell. The string for when you call this method needs to be exactly the same as the string you set in the storyboard, or you'll get an error and the app will crash when you run it.

In the method `dequeueReusableCell(withIdentifier:for:)`, did you notice the words *Reusable Cell?* The cells inside a table view are created once and then can be reused over and over. This helps everything run faster and smoother because creating the cell is what takes the most time. If you had 200 birthdays in your app, but only 10 would fit on your screen at one time, then you need only 10 cells to show your birthdays. When you scroll down to reveal more birthdays, the cells that scroll off the top of the screen are reused. They are filled with new information and show up again at the bottom of the screen. The `UITableView` automatically does this work. When the table view is loaded, `tableView(_:cellForRowAt:)` is called for every visible row. When the user scrolls to look at more cells, it's called again for each row just as it is about to appear on the screen.

Next, we need to find out which `Birthday` should be displayed inside the cell. We want to display one birthday from the `birthdays` array in each row. The first birthday, which is at `birthdays[0]`, should be displayed in row 0. The second birthday, at `birthdays[1]`, should be displayed in row 1, and so on, which means the `indexPath`'s `row` is the same as the position in the `birthdays` array that we want to access. The code at ❷ accesses the correct `Birthday` object from the birthdays array by using `indexPath.row`. Once we have the right `Birthday` object, we assign it to a constant named `birthday` so we can set up the labels in this cell.

Notice that we're using `let` to assign the `birthday` to a constant instead of a variable. We can use `let` because each time `tableView(_:cellForRowAt:)` is called, a new `birthday` constant is created. Each cell gets its own `birthday` constant that is assigned its own `Birthday` object. Since we're not going to change any of the `birthday` constants—we're just going to read their properties—we don't want to make them variables.

Now that you have your cell and your birthday, it's time to fill in the details. You need two labels for each cell to show the birthday person's name and birthdate. You set the cell to the Subtitle style so that it has a Title label and a Subtitle label. Each cell will already contain these labels, so now you don't have to create any labels yourself.

The labels exist as properties of `UITableViewCell` and are called `textLabel` and `detailTextLabel`. The code at ❸ sets the text of the `textLabel` to a string made up of the `firstName` and `lastName` of the birthday with a space between them. At ❹, you use the `string(from:)` method of the `dateFormatter` to display the birthdate in the `detailTextLabel`.

When your cell is completely configured, `tableView(_:cellForRowAt:)` returns the cell at ❺ so that it can be displayed at that `indexPath` of the table view.

PUTTING IT ALL TOGETHER

Now you can add `Birthday` instances to the app using the Add Birthday view controller, and you have a table view to list each `Birthday` in the Birthdays table view controller. But when you try running the app and adding a `Birthday`, it doesn't appear. To make each `Birthday` you add appear in the table view, you need to make the Add Birthday view controller communicate with the Birthdays table view controller. You do this by using *delegation*.

DELEGATION

Delegation can be used when one view controller needs to get information from another view controller. Say you have two view controllers: A and B. The first view controller, A, creates B and presents B on top of itself. A knows about B because it created and presented B, so A can pass information along to B. But B doesn't know about A—it's just popped into being and doesn't know where it came from or how it got there. So how can B talk to A? Through delegation!

Delegation is when someone gives a job or a task to someone else. A *delegate* is like a boss who tells a delegating employee what to do. When the delegating employee is done with their task, sometimes they'll report information back to the delegate boss.

Delegation in Swift is pretty similar, but instead of having a boss and employee, we have a delegate and a delegating object. Since class B is the one being told what to do by class A, it's the delegating object. We give class B a special property called a delegate to tell it who its delegate is—that way, it knows who to communicate with. The delegate can be any class that has a set of methods that have been defined in a *protocol*. A protocol is like an agreement between the two classes that tells them what the delegate can ask the delegating object to do. It has a list of method and property names that the delegate can use with the delegating object.

Class A creates class B, makes itself the delegate of class B, and gives class B a job to do that's in the protocol. Once class B is done with its job, it reports back to class A. Let's see how this works in our app.

The Birthdays table view controller is view controller A, and the Add Birthday view controller is view controller B. We'll create a protocol called `AddBirthdayViewControllerDelegate` and a method for that protocol, `addBirthdayViewController(_:didAddBirthday:)`, which the Add Birthday view controller will use to report back.

Take a look at Figure 11-6. When the user taps the Add button ❶, the Birthdays table view controller creates the Add Birthday view controller ❷ and sets itself as the Add Birthday view controller's delegate.

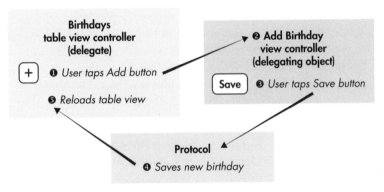

Figure 11-6: A new birthday is added and passed from the Add Birthday view controller to the Birthdays table view controller using delegation.

The `AddBirthdayViewControllerDelegate` protocol is defined to have one method, `addBirthdayViewController(_:didAddBirthday:)`. When the user taps Save ❸, the Add Birthday view controller calls this method ❹ and passes the new birthday to its delegate, the Birthdays table view controller. The Birthdays table view controller takes that birthday, adds it to its `birthdays` array, and then reloads its table view ❺ so that the new birthday will show up in the table.

We'll show you how to make an `AddBirthdayViewControllerDelegate` protocol with the method `addBirthdayViewController(_:didAddBirthday:)` that the Add Birthday view controller can call whenever a birthday is added to the app. The Birthdays table view controller will implement that protocol method so that whenever a birthday is added with the Add Birthday view controller, the Add Birthday view controller can just say to its delegate,

"Hey! Someone just added this birthday," and the Birthdays table view controller will hear the message and say, "Oh! I'll add that to my list and refresh my display so the new one shows up."

So now let's do this in code!

Creating a Protocol

First, we need to create the protocol. In the *AddBirthdayViewController.swift* file, *above* the `AddBirthdayViewController` class, add this code defining the `AddBirthdayViewControllerDelegate` protocol:

AddBirthdayViewController.swift

```
❶ protocol AddBirthdayViewControllerDelegate {

  ❷ func addBirthdayViewController(_ addBirthdayViewController: ↵
         AddBirthdayViewController, didAddBirthday birthday: ↵
         Birthday)

  }

  class AddBirthdayViewController: UIViewController {
      --snip--
```

You define the protocol at ❶ by typing the keyword `protocol` followed by the name `AddBirthdayViewControllerDelegate`. That's a long name, but Swift programmers usually name their protocols after the calling classes and add the word `Delegate` on the end. This is so you'll be able to tell which class is using the protocol by looking at the protocol's name. Since you're a Swift programmer now, you should use the same naming conventions.

In this protocol, `addBirthdayViewController(_:didAddBirthday:)` is the only function, and it's used to pass the `Birthday` object back to the delegate class ❷. Notice that you're including `AddBirthdayViewController` as a parameter in this function. Again, Swift programmers do this based on convention when they implement protocol methods, so you should stick to doing it, too. It's useful to know who sent back a message and for the delegate to have access to that object and its class.

When the Add Birthday view controller calls this method, it will pass itself in as the `addBirthdayViewController` parameter. You'll see how this is done very soon. The other thing to note is the external parameter name `didAddBirthday`. Many delegate protocol methods contain the words *did* and *will* because they're used to describe something that the calling class has either just done or will do.

Now that you have your protocol defined, you need to tell the Birthdays table view controller to adopt this protocol and use the protocol's method.

Making the Birthdays Table View Controller Conform to Protocol

To adopt the protocol, the Birthdays table view controller needs to make itself an `AddBirthdayViewControllerDelegate`. To allow for this, you need to add `AddBirthdayViewControllerDelegate` to the class definition right after the `UITableViewController` superclass. At the top of the class, add a comma after `UITableViewController` and then type **AddBirthdayViewControllerDelegate**:

BirthdaysTableViewController.swift

```
class BirthdaysTableViewController: UITableViewController, ↵
    AddBirthdayViewControllerDelegate {
```

As soon as you do that, a red error appears. This happens because `BirthdaysTableViewController` says it's an `AddBirthdayViewControllerDelegate`, but it hasn't implemented the protocol yet! In order to do that, it needs to implement the `AddBirthdayViewControllerDelegate` protocol definition. Not to worry—we'll fix this soon.

It's important to note here that the `BirthdaysTableViewController` is subclassing the `UITableViewController` superclass. A class can have only one superclass, and that superclass name must be written before any protocols. But while a class can have only one superclass, it can adopt as many protocols as it wants—these will all be listed after the superclass and separated by commas.

Now, to conform to the `AddBirthdayViewControllerDelegate` protocol and fix the error, we need to add the `addBirthdayViewController(_:didAddBirthday:)` method to `BirthdaysTableViewController`. A good place to add that is at the end of the class, right after the navigation section:

```
❶ // MARK: - AddBirthdayViewControllerDelegate

func addBirthdayViewController(_ addBirthdayViewController: ↵
    AddBirthdayViewController, didAddBirthday birthday: Birthday) {

❷   birthdays.append(birthday)
❸   tableView.reloadData()
}
```

When you start typing the function name, Xcode autocomplete suggests this entire method declaration. This is because it knows this class adopts the `AddBirthdayViewControllerDelegate` protocol, and it's expecting you to add this method. Note that unlike with a subclassed method, you don't use the `override` keyword before `addBirthdayViewController(_:didAddBirthday:)` because there is no original method to be overridden.

In this method, you need to do two things. First, you need to add the `Birthday` that was passed in by the Add Birthday view controller to the birthdays array. You do this by using the `append(_:)` method for an array ❷. Next, you need to refresh the table view so that it shows this new birthday by calling the `reloadData()` method on the `tableView` property ❸. When `reloadData()` is called, the table view data source methods will be called again, and the newly added `Birthday` will be displayed at the bottom of the birthday list.

You might have noticed that we added a comment above the method to mark this section: // MARK: - AddBirthdayViewControllerDelegate ❶. This isn't necessary, but it's good coding style to mark off different sections of your class, and it helps to keep your code clean and readable. The first part of the comment, MARK: -, is a special keyword that Xcode recognizes for code comments, and it adds the AddBirthdayViewControllerDelegate section to a drop-down table of contents menu that you can use at the top of your class. This drop-down menu helps you find methods and lets you jump to different places in your code. To use this menu, click BirthdaysTableViewController at the top of the editor pane, as shown in Figure 11-7.

Figure 11-7: Your class has a built-in table of contents for quickly jumping to a section.

Giving the Add Birthday View Controller a Delegate

BirthdaysTableViewController has adopted the AddBirthdayViewControllerDelegate protocol. Now it's time to make the Add Birthday view controller use the AddBirthdayViewControllerDelegate protocol to tell the Birthdays table view controller when it has added a birthday. To do this, the Add Birthday view controller first needs to define a delegate. We arrange for this by adding an optional delegate property of type AddBirthdayViewControllerDelegate to the AddBirthdayViewController class by inserting the following line right below the outlets:

AddBirthdayViewController.swift

```
class AddBirthdayViewController: UIViewController {
    --snip--
    @IBOutlet var birthdatePicker: UIDatePicker!

    var delegate: AddBirthdayViewControllerDelegate?

    override func viewDidLoad() {
```

The delegate has to be an optional because you can't set it until *after* the Add Birthday view controller has been created. You'll learn where to set the delegate shortly.

Now that the Add Birthday view controller has a delegate, in the saveTapped(_:) method, you can pass a Birthday to the delegate using the addBirthdayViewController(_:didAddBirthday:) method. Change saveTapped(_:) to the following:

```
@IBAction func saveTapped(_ sender: UIBarButtonItem) {
    --snip--
    let newBirthday = Birthday(firstName: firstName, ↵
        lastName: lastName, birthdate: birthdate)

❶   delegate?.addBirthdayViewController(self, didAddBirthday: newBirthday)
    dismiss(animated: true, completion: nil)
}
```

After the birthday object is created, the code at ❶ passes it back to the delegate using addBirthdayViewController(_:didAddBirthday:).

Great! You're done making changes to the Add Birthday view controller. It now has a delegate that will listen for the call that a Birthday was saved. Run the app to see what happens.

Hmm . . . not much has changed. When you add a Birthday, you still aren't seeing it show up in the Birthdays table view controller. What gives?

CONNECTING THE TWO CONTROLLERS BY SETTING A DELEGATE

There's one last thing you have to do. The Birthdays table view controller is an AddBirthdayViewControllerDelegate, and the Add Birthday view controller has an AddBirthdayViewControllerDelegate property that holds the delegate it talks to when a Birthday is saved. But we never specifically set the delegate property to be the Birthdays table view controller. So it's time to connect the communication pipeline between our two view controllers.

In the Navigation section of the BirthdaysTableViewController class, there's a method that's been commented out called prepare(for:sender:). Uncomment that method by deleting the /* and */ that surround it.

This method is automatically called whenever the Birthdays table view controller gives up its screen and the app transitions to another view controller using a storyboard segue. We'll use this method to pass the Birthdays table view controller in to Add Birthday view controller to set itself as the Add Birthday view controller's delegate. Write the following in the prepare(for:sender:) method:

BirthdaysTableViewController.swift

```
override func prepare(for segue: UIStoryboardSegue, sender: Any?) {
    // Get the new view controller using segue.destination
❶   let navigationController = segue.destination as! ↵
        UINavigationController
```

```
❷ let addBirthdayViewController = ↵
    navigationController.topViewController as! ↵
    AddBirthdayViewController
❸ addBirthdayViewController.delegate = self
}
```

It takes three lines of code to set the Add Birthday view controller delegate to the Birthdays table view controller. First, you need to be able to get to the AddBirthdayViewController object from the segue parameter. Xcode has left in a comment hinting at how you can do that. A UIStoryboardSegue has a property called destination at the other end of the segue that is being prepared in this method, but the destination for this app isn't the AddBirthdayViewController.

In Chapter 9, you embedded the Add Birthday view controller into a navigation controller so you could have a navigation bar with Cancel and Save buttons. So you don't expect to find the Add Birthday view controller at the other end of the segue. Instead, the destination is a UINavigationController that contains the Add Birthday view controller. The line at ❶ gets you navigationController. The code segue.destination will return a UIViewController, but since our navigationController is a specific type of ViewController, we need to typecast it to a UINavigationController using as.

Next, you can get the Add Birthday view controller, which is the topViewController of the navigationController ❷. The topViewController is just the view controller that's being displayed in the navigationController, but its property is of type UIViewController, so this has to be typecast to an AddBirthdayViewController to indicate that this controller is a specific subclass of UIViewController. Finally, when you have an AddBirthdayViewController, you can set the delegate to self, which is currently the Birthdays table view controller ❸.

Now run the app and add some birthdays! What do you see in the Birthdays table view controller? Birthdays! Birthdays! Birthdays! We're not quite done yet, though. If you quit the app and then run it again, the previous birthdays will disappear. We still need to save the birthdays to the device, which we'll do in Chapter 12.

WHAT YOU LEARNED

In this chapter, you learned how to make a table view controller to display your list of birthdays. You also learned how to add a Birthday in the Add Birthday view controller, and then how to use a delegate to add the Birthday to the birthdays array in the Birthdays table view controller so that it could be displayed.

In Chapter 12, you'll learn how to save the birthdays to your device so that they show up even after you quit the app and then run it again. To save the birthdays, you'll use Core Data, which we set up at the very beginning of our project.

12

SAVING BIRTHDAYS

Now you can add birthdays to your app and display them in a list, which is awesome! However, when you close the app, the birthdays disappear from your device. In this chapter, we'll show you how to save your app's data on your device so it's there even after you quit the app.

STORING BIRTHDAYS IN A DATABASE

Data is stored on the iPhone in a *database*, which is a collection of data that can be quickly saved, updated, and retrieved. You can think of it as an electronic filing system where the data is stored in tables with rows and columns. In the database for our app, there will be a Birthday table to store the birthdays. This will look something like Table 12-1.

Table 12-1: A Birthday Table in a Database

firstName	lastName	birthdate
Jen	Marbury	October 8, 2004
Tezeta	Tulloch	April 28, 2003
Betsy	Nichols	January 27, 2005
Caroline	Greeven	June 12, 2004

Each row will contain one `Birthday` object, with the columns containing its `firstName`, `lastName`, and `birthdate` attributes.

Core Data is an Apple framework that you can use to save and retrieve data in a database. The objects stored in the Core Data database all have to come from subclasses of the `NSManagedObject` class. These subclasses are called *managed objects* because their lifecycles are managed by the Core Data framework. That means you can't create a managed object using the `init()` methods that we covered in Chapter 8. Instead, you need to use a special `NSManagedObject` initializer.

The easiest way to add Core Data to your project is to have Xcode do it automatically. To do this, whenever you create a new project, start with a Single View App and check the Use Core Data box in the new project options. You should have already completed this step when you created the BirthdayTracker project in Chapter 9. When you create a new project using Core Data, Xcode gives you a data model file and setup code in the *AppDelegate.swift* file. You need this code to save data, but you can adjust it to use for your own app.

Every iOS application has a special *application delegate* that is automatically created as an instance of the `AppDelegate` class. The application delegate is in charge of the *application lifecycle*, which refers to the various running states an app can be in. For the BirthdayTracker app, the application delegate will also manage the data storage. We'll show you how to work with the application delegate to save and fetch data in "Saving a Birthday" on page 178.

THE BIRTHDAY ENTITY

In your app, you want to save and retrieve managed `Birthday` objects. To do this, you need to create a `Birthday` *entity* that will model the `Birthday` class. You can think of an entity as a table in the Core Data database.

In your Project navigator, you should see a data model file called *BirthdayTracker.xcdatamodeld*. Click that file and you'll see an empty data model. In the lower-left corner of the model, click the **Add Entity** button. This will create a new entity, which appears under Entities with the default name Entity. Double-click its name to get an editable text field, and then change its name to **Birthday** (see Figure 12-1).

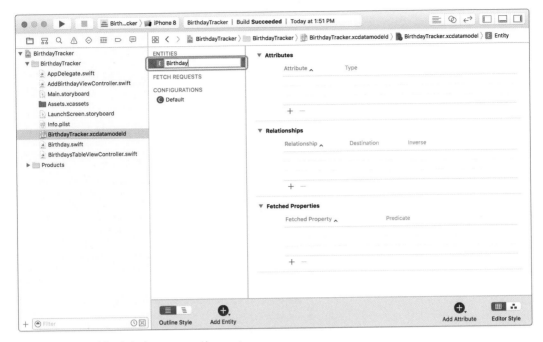

Figure 12-1: Double-click the entity to change its name.

Next, you'll add attributes to the `Birthday` entity so that you can store a `firstName`, `lastName`, and `birthdate` for each `Birthday` object.

THE BIRTHDAY ATTRIBUTES

Just as a class has properties, an entity has attributes. A Core Data entity has to have a corresponding class in Swift with properties that match the entity's attributes. Your `Birthday` class has three properties—`firstName`, `lastName`, and `birthdate`—which means that the `Birthday` entity needs to have three attributes with the same names. We're also going to add a `birthdayId` attribute—a unique string to identify each birthday. We'll need this in Chapter 13 when we remove a birthday and its corresponding user notification from the app.

Let's create the attributes now. Click the **Add Attribute** button to add a new attribute to the `Birthday` entity. Call it `firstName` by typing **firstName** in its editable text field under Attribute. Next, use the Type drop-down menu to set the type to **String** (see Figure 12-2).

When you've done this, add the `lastName` and `birthdayId` attributes, also as **String** types. Finally, add the `birthdate` attribute, but make it a **Date** type. When you're finished, your data model should look like the one shown in Figure 12-3.

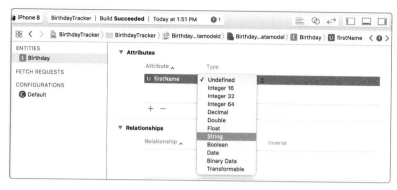

Figure 12-2: Add a firstName attribute of type String to Birthday.

Figure 12-3: The BirthdayTracker data model with a Birthday entity

Now that your data model is set up, Xcode has created a Birthday NSManagedObject subclass behind the scenes to go with it, which will be used to store birthdays. This means that we can remove our original Birthday class from the code. We have a new Birthday class that makes managed Birthday objects to store in the device's database, so we no longer need the temporary Birthday class that we created.

CONTROL-click *Birthday.swift* in the Project navigator to bring up the menu shown in Figure 12-4. Choose **Delete**.

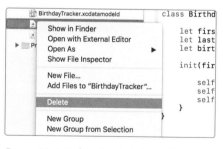

Figure 12-4: Delete the Birthday.swift file.

Next, you'll see a dialog asking if you want to Remove Reference to the file or Move to Trash. Removing a reference to your file removes the file from your project but doesn't actually delete the file in case you need to use it for something else. Since we won't use *Birthday.swift* anymore, you can delete it entirely. Select **Move to Trash**.

THE APPLICATION DELEGATE

We'll show you how to save birthdays on your device soon. To do this, you'll need to access the application delegate in your code. Remember, in our app, the code to manage Core Data is inside the application delegate.

When you create a new iOS application using Xcode, an *AppDelegate* *.swift* file is automatically created for you. This file contains the AppDelegate class, which implements the UIApplicationDelegate protocol, which in turn creates the application delegate for the app. Every app has only one application delegate, and the application delegate is in charge of the app's lifecycle.

On an iOS device, a user typically sees and interacts with only one app at a time. This is called the *foreground* app. When the user hits the home button on their iOS device or switches to another app, the app they were using gets *backgrounded*. That means that the current app is no longer visible and another app can be brought to the foreground. A background app can still execute some code for a short time, but it will eventually be *suspended*, or paused. A backgrounded or suspended app can be brought back to the foreground quickly when the user switches back to it because it's still in the device's memory. When an app is fully closed, it is *terminated*. A terminated app must be relaunched from scratch if the user opens it again.

The application delegate knows when the app has finished launching, been backgrounded, come back to the foreground, or been terminated. The AppDelegate class contains six callback functions that will be called when the application goes into its different lifecycle states:

application(_:didFinishLaunchingWithOptions:) is called when the app is launched. If you want your application to do something as soon as it has launched, you can write code in this callback function.

applicationWillResignActive(_:) is called when the app is leaving the foreground state.

applicationDidEnterBackground(_:) is called when the app has entered the background state, where some code can be executed but the app can still be suspended at any time.

applicationWillEnterForeground(_:) is called when the app is leaving the background state and about to go to the foreground state.

applicationDidBecomeActive(_:) is called when the app is going to the foreground state and has become active again.

applicationWillTerminate(_:) is called when the app is running in the foreground or background and is being closed. This won't be called if the app is suspended when it is closed.

When you create a new project using Core Data, Xcode will automatically have the AppDelegate class manage the data storage for you. In the *AppDelegate.swift* file, you'll see that the AppDelegate class contains a persistentContainer property, which you'll need to save and access data. On the persistentContainer is a NSManagedObjectContext property called viewContext. When we save and fetch birthdays in our code, we'll need to access persistentContainer.viewContext directly. Let's see how that is done.

Accessing the Managed Object Context

The *managed object context* is like a scratch-pad object that is used to create, save, and fetch data from the database. It temporarily stores the data you need. From anywhere in your application, you can access the managed object context using these two lines of code (we'll tell you where to add them later, so for now, just focus on understanding what they do):

```
❶ let appDelegate = UIApplication.shared.delegate as! AppDelegate
❷ let context = appDelegate.persistentContainer.viewContext
```

The purpose of this code is to get the managed object context for your application and to store it into a simple constant that you can use to create and save birthdays. At ❶, you are creating a constant reference to your app's application delegate. You do this by using the shared property of UIApplication to return your application instance (that is, your currently running app). Once you have the current application instance, you cast the delegate property in that instance as an AppDelegate and store it in the constant appDelegate. The line at ❷ retrieves the viewContext, which is in the persistentContainer of appDelegate, and stores it in a constant called context.

Now that you've accessed the managed object context, you're ready to save some birthdays! You use the context to create a new birthday, and then when you want to save the birthday, you just save the context.

Saving a Birthday

Let's save a birthday on the iPhone! Open *AddBirthdayViewController.swift*. The first step is to import Core Data, which you need to do for any file in which you want to use Core Data. Add the following to the top of the file.

AddBirthdayViewController.swift

```
import UIKit
import CoreData
```

Next, take a look at the saveTapped(_:) method. Delete the following lines:

```
❶ let newBirthday = Birthday(firstName: firstName, ↵    // ← Remove this code
      lastName: lastName, birthdate: birthdate)           // ← Remove this code
❷ delegate?.addBirthdayViewController(self, ↵             // ← Remove this code
      didAddBirthday: newBirthday)                        // ← Remove this code
```

We're not going to use the initializer to create newBirthday anymore, so you can get rid of the line at ❶. In addition, we don't need to use a delegate to pass a birthday to the Birthdays table view controller (you'll see why shortly), so you can also get rid of the line at ❷.

Now we'll add code inside the `saveTapped(_:)` method. We need to get the managed object context to create and save a `Birthday`. First, add the two lines of code we talked about in "Accessing the Managed Object Context" on page 178:

```
let firstName = firstNameTextField.text ?? ""
let lastName = lastNameTextField.text ?? ""
let birthdate = birthdatePicker.date

let appDelegate = UIApplication.shared.delegate as! AppDelegate
let context = appDelegate.persistentContainer.viewContext

dismiss(animated: true, completion: nil)
```

After you've accessed the context, you can use it to create a `Birthday`. Add the following lines to `saveTapped(_:)` right after setting `context`.

```
let appDelegate = UIApplication.shared.delegate as! AppDelegate
let context = appDelegate.persistentContainer.viewContext

❶ let newBirthday = Birthday(context: context)
❷ newBirthday.firstName = firstName
❸ newBirthday.lastName = lastName
❹ newBirthday.birthdate = birthdate as NSDate?
❺ newBirthday.birthdayId = UUID().uuidString

❻ if let uniqueId = newBirthday.birthdayId {
      print("The birthdayId is \(uniqueId)")
  }

dismiss(animated: true, completion: nil)
```

Each `NSManagedObject` subclass comes with a default initializer that takes a context and will create a new managed object. At ❶, we create a birthday by using a new `Birthday` initializer and passing in the `context` created in the line above. After `newBirthday` is created, we can set its `firstName` ❷, `lastName` ❸, and `birthdate` ❹ properties. Notice how this is different from our old initializer, where we passed in all of the `Birthday` class's properties. Here, we first create the `newBirthday` and then set its properties line by line. One extra thing that we have to do at ❹ (as of Xcode Version 8.2.1) is to cast the `birthdate` attribute to an `NSDate` object. `NSDate` was used in older versions of Swift and has been updated to `Date`. However, dates in Core Data have not yet been updated to use the new `Date` class, so we have to cast our `birthdate` attribute to `NSDate` to ensure we get the right value from the database.

We also want to set that `birthdayId` field to be a unique identifier for each birthday. This is kind of like how the United States government issues each of its citizens a Social Security number. No two people can have the same number. In computer programming, objects often need to have unique identifiers, which are called *universally unique identifiers (UUIDs)*. Swift has a UUID class that will make a UUID String for us. We use this class at ❺ when we set the birthdayId of newBirthday to UUID().uuidString. This property of the UUID class will return a new unique value every time it's called. If you want to see the value of the birthdayId, you can add a print statement ❻, and you'll see something like the following printed every time you add a birthday:

```
The birthdayId is 79E2B0EF-2AD5-4382-A38C-4911454515F1
```

Next, we need to save newBirthday. To do that, we call the save() method on the context. This is kind of like saving changes to a computer document after you're done working on it. The managed object context is like your document, and you've added a birthday to it, so now you want to save that document. Add these lines after setting the properties:

```
if let uniqueId = newBirthday.birthdayId {
    print("The birthdayId is \(uniqueId)")
}
```

```
❶ do {
❷    try context.save()
❸ } catch let error {
❹    print("Could not save because of \(error).")
}
dismiss(animated: true, completion: nil)
```

Now this is something new! We've wrapped our method to save the context inside a do-try-catch block, which is used in Swift to handle errors. In most simple applications, you'll only use the do-try-catch block around methods called on a managed object context, so this book will just cover how to use it in that situation. When you want to call a method such as save() on a context, you need to wrap the method in a block that starts with the keyword do ❶. This tells Swift to run the code inside of the do block's braces. Next, you need to put the keyword try in front of the method call ❷. The try keyword tells Swift that it should *try* to run the method, but if the method doesn't work, it will throw an error that Swift needs to *catch*.

The try keyword is used only in front of methods that throw errors, like this context.save() method. A method that throws an error will have the keyword throws after the input parameters in its definition. For example:

```
func save() throws
```

If you try to call the context.save() method without using do-try-catch, Xcode will give you an error.

Finally, the last part is a catch block, to catch any errors thrown by the context.save() method ❸. If the context.save() method fails and you want to find out what happened, you can print the error that was thrown and then caught ❹.

Now you're saving all of the birthdays that are entered into the app. But before we run the app again, we still need to have our Birthdays table view controller grab all of the birthdays out of the database to display them.

Getting the Birthdays

The Add Birthday view controller saves each birthday that is added to your app onto your device. Now let's *fetch* the birthdays—that is, get the `Birthday` objects out of Core Data—so that they can be displayed in the Birthdays table view controller.

First, add `import CoreData` to the top of the `BirthdaysTableViewController` file, just like you did to the `AddBirthdayViewController`. This `import` statement must be included at the top of every file that uses the framework, or Xcode won't recognize classes or methods used by Core Data.

Next, we need to write the code to fetch the birthdays we want to display. The list of birthdays should be refreshed every time the Birthdays table view controller's view appears on the screen. That way, when you add a birthday and then dismiss the Add Birthday view controller, the Birthdays table view controller will appear showing the new birthday as part of the list.

There is a built-in method called `viewWillAppear(_:)` in the `UIViewController` class where we can fetch the birthdays and put them in the `birthdays` array each time the Birthdays table view controller comes onto the screen. Add the following code right after the `viewDidLoad()` method:

BirthdaysTableViewController.swift

```
override func viewDidLoad() {
    --snip--
}

❶ override func viewWillAppear(_ animated: Bool) {
❷     super.viewWillAppear(animated)

❸     let appDelegate = UIApplication.shared.delegate as! AppDelegate
❹     let context = appDelegate.persistentContainer.viewContext

❺     let fetchRequest = Birthday.fetchRequest() as NSFetchRequest<Birthday>
       do {
❻         birthdays = try context.fetch(fetchRequest)
       } catch let error {
           print("Could not fetch because of error: \(error).")
       }
❼     tableView.reloadData()
}
```

The function `viewWillAppear(_:)` ❶ is a `UIViewController` lifecycle method similar to `viewDidLoad()`. Whereas `viewDidLoad()` will be called only once when the view controller is first created, `viewWillAppear(_:)` will be called every time the view appears on the screen. This makes it a very useful place to put code that you want to execute each time a view appears or reappears.

If you are going to implement viewWillAppear(_:), make sure to call super.viewWillAppear(_:) ❷ so that you still get the built-in functionality of the UIViewController's viewWillAppear(_:) method. In this case, you want to pass the animated parameter into that method as well. The animated parameter is a Boolean that tells the app whether the view will animate (that is, slide onto the screen).

To fetch data from the database, you need to access the managed object context of the app delegate. The lines at ❸ and ❹ get you the context that you'll use to fetch the data. This is the same way that you got the context to save a Birthday in the Add Birthday view controller.

Next, you need to create an NSFetchRequest object. The line at ❺ creates an NSFetchRequest that will get all of the Birthday objects out of Core Data. It uses the class method fetchRequest() that Xcode created automatically in your *Birthday+CoreDataProperties.swift* file. Note that when you create the fetchRequest, you need to cast it as an NSFetchRequest<Birthday> data type so that it knows what type of objects to get out of the database.

Once you have the fetchRequest, you can have your managed object context perform its fetch(_:) method with it. The fetch(_:) method ❻ will return an array of objects of the data type specified in the fetchRequest. In this case, we'll get back an array of Birthday objects that we can assign to the birthdays array. This line is wrapped in a do-try-catch error-handling block, much like the one we used to save the birthday in the Add Birthday view controller. Swift uses this type of error handling when fetching objects out of Core Data so that the error can tell you what happened if the fetch doesn't work.

Finally, after the birthdays have been fetched, we need to reload the table view so that we can see the new birthdays ❼.

We still have to take care of a few more things before we can run the app and test out our saved birthdays.

CODE CLEANUP

You'll find that when you write your apps, it's very common to do something one way and then figure out that there is a better way to do it. When you improve code you've already written, that's called *refactoring* your code. Let's start by cleaning up and getting rid of old code we don't need anymore.

In Chapter 11, we used delegation to have the Add Birthday view controller tell the Birthdays table view controller each time a Birthday was added so that it could be displayed. Now we don't need to do that. Instead, we'll have the Birthdays table view controller fill its birthdays array by pulling the saved Birthday objects out of the database every time it comes on the screen. This means that we can get rid of the AddBirthdayViewControllerDelegate and all of the code that goes with it!

To do so, delete the entire `AddBirthdayViewControllerDelegate` protocol and its function, `addBirthdayViewController(_:didAddBirthday:)`:

AddBirthdayViewController.swift

```
protocol AddBirthdayViewControllerDelegate {          // ← Remove
    func addBirthdayViewController(_ ↵                // ← Remove
        addBirthdayViewController: AddBirthdayViewController, ↵ // ← Remove
        didAddBirthday birthday: Birthday)            // ← Remove
}                                                     // ← Remove
```

As soon as you delete this, you'll see a red error next to the delegate property in the `AddBirthdayViewController` class. Delete that line of code as well:

```
var delegate: AddBirthdayViewControllerDelegate?   // ← Remove
```

Next, click the `BirthdaysTableViewController` to open that file. Because the `AddBirthdayViewControllerDelegate` protocol no longer exists, you can't have the `BirthdaysTableViewController` class adopt this protocol, so there will be an error next to the `BirthdaysTableViewController` definition. Remove the comma and `AddBirthdayViewControllerDelegate` from this line of code:

BirthdaysTableViewController.swift

```
class BirthdaysTableViewController: UITableViewController ↵
    , AddBirthdayViewControllerDelegate ↵          // ← Remove
    {
```

so the `BirthdaysTableViewController` declaration should now look like this:

```
class BirthdaysTableViewController: UITableViewController {
```

Now you can remove two sections in the *BirthdaysTableViewController.swift* file. Remove all of the code below and including the comment `// MARK: - AddBirthdayViewControllerDelegate` because `AddBirthdayViewControllerDelegate` no longer exists and its methods will never be called:

```
// MARK: - AddBirthdayViewControllerDelegate            // ← Remove

    func addBirthdayViewController(_ ↵                  // ← Remove
        addBirthdayViewController: AddBirthdayViewController, ↵ // ← Remove
        didAddBirthday birthday: Birthday) {            // ← Remove
        birthdays.append(birthday)                      // ← Remove
        tableView.reloadData()                          // ← Remove
    }                                                   // ← Remove
```

Then take a look at the Navigation section. In the `prepare(for:sender:)` function, all we are doing is setting the Birthdays table view controller as the delegate for the Add Birthday view controller. This is no longer necessary, so we can get rid of this method and the entire // MARK: - Navigation section as well:

```
// MARK: - Navigation                                                  // ← Remove

    // In a storyboard-based application, you will often want           // ← Remove
    // to do a little preparation before navigation                     // ← Remove
    override func prepare(for segue: UIStoryboardSegue, ↵               // ← Remove
        sender: Any?) {                                                 // ← Remove
        // Get the new view controller                                  // ← Remove
        // using segue.destinationViewController                        // ← Remove
        let navigationController = segue.destination as! ↵              // ← Remove
            UINavigationController                                      // ← Remove
        let addBirthdayViewController = ↵                               // ← Remove
            navigationController.topViewController as! ↵                // ← Remove
            AddBirthdayViewController                                   // ← Remove
        addBirthdayViewController.delegate = self                       // ← Remove
    }                                                                   // ← Remove
```

Since the properties in the Birthday NSManagedObject class are optionals, we'll need to unwrap them before we can display a Birthday in UITableViewCell. Delete these two lines inside the method tableView(_:cellForRowAt:):

```
override func tableView(_ tableView: UITableView, ↵
    cellForRowAt indexPath: IndexPath) -> UITableViewCell {
    let cell = tableView.dequeueReusableCell(withIdentifier: ↵
        "birthdayCellIdentifier", for: indexPath)

    let birthday = birthdays[indexPath.row]

    cell.textLabel?.text = birthday.firstName + " " + ↵                 // ← Remove
        birthday.lastName                                              // ← Remove
    cell.detailTextLabel?.text = ↵                                     // ← Remove
        dateFormatter.string(from: birthday.birthdate)                 // ← Remove

    return cell
}
```

Next add the following to the same method, tableView(_:cellForRowAt:):

```
let birthday = birthdays[indexPath.row]

❶ let firstName = birthday.firstName ?? ""
❷ let lastName = birthday.lastName ?? ""
  cell.textLabel?.text = firstName + " " + lastName

❸ if let date = birthday.birthdate as Date? {
❹     cell.detailTextLabel?.text = dateFormatter.string(from: date)
  } else {
```

```
❺ cell.detailTextLabel?.text = ""
}

return cell
```

We use the nil coalescing operator to set `birthday.firstName` as a constant `firstName` if it exists and to leave `firstName` as an empty string if there is no `birthday.firstName` ❶. At ❷, we do the same thing for `lastName`. Finally, to display the `birthdate`, we use optional binding in an `if let` statement to set the `birthday.birthdate` into a constant called `date` if it exists and to display this date in the `cell.detailTextLabel` at ❸ and ❹. Note that at ❸, we need to cast the `NSDate` `birthdate` to a `Date` object, which is easily done with `as Date?`. If the `birthdate` doesn't exist, we just set the `detailTextLabel?.text` to an empty string ❺.

Now run your app and add some birthdays! Then stop the app and run it again. The birthdays you just added should show up the second time you run the app. They'll stay in the app forever—that is, until you delete the app.

ADDING MORE FEATURES TO OUR APP

Our app stores birthdays now, but it still seems incomplete. Even though our app does the basic thing we wanted it to do, it doesn't function very well. For instance, the birthday list isn't organized, so when a user wants to find a specific birthday, they have to search for it line by line. That's annoying! And users can add as many birthdays as they want, but there isn't any way for them to delete a birthday if they made a mistake. How frustrating!

To fix these issues, we'll add more features to our app by building on top of our existing code. Once we're done with that, you can even keep going and add more!

ALPHABETIZING BIRTHDAYS

Wouldn't it be great if the birthdays were in an alphabetical list? It's very easy to have the `fetchRequest` return a sorted list of objects. To return an alphabetized list of `Birthday` objects, add the following three lines to `viewWillAppear(_:)` right after the code where you create the `fetchRequest`:

BirthdaysTableViewController.swift

```
override func viewWillAppear(_ animated: Bool) {
    --snip--
    let fetchRequest = Birthday.fetchRequest() as NSFetchRequest<Birthday>

❶  let sortDescriptor1 = NSSortDescriptor(key: "lastName", ascending: true)
❷  let sortDescriptor2 = NSSortDescriptor(key: "firstName", ascending: true)
❸  fetchRequest.sortDescriptors = [sortDescriptor1, sortDescriptor2]
    do {
        birthdays = try context.fetch(fetchRequest)
```

We'll alphabetize the list of `Birthday` objects first by last name and then by first name, in case some people have the same last names. An `NSFetchedRequest` comes with a property just for this purpose called `sortDescriptors`. This is an array of `NSSortDescriptor` objects. You use the `NSSortDescriptor` class to create a `sortDescriptor`, which orders a group of items for you. Each `sortDescriptor` has a *key* and a Boolean for whether the list should be ascending (`true`) or not, in which case it would be descending (`false`). The key is the attribute you want your objects to be sorted by. At ❶, we create `sortDescriptor1` and pass in `lastName` for the key. To sort the last names in alphabetical order from A to Z, we pass in true for `ascending`. Similarly, the line at ❷ creates `sortDescriptor2` to sort by `firstName` from A to Z. If we pass in a string data type as our key, Swift knows we want the strings sorted alphabetically. If we passed in "birthdate" instead, Swift would sort the birthdays by date from oldest to youngest. At line ❸, we set the `sortDescriptors` on the `fetchRequest` to be an array with `sortDescriptor1` as the first element, followed by `sortDescriptor2`. The `sortDescriptors` will be sorted in the order they are listed.

Now run the app and let's see what you get! You should see your friends' birthdays in an alphabetized list like the one shown in Figure 12-5.

Can you change the order of the list so that it's sorted by the birthdates instead? Give it a try!

Figure 12-5: An alphabetical list of birthdays

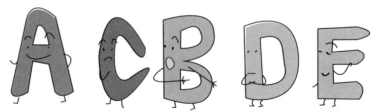

REMOVING BIRTHDAYS

If you get a birthday wrong, it would be nice to be able to remove it and then add it back in again with the correct information. Let's add the capability to remove a birthday now.

In the `BirthdaysTableViewController` class, we left in two commented-out methods toward the bottom of the file: `tableView(_:canEditRowAt:)` and `tableView(_:commit:forRowAt:)`. These methods allow us to enable the built-in "swipe to delete" functionality of a table view. We'll make it so that when you run BirthdayTracker and look at a list of birthdays, you'll be able to put your finger on one and slide to the left. This action will reveal a Delete button like the one shown in Figure 12-6 that you can tap to remove the birthday from the app.

Uncomment the methods `tableView(_:canEditRowAt:)` and `tableView(_:commit:forRowAt:)` by removing the /* and */ that surround them.

Next, make sure that the method `tableView(_:canEditRowAt:)` returns `true`. This just means that you'll be able to edit the table or, in our case, remove rows. If you have it return `false`, then you won't be able to swipe the table to remove a row. The function should look like this:

Figure 12-6: Swiping left to remove a birthday from BirthdayTracker

BirthdaysTableViewController.swift

```
override func tableView(_ tableView: UITableView, ↵
    canEditRowAt indexPath: IndexPath) -> Bool {
    return true
}
```

You'll have to add some code to the method `tableView(_:commit:forRowAt:)` to actually remove the row from the table and also remove the `Birthday` object from the database and the birthdays array. If you only removed the row from the table view, then the computer would be confused because the number of rows in the table would no longer match `birthdays.count` and the app would crash. First, remove the following lines that were provided by Xcode in `tableView(_:commit:forRowAt:)`:

```
// Override to support editing the table view
override func tableView(_ tableView: UITableView, commit editingStyle: ↵
    UITableViewCellEditingStyle, forRowAt indexPath: IndexPath) {

    if editingStyle == .delete {                            // ← Remove
        // Delete the row from the data source              // ← Remove
        tableView.deleteRows(at: [indexPath], with: .fade)  // ← Remove
```

```
    } else if editingStyle == .insert {            // ← Remove
        // Create a new instance of the appropriate class,  // ← Remove
        // insert it into the array, and add a new row       // ← Remove
        // to the table view                                 // ← Remove
    }                                                        // ← Remove
}
```

Then add the following code:

```
override func tableView(_ tableView: UITableView, commit editingStyle: ↵
    UITableViewCellEditingStyle, forRowAt indexPath: IndexPath) {
❶  if birthdays.count > indexPath.row {
❷      let birthday = birthdays[indexPath.row]

❸      let appDelegate = UIApplication.shared.delegate as! AppDelegate
❹      let context = appDelegate.persistentContainer.viewContext
❺      context.delete(birthday)
❻      birthdays.remove(at: indexPath.row)
❼      tableView.deleteRows(at: [indexPath], with: .fade)
    }
}
```

At ❶, we first do a safety check to make sure that the birthdays array has at least as many birthdays in it as the row number of the indexPath that we are trying to remove. To do this, we use the > operator, not the >= operator, because the birthdays.count must be greater than indexPath.row. For example, if the birthdays array only has two birthdays and we are trying to get the birthday at birthdays[2], which would be the third birthday, then the app will crash. Remember that the rows of indexPath start at 0.

The line at ❷ sets the birthday at the correct index in the birthdays array to birthday so that it can be deleted. Then we access the managed object context of the application delegate at ❸ and ❹. At ❺, the object gets deleted from the context. When we delete the object from the database, we also want to make sure to delete it from the birthdays array of the Birthdays table view controller ❻. Finally, the method deleteRows(at:with:) ❼ takes two parameters, an array of NSIndexPaths to know which rows to remove and a type of UITableViewRowAnimation. The animation specifies how you want the rows to look when they are being removed. You can choose from the options none, bottom, top, left, right, middle, or fade. We want to remove only the row that we deleted with a fade-out animation. To do this, we pass in an array with our indexpath as the first parameter enclosed with square brackets, [indexpath], and .fade as our second parameter.

Now run the app and delete some of your birthdays. You should see the rows removed from the table. However, if you quit the app and then run it again, the deleted birthdays reappear. What gives?

Well, you deleted the birthdays from the managed object context, but those changes were not automatically saved. Whenever you add, update, or remove objects in the context, you also need to save the context or the changes won't stay on the device. Remember that the context is like a computer document that needs to be saved. To do that, add the following lines right after you remove the birthday:

```
context.delete(birthday)
birthdays.remove(at: indexPath.row)
do {
    try context.save()
} catch let error {
    print("Could not save \(error).")
}
tableView.deleteRows(at: [indexPath], with: .fade)
```

Those lines should look familiar since they're the same lines that saved the managed object context after you added a Birthday in the Add Birthday view controller.

This time when you run the app and delete a Birthday, it should stay deleted!

WHAT YOU LEARNED

In this chapter, you learned how to save, fetch, and remove Birthday objects in a database using the Core Data framework so that your birthdays will be there every time you run your app. Your birthdays also now display in alphabetical order.

In Chapter 13, we'll show you how to use local notifications to ping users on their friends' birthdays.

13

GETTING BIRTHDAY NOTIFICATIONS

Now let's finish BirthdayTracker by adding *local notifications*. A local notification is an alert that is sent to your phone from an app, even when the app isn't running. The BirthdayTracker app will use a local notification to alert the user when they should wish a friend a happy birthday.

THE USER NOTIFICATIONS FRAMEWORK

Just as you used Apple's Core Data framework to save birthdays on your phone in a database, you'll use Apple's User Notifications framework to send notifications to the user. Using this framework is easy! You just need to add an `import` statement at the top of any class that deals with user notifications, like this:

```
import UserNotifications
```

We'll use the framework in three files—*AddBirthdayViewController.swift*, *AppDelegate.swift*, and *BirthdaysTableViewController.swift*—so add import UserNotifications to each of them, below the other import statements.

REGISTERING FOR LOCAL NOTIFICATIONS

Next, you need to have your app ask the user for permission to send notifications when it's someone's birthday. If you don't have permission for notifications, they won't be sent. You can get permission by having your app request authorization for notifications in your application delegate. This needs to be done as soon as the app starts, which is when it finishes launching. Luckily, there is a method in the AppDelegate class called application(_:didFinishLaunchingWithOptions:) that we can use to do this.

First, make sure that you added the line import UserNotifications at the top of your *AppDelegate.swift* file. Next, add the following lines in application(_:didFinishLaunchingWithOptions:) to request permission to send local notifications.

AppDelegate.swift

```
func application(_ application: UIApplication, didFinishLaunchingWithOptions ↵
    launchOptions: [UIApplicationLaunchOptionsKey: Any]?) -> Bool {

❶ let center = UNUserNotificationCenter.current()
❷ center.requestAuthorization(options: ❸[.alert, .sound], ↵
       completionHandler: ❹{ (granted, error) in

    ❺ if granted {
           print("Permission for notifications granted!")
       } else {
           print("Permission for notifications denied.")
       }
   })

   return true
}
```

The line at ❶ gets the current UNUserNotificationCenter and stores it in a constant called center. The *notification center* is used to schedule and manage the notifications that you send from your app. In this chapter, we'll use three methods from the UNUserNotificationCenter class:

requestAuthorization(options:completionHandler:) asks the user for permission to send notifications.

add(_:withCompletionHandler:) requests to add a new notification to send to the user.

removePendingNotificationRequests(withIdentifiers:) removes an existing notification.

We use the first of these methods at ❷ to ask the user to grant permission for the app to send notifications. We'll use the other two methods later in this chapter.

The method requestAuthorization(options:completionHandler:) takes two parameters: options and completionHandler. In the options parameter, you pass in an array of the UNAuthorizationOptions that you want to be available on your notifications. There are four types of UNAuthorizationOptions that you can use for your notifications: badge, sound, alert, and carPlay. The badge option adds a badge on your app icon so the user can quickly see when there's something new in your app. This is typically a number indicating how many new or waiting notifications are in the app. The sound option adds a sound to be played when your noti-

fication is sent to the phone. The alert option displays a notification as either an alert that pops up in the middle of the screen or a banner that comes in at the top of the screen. You, the app developer, don't get to decide how the notification will appear or if the user will turn on the sound for their notifications. This is something that the user controls in their Settings app. The fourth option, carPlay, allows notifications on a CarPlay-enabled device in a car.

We want to display the notifications as alerts for the user and play a sound when each notification comes in, so we pass in [.alert, .sound] for our options ❸. The completionHandler parameter is a clo-sure that is passed in and called after the user either grants or denies permission for the app to send notifications. The completionHandler closure has two param-eters, granted and error ❹. The granted parameter is a Boolean value that lets you know if permission was granted (in which case it would be true) or denied (false). We're not going to change the behavior of our app if the user refuses to let us send notifications, but we'll print a statement in the console ❺ so you can see if permis-sion was granted or denied when you test the app. The second parameter, error, is the Error class type and lets you know if there was an error of some sort.

Now that you have requested autho-rization for notifications, the first time the user runs the app, it will display an alert dialog asking if they want to allow it to send notifications, as shown in Figure 13-1.

Figure 13-1: The app will ask per-mission from the user to deliver notifications.

If the user selects the Don't Allow option here, they won't receive any notifications on people's birthdays. If they select Allow, they will receive notifications. The user will only be asked this the first time the app is run after a fresh installation. However, they can change the notifications settings at any time in the Settings app.

When the user opens the Settings app and scrolls to the apps section, they'll see a listing for the BirthdayTracker app, labeled *Birthdays*, at the bottom of the list (Figure 13-2). You can also see this in the simulator.

Drilling down into the BirthdayTracker app settings will lead the user to the Notifications settings screen (Figure 13-3).

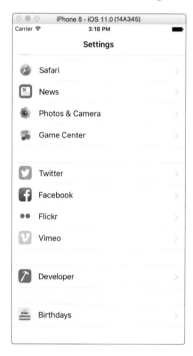

Figure 13-2: From the Settings app, the user can drill down to specify notification settings for their apps.

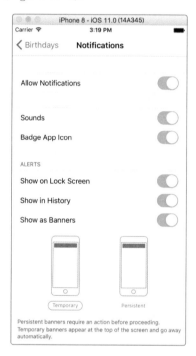

Figure 13-3: Notification settings for our app

On this screen, the user can specify whether they want to see notifications for the app and what kind of notifications they want (temporary or persistent).

SCHEDULING A NOTIFICATION

Each time we create a birthday, we'll want to schedule a notification to be sent to us every year on the birthday person's birthdate. To do this, we'll add some code to the saveTapped(_:) method in the AddBirthdayViewController class.

In that method, first we need to create a message string to be sent in the notification. Our message will be a string that says, "Wish *firstName lastName* a Happy Birthday today!" Add the following code right after a birthday is saved in the saveTapped(_:) method in *AddBirthdayViewController.swift*:

AddBirthdayViewController.swift

```
do {
    try context.save()
    let message = "Wish \(firstName) \(lastName) a Happy Birthday today!"
} catch let error {
    print("Could not save because of \(error).")
}
```

Now that we have our message, we need to create and schedule the notification that will be sent to the user's device on their friend's birthday. First, make sure that import UserNotifications is at the top of the file. Then add the following right under the message constant you just wrote:

```
    let message = "Wish \(firstName) + \(lastName) a Happy Birthday today!"
❶ let content = UNMutableNotificationContent()
❷ content.body = message
❸ content.sound = UNNotificationSound.default()
} catch let error {
    print("Could not save because of \(error).")
}
```

The line at ❶ creates a UNMutableNotificationContent that is stored into a constant called content. A UNMutableNotificationContent contains data for a user notification, such as a message or sound. At ❷, we set the content.body property to the birthday reminder message called message. Then, at ❸, we set content.sound to be the default notification sound, which is the same sound that occurs when you receive a text message.

After we create the content of the notification, we need to create the notification's *trigger*. Triggers are of the UNCalendarNotificationTrigger class and let the app know when and how often to send the notification. We'll schedule the birthday notification to be sent at 8 AM every year on the person's birthday. Swift lets us get just the month and day of the triggerDate by using the Calendar and DateComponents classes.

Add the following code to create a trigger after setting content.sound:

```
    let content = UNMutableNotificationContent()
    content.body = message
    content.sound = UNNotificationSound.default()
❶ var dateComponents = Calendar.current.dateComponents([.month, .day], ↵
        from: birthdate)
❷ dateComponents.hour = 8
❸ let trigger = UNCalendarNotificationTrigger(dateMatching: dateComponents, ↵
        repeats: true)
} catch let error {
```

To do this, first we get the month and the day DateComponents from birthDate by using the Calendar method dateComponents(_:from:). We pass in just [.month, .day] for the components ❶, and not the year. This is because we want the trigger to go off every year, not just on the year the person was born—which is in the past, so it would never happen anyway! We want to send the birthdate notification at 8 AM, so next we set dateComponents .hour to 8 ❷.

At ❸, we create the UNCalendarNotificationTrigger with its initializer. This initializer takes two parameters: the dateComponents and a Boolean that says whether you want the trigger to be repeated or not. We want the trigger to be repeated every year, so we pass in true. Swift is smart about how often you want a trigger to be repeated. If you passed in DateComponents that were just an hour and a minute, for example, it would fire the notification every day at that hour and minute. Because we passed in a month and a day, the trigger will repeat every year.

THE CALENDAR AND DATECOMPONENTS CLASSES

The Calendar and DateComponents classes make it super easy to create dates and times. DateComponents has integer properties that you can set for the year, month, day, hour, minute, and second of a date and time, or a time interval. The Calendar class has methods to convert DateComponents into a Date or vice versa. To try creating a date, open your Swift playground. We'll create a date and time of May 10, 1971, at 8:23 AM:

```
❶ var myDateComponents = DateComponents()
❷ myDateComponents.month = 5
  myDateComponents.day = 10
  myDateComponents.year = 1971
❸ myDateComponents.hour = 8
  myDateComponents.minute = 23

❹ let date = Calendar.current.date(from: ↵    "May 10, 1971, 8:23 AM"
     myDateComponents)
```

First, we create a variable called myDateComponents ❶, which we'll use to create our date. After creating myDateComponents, we can set integers for its various properties. The months of the year are all represented by integers in numeric order, from 1 for January to 12 for December. For May, we set myDateComponents.month to 5 ❷. For 8 AM, we use 8 for myDateComponents.hour ❸. The myDateComponents properties use a 24-hour clock so that each hour of a 24-hour day is labeled in numeric order, starting with 0 for midnight. So all the hours before noon would be the same as on a 12-hour clock, but for 2 PM, which is two hours after noon, we would count two hours past 12 and set myDateComponents to 14. For another example, 11 PM would be 23. Finally, we can make a date from myDateComponents by using the date(from:) method on the Calendar class ❹. To use this method, we first need a Calendar instance. We use Calendar.current, which returns the type of calendar being used by the device. In most Western countries, this is the Gregorian calendar, which has 12 months and a 7-day week.

To get DateComponents out of a Date, we use the Calendar method myDateComponents(_:from:). This method takes two parameters: the first is an array of the DateComponents that you want out of the Date, and the second is the Date itself. The myDateComponents(_:from:) method is useful if you want to create a new Date object that is today's date, but at 8 AM, for example.

Write the following in your playground:

```
❶ let today = Date()                              "Dec 9, 2017, 11:03 AM"
❷ var myDateComponents = ↵
      Calendar.current.dateComponents([ ↵
      .month, .day, .year], from: today)
❸ myDateComponents.hour = 8

❹ let todayEightAm = ↵                            "Dec 9, 2017, 8:00 AM"
      Calendar.current.date( ↵
      from: myDateComponents)
```

The line at ❶ creates the current date and time and assigns it to a constant called today. Next, we get the myDateComponents for the month, day, and year out of today ❷. Note that we pass in only the DateComponents properties that we care about. We don't need the hour, minutes, or seconds, for example. We make myDateComponents a variable instead of a constant because we are going to set the hour property, which we do at ❸. Finally, we create a new date called todayEightAm using myDateComponents ❹. You should see that the new Date is the same as today, except the time is 8:00 AM.

Now that we have our notification content and trigger, we are almost ready to create a UNNotificationRequest object to schedule the notification. But to create a UNNotificationRequest, first we need an identifier. This is a string that can be used to identify the notification.

We'll also use this identifier to remove a scheduled notification if we delete a birthday from the app. After all, you wouldn't want to be getting notifications for birthdays that you deleted!

In Chapter 12, we added a birthdayId property to Birthday, so we'll use birthdayId as the identifier of our notification. First, we need to unwrap the optional birthdayId property and store it in a constant called identifier. Then, we can create a notification request using the identifier and the trigger. Add the following code right after trigger is created:

AddBirthdayViewController.swift

```
do {
    --snip--
    let trigger = UNCalendarNotificationTrigger(dateMatching: dateComponents, ↵
        repeats: true)
    if let identifier = newBirthday.birthdayId {

    ❶ let request = UNNotificationRequest(identifier: identifier, ↵
          content: content, trigger: trigger)
    ❷ let center = UNUserNotificationCenter.current()
    ❸ center.add(request, withCompletionHandler: nil)
    }
} catch let error {
```

At ❶, we create the UNNotificationRequest using the identifier, content, and trigger. After request is created, it must be added to the UNUserNotificationCenter. To do this, we create a constant called center ❷, which is the current UNUserNotificationCenter of the app. Then we use the method add(_:withCompletionHandler:) to add the request for our scheduled notification ❸. This method takes two parameters, a UNNotificationRequest and a closure as a completionHandler that performs some action after the notification has been added. We pass in our request for the first parameter, and since we don't need to do anything when the request has been added, we pass in nil for the completionHandler.

Whew! We've just finished writing the method to schedule a notification! Now if you run your app and create Birthday objects, you'll receive a notification when it's someone's birthday!

To test your notifications, you'd need to add a birthday for the next day and wait until 8 AM for your notification to appear. But waiting a whole day to test your code is too long! To test your code right now, tweak it to make the notification go off much sooner. Set the hour and minute of myDateComponents to be 10 minutes from the present time. So if it's 1:35 PM, change the code that you just wrote to the following:

```
var dateComponents = Calendar.current.dateComponents([.month, .day], ↵
    from: birthDate)
```

```
dateComponents.hour = 13
dateComponents.minute = 45

let trigger = UNCalendarNotificationTrigger(dateMatching: dateComponents, ↵
    repeats: true)
--snip--
}
```

Then run the app, add a birthday with today's date, turn off the app by clicking the stop button (but keep the simulated iPhone's window open), and wait 10 minutes. You should see a notification appear like the one in Figure 13-4. After testing, don't forget to change your code back so that the notifications go off first thing in the morning!

Figure 13-4: A banner-style birthday notification

REMOVING A NOTIFICATION

When we remove a birthday from the app, we'll also want to cancel its corresponding notification, which we can do in the `BirthdaysTableViewController` by adding some code. A good place to do this is right after the user selects a birthday to delete, in `tableView(_:commitEditingStyle:forRowAtIndexPath:)`. Add the following lines to that method:

BirthdaysTableViewController.swift

```
let birthday = birthdays[indexPath.row]

// Remove notification
❶ if let identifier = birthday.birthdayId {
❷     let center = UNUserNotificationCenter.current()
❸     center.removePendingNotificationRequests(withIdentifiers: [identifier])
}

let appDelegate = UIApplication.sharedApplication().delegate as! AppDelegate
let context = appDelegate.managedObjectContext
```

To remove the notification for a birthday, first we unwrap the `birthdayId` to use it as an `identifier` ❶. Next, we get the `UNUserNotificationCenter` ❷ and remove the notification ❸. The remove method takes an array of identifiers so that you can remove more than one notification at a time, but since we want to remove only one, we pass it `[identifier]`, which is an array but has only one value.

> **NOTE** *The BirthdayTracker app is now complete! Remember that the final project files are available from* https://www.nostarch.com/iphoneappsforkids/, *so you can compare yours to double-check that everything is in the right place.*

WHAT YOU LEARNED

In this chapter, we showed you how to use the User Notifications framework to ping your users on their friends' birthdays. You learned how to add a notification that will be sent at a specific time every year and also how to remove that notification if the user removes a birthday from the app.

In Part 3, you'll build another exciting app—a game called Schoolhouse Skateboarder, which features graphics, sounds, and more!

PART 3

SCHOOLHOUSE
SKATEBOARDER

14

SETTING THE STAGE

Over the next several chapters, we'll put your new skills to good use to build a game called *Schoolhouse Skateboarder*, where the player controls a skateboarder who has to jump over obstacles and collect gems.

In this chapter, you'll set up your Xcode project file, add images for the player, and display a schoolyard background. Figure 14-1 is a preview of how the game will look on an iPhone. Players try to survive as long as possible by tapping to jump over obstacles, collecting gems and scoring points along the way. They lose when they tip over or fall down a hole.

Figure 14-1: The finished game

WHERE DO I GET ART AND SOUND EFFECTS?

We've already created all the art and sound effects you need to make Schoolhouse Skateboarder (available from *https://www.nostarch.com/ iphoneappsforkids/*). You don't need anything else to follow along. If you want to customize it, you can make the game your own by replacing the skateboarder image with a character of your choosing, or you might have someone grabbing hamburgers instead of gems.

Hopefully, by the end of this book, you'll be inspired to design your own games. It can be rewarding to create the entire game by yourself, including the artwork and sound effects. You have complete control over every aspect of *your* game.

There are also plenty of places on the web where you can find free game art to use:

http://opengameart.org/   Free game art, sounds, and music

http://freetems.net/   Free game art and music

http://www.bfxr.net/   Free retro game sound creation tool

MAKING GAMES WITH XCODE'S SPRITEKIT

SpriteKit is iOS's built-in game engine for making two-dimensional, or 2D, games. A *game engine* is a set of tools that lets you quickly and easily make animations, use audio and sound effects, create a menu system, and more. Programmers use game engines so they can focus on what's truly important—making the game fun.

Typically, a game consists of many sprites. A *sprite* is a 2D image used in a game. Sprites can be full-screen images that provide the backdrop for the game, or they can be smaller images that move around and do things. Background sprites set the stage. For example, in a space shooter game, the background sprites might show a space scene with stars and planets, and there would be smaller sprites for the player's spaceship, enemy ships, bullets, asteroids, and power-ups.

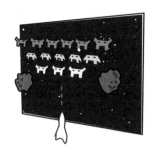

As far as game engines go, SpriteKit is top notch. Tasks that would take many lines of code in other game engines can be accomplished with just a line or two in SpriteKit, and it's fun to use!

NOTE   *iOS also has a 3D game engine called SceneKit, but since we're building a 2D game, we'll stick with SpriteKit.*

CREATING THE GAME PROJECT

The first thing we need to do is create a new SpriteKit project for our game. Open Xcode and select **File ▸ New ▸ Project...**. In the project template dialog, select **iOS**, choose the **Game** template, and then click **Next**.

Now, name your project SchoolhouseSkateboarder in the Product Name field. Choose **SpriteKit** as the Game Technology. Then click **Next** to create your game project.

Without changing a thing, you can run this project and you'll see a black screen with a label that says *Hello, World!*. Each time you click your mouse anywhere in the simulator, a spinning box will appear on the screen (see Figure 14-2), and the label will shrink for a second. If the label appears sideways, you can rotate the simulator window by selecting **Hardware ▸ Rotate Left** from the simulator's menu.

Whenever you make a new project using the Game template, Xcode adds this simple interaction so you can make sure everything's working.

Since we don't want a giant *Hello, World!* label in our game, let's remove that first. That label exists in the *scene editor*, a tool used to visually design a SpriteKit scene, similar to the way storyboards are used to design UIKit views. You can drag objects into the scene editor, move them around, and change their size, color, and other properties. This can be a useful tool, but it has many limitations compared to what can

Figure 14-2: Running the project created by the Game template before making any changes

be done in code. Therefore, apart from removing the *Hello, World!* label, we won't be using the scene editor for Schoolhouse Skateboarder. To open the scene editor, click the file named *GameScene.sks* in the Project navigator. Once it loads, you should see a black scene with the *Hello, World!* label. Click the label, and then press DELETE. See Figure 14-3.

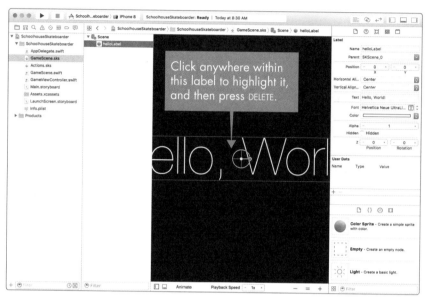

Figure 14-3: Deleting the Game template's Hello, World! *label*

Now that we've created the project and removed the *Hello, World!* label, we can get down to business—the business of fun, that is!

ADDING IMAGES

First, you'll want to add all of the images to your project as assets. (An asset is just a thing in your game, such as a sprite or a sound effect.)

Download the ZIP file from *https://www.nostarch.com/iphoneappsforkids/*. Once the download is complete, you'll have a folder named *ch14-images* inside your *Downloads* folder with all the image files you need.

To add the image files to your project, you'll need to drag them from Finder into Xcode and drop them into an asset catalog. (An asset catalog is a special type of folder in an Xcode project that holds and organizes project resources such as image files and icons.) It is helpful for images because it groups together related image files. Once the files are in the asset catalog, you can use them anywhere in your code by referring to their filenames. The Game template we used comes with one asset catalog already, called *Assets.xcassets*, which is the catalog we'll use.

Click *Assets.xcassets* in the Project navigator. You should see the existing assets, AppIcon, and spaceship image. You can delete the spaceship image, since we won't be using it. Click it and then press DELETE.

Now open Finder and navigate to the folder where the image files were downloaded. Press ⌘-A to select them all. Once they're highlighted, drag them into the Xcode asset catalog, as shown in Figure 14-4.

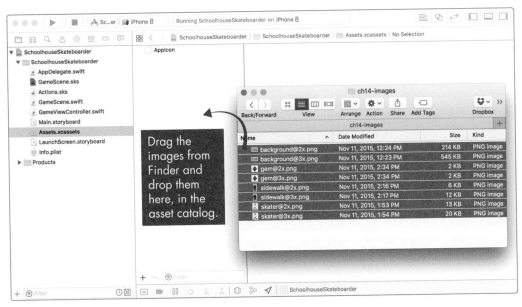

Figure 14-4: Adding the image files to your project's asset catalog

You might have noticed that all of the image files are *.png* files. *PNG* stands for *Portable Network Graphics*, and it is the most common image file type used in iOS applications because it has the smallest file size for the best quality image. You could use *.jpg* files, but *.png* files are recommended.

THE SCENERY: DISPLAYING A BACKGROUND IMAGE

Now that you've added all the images to the project, let's write some code to display the background image in our app.

When you created a new project using the Game template, some help-ful code was automatically added to your project. Click the file named *GameScene.swift* in the Project navigator. You should see a bunch of code already there. This code is there for two reasons. First, it gives you an example of how to create a shape (the spinning box) and how to perform an action (making the box spin). Second, it lets you immediately run a new project and make sure that everything is set up properly.

At this point, we're going to remove most of that code and add our own code. Go ahead and delete everything in *GameScene.swift*, except for the declaration of the `didMove(to:)` function and the `update(_:)` function, so that it looks like this:

GameScene.swift

```
import SpriteKit

class GameScene: SKScene {

    override func didMove(to view: SKView) {
    }

    override func update(_ currentTime: TimeInterval) {
        // Called before each frame is rendered
    }
}
```

Most of the logic in our game will be in the `GameScene` class. Think of a scene as one view or screen in your app. The `GameScene` class will manage everything that happens within the scene—how the sprites should be displayed, how the player will interact with the game, and how scoring will happen. Complex games may have many separate scenes—for example, a title scene, a menu scene, a game scene, and a settings scene. Our game will have just one scene: the game scene.

Scene classes will usually have setup functions (stuff that happens once), a game loop or update functions (stuff that happens over and over again during the game), and user interaction functions (stuff that happens only when the user taps or swipes).

The setup function `didMove(to:)` is called when your game first starts. It's great for code that sets up the scene, such as the code that adds the initial sprites or sets the player's score and lives. It's similar to the `viewDidLoad()` method that you used to set up the date picker in the `AddBirthdayViewController` in Chapter 10, and it's called just once.

Before we add the background image to the scene, we have to set the `anchorPoint` of the scene. Add this line of code to the `didMove(to:)` method (the gray lines indicate some of the existing code, for placement):

```
override func didMove(to view: SKView) {

    anchorPoint = CGPoint.zero

}
```

Setting the scene's anchor point determines how sprites will be positioned in the scene. When you pin a piece of paper to a corkboard with a pushpin, the pushpin is the anchor point. The piece of paper will be positioned where you put the pushpin, and if the paper rotates, it will rotate around the pushpin. This is exactly how the `anchorPoint` property works

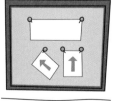

with sprites and scenes in SpriteKit. The Game template's GameScene has its anchor point in the middle of the scene, but we want the anchor point to be in the lower left of the scene, so we set it to CGPoint.zero, or (0, 0). For some games, such as a space shooter, it's better to have the anchor point in the middle of the scene. But for our game, where the ground is on the bottom of the screen, moving the anchor point to the lower left will make it easier to work with. See Figure 14-5 for an illustration of various anchor points.

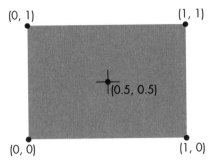

Figure 14-5: Various locations of anchor points ranging from (0, 0) to (1, 1)

In our scene, when we place a sprite at an x-position of 0, it will be at the left edge of the screen. And when we place a sprite at a y-position of 0, it will be at the bottom edge of the screen.

NOTE   *We'll be building each code file for the projects step-by-step. The final versions are available from* https://www.nostarch.com/iphoneappsforkids/.

ANCHOR POINTS FOR SPRITES

You can also set the anchor point of a sprite, changing how that sprite gets positioned and how it rotates. See Figure 14-6 for an example of rotating a sprite with different anchor points.

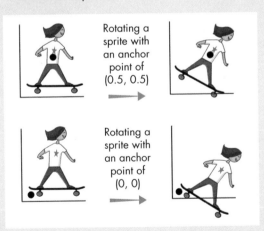

Figure 14-6: The anchor point of a sprite determines how it will rotate.

Sprites normally have their anchor point in the center. We won't be changing any sprite anchor points, so we will always position sprites using their center point.

Now, to load our background image, add the following lines of code to the `didMove(to:)` function:

```
override func didMove(to view: SKView) {

    anchorPoint = CGPoint.zero

❶   let background = SKSpriteNode(imageNamed: "background")
❷   let xMid = frame.midX
❸   let yMid = frame.midY
❹   background.position = CGPoint(x: xMid, y: yMid)
❺   addChild(background)
}
```

Let's walk through the five lines of code we just added. The line at ❶ creates a sprite called `background`, using either the *background@2x.png* file or the *background@3x.png* file. Both files were added to the asset catalog earlier and Xcode will choose the right file automatically. You simply have to refer to it in code as `"background"` or `"background.png"`. To understand how Xcode picks the right file, see "Sizing Images for Different Screen Resolutions" on page 213. Note that the variable name does not have to match the image name—you can use whatever you want for the variable name. The image name, however, must match a file that you added to an asset catalog in your project. `SKSpriteNode` is the sprite class in SpriteKit, so when we create a sprite in our game, we'll be creating an `SKSpriteNode`, as we did here.

The lines at ❷ and ❸ create the constants `xMid` and `yMid`, which will represent the middle position of the screen. `frame` is a property of GameScene—it's a CGRect (a rectangle) that represents the entire screen. Every scene and sprite has a frame that describes where it is on the screen. A frame has an x-position, a y-position, a width, and a height (see Figure 14-7). The `midX` property gives us the middle x-position of the screen's frame, and `midY` gives us the middle y-position.

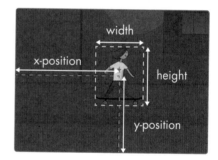

Figure 14-7: A frame describes the position and size of a sprite.

The line at ❹ sets the position of our background image to the middle of the screen by creating a CGPoint using `xMid` and `yMid` and assigning it to the sprite's `position` property.

A CGPoint is a struct that holds two CGFloat values, which represent x- and y-coordinates. When you're dealing with screen coordinates, you typically use CGFloat as the data type instead of Float or Double. A single CGPoint can hold two values, one for *x* and one for *y*, which makes it convenient for dealing with screen coordinates in a 2D game where everything is positioned using both x- and y-positions.

Anything that begins with CG *comes from the* Core Graphics framework, *an Apple framework used for graphics. You'll notice this kind of naming system a lot in Swift— the first two or three letters of a class or struct often tell you what that object is used for or where it comes from. For example, all the SpriteKit classes, such as* SKSpriteNode, *start with* SK.

The line at ❺ adds the background image to the scene by calling the function addChild(_:). This sprite is now a *child* of the scene, which means it is attached to this scene. For instance, if the scene grows, shrinks, or goes away, this child sprite will, too. In a SpriteKit game, the scene is always the parent object, and every sprite is added as a child of that scene or as a child of another sprite. Whenever you add a sprite, it's important to think about what that sprite's parent should be. For example, the skater sprite is a child of the scene, but if we wanted to add interchangeable hats onto the skater, we would use a hat sprite that is a child of the skater sprite. That way, whenever the skater jumped, the hat would stay on the skater, and we wouldn't have to also move the hat separately.

HOW IT WILL BE PLAYED: SCREEN ORIENTATION

It takes more work to create a game that runs in both portrait and landscape modes, so it's often best to decide which orientation is best for your game and just pick that one. Since our game is an action game that scrolls horizontally, landscape orientation (where the device is on its side, as shown in Figure 14-8) makes the most sense.

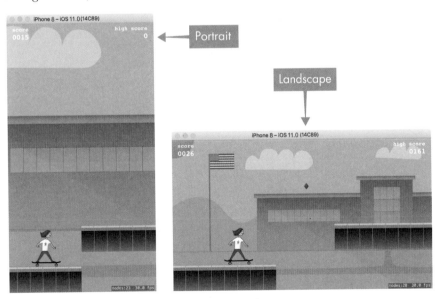

Figure 14-8: How our game looks in portrait versus landscape orientation

Try running the project now, using the iPhone 8 simulator, and you'll notice it may default to portrait orientation. Let's change the project settings so the game runs only in landscape. Go to the Project navigator and click the **SchoolhouseSkateboarder** project—it's at the top of the Project navigator with a blue icon next to it, as you can see in Figure 14-9.

Figure 14-9: Access the project settings by clicking the project entry in the Project navigator.

In Figure 14-10, you can see a list of projects and targets.

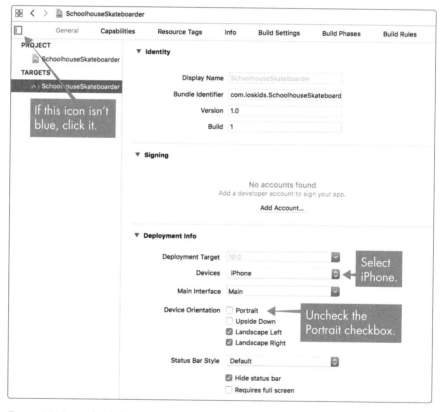

Figure 14-10: Uncheck the Portrait option, leaving both Landscape orientation options checked.

If you don't see the list of Projects and Targets on your screen, click the square icon in the upper-left corner of the window, as shown in Figure 14-10. This list will appear and the icon will turn blue to indicate that the list area is now being shown. Make sure the **SchoolhouseSkateboarder** target is selected. Now find the **Portrait** checkbox and uncheck it. Leave the Landscape orientation options checked. Since our game will run only on iPhones (and iPod touches), select **iPhone** as the Devices setting.

Run the game again, and you'll see it launches in landscape orientation. We're getting closer, but the background image doesn't yet fill the screen. We'll see how to fix this in a bit.

With the game now running in landscape orientation, you need to make sure that your simulator is also in landscape orientation. To rotate it, select **Hardware ▸ Rotate Right** from the simulator's menu, as shown in Figure 14-11.

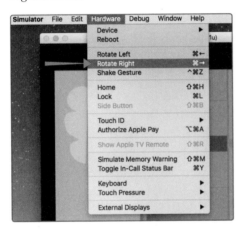

Figure 14-11: Rotating the simulator orientation to match the game

SIZING IMAGES FOR DIFFERENT SCREEN RESOLUTIONS

Before we dive into the code, we should decide which devices and screen resolutions we'll support. The more devices you support, the more you'll have to deal with different screen sizes, which means you need to do extra work to ensure the artwork assets you create will display properly on each device. Games tend to require more effort in this area than UIKit-based apps like our Birthday Tracker because game artwork will look stretched out if you just scale it up or down. To avoid that problem, you'll have to work with a different set of images for each device you want to support.

Xcode has a system for naming image files to help you tell which images are for which devices. For example, suppose you wanted to add an image of a skater to your game, and you had a skater image file that was 100 pixels wide and 100 pixels tall (100×100). You would name that image *skater.png*. You'd also need to create an image named *skater@2x.png* that is 200×200 pixels, and another image named *skater@3x.png* that is 300×300 pixels. These three files should be the same image in three different sizes. If the game is run on an iPhone 4, the *@2x* file will automatically be used thanks to the handy *@2x* suffix. If the game runs on an iPhone 6 Plus, the *@3x* file will automatically be used. In your code, you can just refer to the file as skater, and as long as you've correctly named the images in your project, Xcode will display the correct image.

For Schoolhouse Skateboarder, we'll support everything from the iPhone 4 on. That means we'll need to support the following four screen resolutions: 960×640, 1136×640, 1334×750, and 1920×1080.

NOTE *All the images we're using have a suffix, such as @2x or @3x. An image without a suffix, such as* skater.png, *is considered to be a 1x image. You only need to include 1x-sized images for older devices that have a non-retina display, such as an iPhone 3GS or a first-generation iPad mini. Therefore, all of our image files will have the @2x or @3x suffix.*

Our background image files are named *background@2x.png* and *background@3x.png*. If you look at the *Assets.xcassets* asset catalog, you'll notice that Xcode grouped these two images together. If you drag images at the same time into an Xcode asset catalog, Xcode automatically recognizes that they are different sizes of the same image because of how they are named and groups them together. See Figure 14-12.

Figure 14-12: Images with multiple sizes are grouped together in the asset catalog.

We have one last bit of prep to take care of before moving on from the background image. You may have noticed that when you run the game using the iPhone 8 simulator, the background image doesn't fill the entire screen, as shown in Figure 14-13. This is because of the way the Game template handles sizing a game scene. The game scene's size will be set based on the settings in the *GameScene.sks* scene editor file that was included in our project. We won't be using the scene editor in this project, so we need to add code in order to make sure our scenes are sized properly.

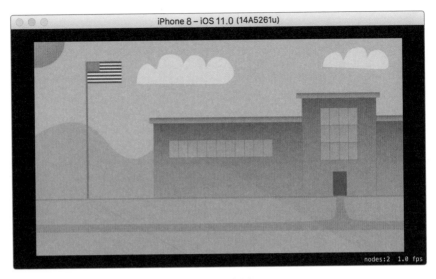

Figure 14-13: The background image doesn't fill the entire screen.

Click the *GameViewController.swift* file in the Project navigator and find the viewDidLoad() method. Add the following lines of code that set the scene's size:

GameViewController.swift

```
override func viewDidLoad() {
    --snip--
        scene.scaleMode = .aspectFill

        // Adjust the size of the scene to match the view
        let width = view.bounds.width
        let height = view.bounds.height
        scene.size = CGSize(width: width, height: height)

        // Present the scene
        view.presentScene(scene)

    --snip--
}
```

The code in the viewDidLoad() method creates an instance of the GameScene class and displays it. Since the GameScene is the main scene of our game, we want it to always fill the entire screen. The code that we added here determines the size (width and height) of the view being displayed, and sets the size of the new scene so that it fills the entire view.

Run the project again. The background image should fill the entire screen now.

WHAT YOU LEARNED

In this chapter, you started making the Schoolhouse Skateboarder game and learned about SpriteKit. You learned how to create a game project in Xcode and import assets, such as images, into the project. You also learned about supporting various device screen resolutions through standard file naming practices and about how to pick what image types you'll need in a game. Finally, you created and displayed a background image sprite.

Now that we've set up a SpriteKit game project with the resources we need and tackled the questions of screen orientation and resolution, it's time to program some action. In Chapter 15, we'll add our hero and the ground that she skates on, make everything move, and let the player tap on the screen to make her jump.

15

MAKING SCHOOLHOUSE
SKATEBOARDER A REAL GAME

In this chapter, we'll add our hero, the skateboarder. We'll use a little trick to make it look like she's moving: we'll move the ground beneath her. Then we'll add jumping to the game so that when the player taps on the screen, the skater jumps. To do all of this, we'll create our own custom sprite subclass, and we'll add a game loop where all the action happens.

OUR HERO, THE SKATEBOARDER

It's time to add the skater to our game. As we did with the background image, we'll create a sprite, position it on the screen, and then add it to the scene. To make a sprite, we use the SKSpriteNode class.

Our skater will need some additional properties to keep track of things, such as her current velocity (speed) and whether she is on the ground. Since `SKSpriteNode` doesn't have these properties, we'll create our own subclass of `SKSpriteNode` called `Skater`. This will allow us to add whatever extra properties we want to this sprite, in addition to all of the built-in `SKSpriteNode` properties.

CREATING A SKATER SPRITE CLASS

To create the `Skater` class, right-click the *SchoolhouseSkateboarder* folder in the Project navigator and choose **New File…**. On the next screen, choose the template called **Cocoa Touch Class** in the Source section of the iOS templates, and then click **Next**. Type `Skater` for the class name and `SKSpriteNode` for the class we want to subclass.

Click **Next**, and then on the final screen, click **Create** to confirm the file location. Now you'll see your new `Skater` class has appeared in both the Project navigator and the Editor pane.

IMPORTING SPRITEKIT

When you create a subclass of a SpriteKit class, such as `SKSpriteNode`, you need to add a statement at the top of your code to import SpriteKit for this class instead of UIKit. To import the SpriteKit library, change the line at the top of your new `Skater` class (*Skater.swift*) from this:

```
import UIKit
```

to this:

```
import SpriteKit
```

Importing SpriteKit makes all the SpriteKit classes and methods available within the *Skater.swift* file. If you try to use SpriteKit classes or methods in a file without first importing SpriteKit, you'll see errors like "Use of undeclared type."

ADDING CUSTOM PROPERTIES TO THE SKATER CLASS

Now that we've imported the SpriteKit library, let's add some properties to our new `Skater` class inside the existing braces:

Skater.swift

```
import SpriteKit

class Skater: SKSpriteNode {
❶ var velocity = CGPoint.zero
❷ var minimumY: CGFloat = 0.0
❸ var jumpSpeed: CGFloat = 20.0
❹ var isOnGround = true
}
```

Soon we'll be adding code to our game scene to make the skater jump, so we need these properties to keep track of the skater's movements.

The variable named `velocity`, a `CGPoint`, is initialized with `CGPoint.zero` at ❶. This is a shortcut to specify a point with x and y values both equal to 0.0. It's the same as using `CGPoint(x: 0.0, y: 0.0)`. Velocity means speed, so this variable will keep track of the skater's speed in both the x-direction (right-left) and y-direction (up-down). For example, when the skater jumps up, the velocity's y value will determine how fast she is moving upward.

The variable `minimumY` is a `CGFloat` that we'll use to specify the y-position of the ground ❷. So when the skater jumps, we know what y-position she should stop at when coming back down.

The variable `jumpSpeed` is a `CGFloat` that we'll use to specify how fast the skater can jump ❸. We've given it an initial value of 20.0. This is just a guess for now. We may have to change this value later if we find that the skater jumps too quickly or too slowly.

NOTE   *Notice that we specified the type `CGFloat` when we wrote `var minimumY: CGFloat = 0.0` and `var jumpSpeed: CGFloat = 20.0`. You will always need to do this when creating a `CGFloat` variable or constant, or else Xcode will infer that the type is `Double`.*

Finally, the variable `isOnGround` is a `Bool` that we'll use to keep track of whether the skater is currently on the ground ❹. If she's on the ground, she can jump. If she's not on the ground (that is, if she's already jumping), she can't jump again until she comes back down.

CREATING AN INSTANCE OF THE SKATER IN THE SCENE

Now it's time to switch back to our *GameScene.swift* file and add a skater sprite. Add the following code just inside the `GameScene` class's braces, above the `didMove(to:)` method:

GameScene.swift

```
import SpriteKit

class GameScene: SKScene {

    // The hero of the game, the skater, is created here
    let skater = Skater(imageNamed: "skater")

    override func didMove(to view: SKView) {
```

This line creates a new class property named skater, which is an instance of our new class Skater. It uses the image *skater.png,* which you should have already downloaded and added to your asset catalog in Chapter 14. Since skater is a class property (created inside the class declaration but outside of any function), it will be available to use inside any method within the GameScene class.

Note that creating a sprite doesn't make it show up on the screen. You'll always need to add the sprite as a child of the scene or as a child of another sprite, which we'll do soon. You'll see this common pattern with sprites: 1) create the sprite, 2) position the sprite and set any initial values, and 3) call the addChild() method to add the sprite to the scene. So far we've just created the sprite. Next, we'll set the sprite's position and values before calling the addChild() method to add the skater to our scene.

SETTING UP THE SKATER

To set our skater sprite's position and other initial values, we'll create a separate method called resetSkater(). We want to have this setup code in a separate method so that any time we need to reset the skater to her initial position (such as when the game has to restart), we can reuse this method.

Write the following method below the existing didMove(to:) method:

GameScene.swift

```
override func didMove(to view: SKView) {
--snip--
}

func resetSkater() {

    // Set the skater's starting position, zPosition, and minimumY
❶   let skaterX = frame.midX / 2.0
❷   let skaterY = skater.frame.height / 2.0 + 64.0
❸   skater.position = CGPoint(x: skaterX, y: skaterY)
❹   skater.zPosition = 10
❺   skater.minimumY = skaterY
}

override func update(_ currentTime: TimeInterval) {
    // Called before each frame is rendered
}
}
```

This method performs some basic setup for the skater sprite. First, we determine the skater's x-position, skaterX, by finding the x value at the middle of the scene's frame with frame.midX and dividing that by two ❶. This will put the skater in the left side of the scene, which will give the player time to respond to obstacles that come from the right side. If we position the skater exactly in the middle of the screen, the player might not have enough time to see the obstacles before they have to jump over them. Remember, the skater will stay in the same x-position on the screen since we will be animating the ground beneath her to make it look like she's moving.

At ❷, we calculate the y-position for our skater by adding half of the skater sprite's height to 64. In SpriteKit, y-positions increase as you go up the screen (unlike in UIKit apps, where a y-position of 0.0 represents the top of the screen). Also, when we set a sprite's position, we're actually setting where the *center* of that sprite should be. Therefore, if we place a sprite at a y-position of 0.0, half of it would be on the screen, and half would be off. So to place an object at the bottom of the screen (but not hanging off the screen), we need to set its y-position to half of its height. Finally, to account for the height of our sidewalk, which will be 64, we add 64 to the y-position of the skater. Figure 15-1 shows how y-positions work in SpriteKit.

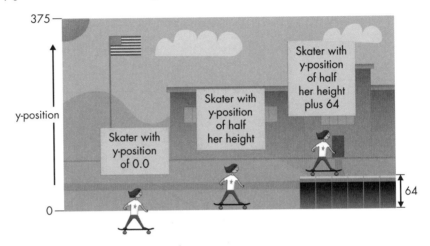

Figure 15-1: Setting the y-position of a sprite

Now that we've calculated the skater's x- and y-positions, we set our skater's starting position by creating a CGPoint that uses these values ❸.

The zPosition of the skater sprite is set to 10 ❹. To understand zPosition, imagine you're assembling a stack of papers. Papers that are higher up in the stack have a higher zPosition and will be *on top* of anything that has a lower zPosition. It's possible for two or more sprites to have the same zPosition, in which case the sprite that was added later would be on top.

When we added our background sprite, we didn't set a zPosition, so it's at the default zPosition of 0 (the bottom of the stack). Since we want our skater to be on top of the background image, we're setting a zPosition of 10. This way, we still have some room to put other objects in between the skater and the background (unlike if we'd set the skater's zPosition to just 1). If we wanted to add a dog walking around the scene, we could put it at a zPosition of 5, and it would be behind the skater but in front of the background image.

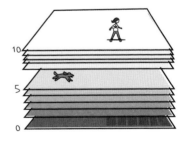

Finally, at ❺, we set the skater sprite's minimumY variable to be the same as her y-position. Over the course of playing the game, the skater will jump, so her y-position will change, but now we'll always have this minimumY variable to indicate what the skater's y-position should be when she's on the ground.

SEEING THE SKATER ON THE SCREEN

Now we're ready to add the skater to the scene! Add these lines inside the didMove(to:) method, below the existing code in that method:

```
override func didMove(to view: SKView) {
    --snip--
    addChild(background)

    // Set up the skater and add her to the scene
    resetSkater()
    addChild(skater)
}
```

Now when the game scene is first presented, our skater sprite will be set up and added as a child of the scene. Your entire GameScene class should now look like this:

GameScene.swift

```
import SpriteKit

class GameScene: SKScene {

    // The hero of the game, the skater, is created here
    let skater = Skater(imageNamed: "skater")

    override func didMove(to view: SKView) {

        anchorPoint = CGPoint.zero

        let background = SKSpriteNode(imageNamed: "background")
        let xMid = frame.midX
        let yMid = frame.midY
        background.position = CGPoint(x: xMid, y: yMid)
        addChild(background)

        // Set up the skater and add her to the scene
        resetSkater()
        addChild(skater)
    }

    func resetSkater() {

        // Set the skater's starting position, zPosition, and minimumY
        let skaterX = frame.midX / 2.0
        let skaterY = skater.frame.height / 2.0 + 64.0
        skater.position = CGPoint(x: skaterX, y: skaterY)
        skater.zPosition = 10
        skater.minimumY = skaterY
    }

    override func update(_ currentTime: TimeInterval) {
        // Called before each frame is rendered
    }
}
```

Now, using the iPhone 8 simulator, run the game by pressing ⌘-R. You should see something like Figure 15-2.

Figure 15-2: Our hero makes her first appearance!

Congratulations! You have set up the skater sprite and the skater's starting position. Looks great, right? We'll add the sidewalk and make her skate along it pretty soon, too, but first let's talk about SpriteKit's debugging tool.

UNDERSTANDING SPRITEKIT'S DEBUGGING INFORMATION

Notice the small text in the bottom-right corner of your simulator? It should say something like nodes:3 25.0 fps. This is helpful information about what's happening in your game. In SpriteKit, most things that are displayed on the screen are called *nodes*. This display is telling us there are currently three SpriteKit nodes being displayed. This makes sense, since we have our GameScene itself, the background image, and the skater sprite.

Knowing how many nodes are currently displayed can help you debug problems with your code. For example, if your game is slowing down, you might look at the debugging info and see that the number of nodes keeps going up. This would tell you that perhaps you're adding too many sprites and not removing them when you're done with them.

The display is also telling us that the game is currently running at 25 frames per second (your actual number may differ depending on your computer's speed). Movies are made up of many *frames*, or images, that give the appearance of animation or movement when they are played back quickly. The same is true of games! Our game is updating the scene and its nodes 25 times per second. None of our nodes are moving, so you can't actually tell, but every second the screen is being completely redrawn 25 times. When we add our sidewalk bricks and make them move in the next section, the magic of animation will make this very clear.

HITTIN' THE BRICKS

As the skater skates along the sidewalk, she won't actually move to the right. Rather, we'll keep adding bricks onto the right side of the screen that move to the left side. This is a nice trick to create the illusion that the skater is moving to the right.

CREATING SIDEWALK BRICKS

Each time we add a brick into the scene, we'll also add it into an array that we'll be using to keep track of all our bricks. Once a brick moves off the left edge of the screen, we'll remove it from the array and also remove it from the scene. It's important to remove sprites that you no longer need, or your node count will keep going up and up. Your game will slow down because the game engine is still keeping track of every node in the scene!

Add the code to create this class property at the top of GameScene, just above where we created the skater:

GameScene.swift

```
class GameScene: SKScene {

    // An array that holds all the current sidewalk bricks
    var bricks = [SKSpriteNode]()

    // The hero of the game, the skater, is created here
```

This creates a class variable named bricks and assigns to it an empty array of sprites (since our bricks will be sprites). Just below that, add the following code:

```
class GameScene: SKScene {
    --snip--
    var bricks = [SKSpriteNode]()

    // The size of the sidewalk brick graphics used
    var brickSize = CGSize.zero

    // The hero of the game, the skater, is created here
```

This brickSize variable does exactly what its name says and sets up each brick's size. It will come in handy later when we're moving our bricks around. We set brickSize to CGSize.zero now, since we don't know yet what the actual brick size will be. Once we create the brick sprites, we'll set the brickSize to the actual size of those sprites.

We need one more class property, scrollSpeed, to keep track of how fast the bricks are moving. Add the following code below the brickSize declaration:

```
    --snip--
    var brickSize = CGSize.zero
```

```
// Setting for how fast the game is scrolling to the right
// This may increase as the user progresses in the game
var scrollSpeed: CGFloat = 5.0

// The hero of the game, the skater, is created here
```

Again, remember that you need to specify the CGFloat data type. Otherwise, Xcode will infer that the variable is a Double.

Now we're going to add a method that will create a new sidewalk brick. Since we'll be displaying a lot of sidewalk bricks, this method will be a timesaver. In games, when something new comes on the screen, it is said to have *spawned*, so we'll use that word to refer to our method. Just below the resetSkater() method, add the following method:

```
❶ func spawnBrick(atPosition position: CGPoint) -> SKSpriteNode {

    // Create a brick sprite and add it to the scene
❷   let brick = SKSpriteNode(imageNamed: "sidewalk")
❸   brick.position = position
❹   brick.zPosition = 8
❺   addChild(brick)

    // Update our brickSize with the real brick size
❻   brickSize = brick.size

    // Add the new brick to the array of bricks
❼   bricks.append(brick)

    // Return this new brick to the caller
❽   return brick
}
```

At ❶, our spawnBrick(atPosition:) method takes a CGPoint for input (so it knows where to place the brick) and returns the newly created brick sprite. Note that we are using a custom parameter label of atPosition for the position parameter. This is so when we call the method, it's more readable—we can see that we're asking for a brick to be spawned at a specific position.

We create the brick sprite as an SKSpriteNode using an image named *sidewalk.png* ❷. At ❸, the new brick sprite is placed at the position that was passed in to the method. At ❹, the brick sprite is given a zPosition of 8. Remember that we put our background image at a zPosition of 0 and our skater sprite at a zPosition of 10, so these sidewalk bricks will always be on top of the background image but behind the skater.

After that, our brick is added to the scene ❺ (or it won't show up). The line at ❻ sets our brickSize class property equal to this new brick's size based on the actual size of *sidewalk.png*, which will be helpful to have a bit later in our code. At ❼, our brick sprite is added to the array of bricks we created earlier. Finally, at ❽, the new brick sprite is returned to the code that called this method.

UPDATING SIDEWALK BRICKS

Now that we have some code to create bricks, we need a method that will go through all the onscreen bricks and move them to the left. This method will be called a lot (25 times per second or more), so it only needs to move the bricks by a tiny bit each time. We'll pass in the amount the bricks move as a parameter so it can be adjusted as the skater speeds up. (This is how we'll make the game harder over time!) Add the following method declaration below the spawnBrick(atPosition:) method:

GameScene.swift

```swift
func updateBricks(withScrollAmount currentScrollAmount: CGFloat) {
}
```

This method will be our largest yet, so we'll walk through it one chunk at a time. Inside the method's braces, add the following:

```swift
func updateBricks(withScrollAmount currentScrollAmount: CGFloat) {

    // Keep track of the greatest x-position of all the current bricks
    var farthestRightBrickX: CGFloat = 0.0

}
```

This is a variable we'll use to keep track of the x-position of the brick that is farthest to the right. That way we'll know when it's time to add another brick on the right edge, and where to position that new brick. Below that, add the following block of code:

```swift
func updateBricks(withScrollAmount currentScrollAmount: CGFloat) {
    --snip--
    var farthestRightBrickX: CGFloat = 0.0

❶ for brick in bricks {

    ❷ let newX = brick.position.x - currentScrollAmount

        // If a brick has moved too far left (off the screen), remove it
    ❸ if newX < -brickSize.width {

        ❹ brick.removeFromParent()

        ❺ if let brickIndex = bricks.index(of: brick) {
            ❻ bricks.remove(at: brickIndex)
            }

    ❼ } else {

            // For a brick that is still onscreen, update its position
        ❽ brick.position = CGPoint(x: newX, y: brick.position.y)
```

```
                        // Update our farthest-right position tracker
    ❾ if brick.position.x > farthestRightBrickX {
        ❿ farthestRightBrickX = brick.position.x
        }
    }
  }
}
```

This code loops through our array of bricks at ❶ using a for-in loop. The line at ❷ calculates a new x-position for the brick sprite by subtracting the passed-in currentScrollAmount from its x-position. This newX represents a new spot that's a little to the left of where this brick is currently positioned.

Next, at ❸, we use an if statement to see if this newX position would move the brick offscreen by checking if it is less than the negative of the brick's width (-brickSize.width). Why not just check if the newX is less than 0.0? Remember that when you set a sprite's position, you're telling the computer where to put the *center* of the sprite. So at an x-position of 0.0, the brick is still partially on the screen. Checking that the brick's position is less than -brickSize.width ensures that the brick is fully offscreen before we remove it. Figure 15-3 illustrates how the bricks are moving.

This brick has moved fully offscreen and must now be moved back to the far right.

This brick, with an x-position of 0.0, is still partially onscreen.

Bricks are moving to the left.

Figure 15-3: The bricks are moved to the left until they are off the screen.

Sprites that are no longer needed should be removed so the app won't have to waste resources keeping track of extra nodes. Line ❹ does just that. To remove any sprite from the scene, we call the removeFromParent() method on the sprite. When removed from the scene, the sprite will disappear. That's why we want to be sure it's completely offscreen before removing it, or it would look like it just vanished.

There is one more bit of cleanup we need to do when removing a brick sprite: we need to remove it from our bricks array, because we want this array to contain only onscreen bricks. The line at ❺ checks if this brick sprite is in our bricks array by testing if its index in the array is found. Then, the line at ❻ uses this index to remove the sprite from the bricks array.

Now that we've taken care of bricks that have moved offscreen, we can use an else block at ❼ to deal with bricks that are still onscreen. The line at ❽ sets a new x-position for the brick sprite by creating a CGPoint using the newX that we calculated. We want the bricks to move only to the left, not up or down, so we won't be changing their y-positions.

The last thing we need to do inside the else block is to update our farthestRightBrickX variable. To do this, we check if the current brick sprite's new x-position is greater than the value of farthestRightBrickX at ❾. If it is, we set farthestRightBrickX equal to this brick sprite's x-position at ❿. This way, when the for-in loop is finished and we've iterated through all the bricks in our array, the value of farthestRightBrickX will be equal to the x-position of whichever brick was found to be farthest to the right.

FILLING THE SCREEN WITH BRICKS

After repositioning all the bricks, we need to see if it's time to add any new bricks. Since our bricks scroll from right to left, we'll continually have bricks that go offscreen to the left and are removed, and new bricks that need to spawn on the right side of the screen. If we didn't keep spawning new bricks, our skater would quickly run out of sidewalk!

To spawn new bricks on the right, we need to add one more chunk of code to our method updateBricks(withScrollAmount:). Add the following below the for-in loop you just added:

GameScene.swift

```
func updateBricks(withScrollAmount currentScrollAmount: CGFloat) {
    --snip--
    for brick in bricks {
        --snip--
    }

    // A while loop to ensure our screen is always full of bricks
 ❶ while farthestRightBrickX < frame.width {

     ❷ var brickX = farthestRightBrickX + brickSize.width + 1.0
     ❸ let brickY = brickSize.height / 2.0
    }
}
```

We already know the x-position of the farthest-right brick from our previous chunk of code. Now we use a while loop at ❶ to spawn a brick any time we find that our farthest-right brick position is less than the scene's width. This loop will keep executing until we have sidewalk bricks that fill the screen, all the way to the right edge. Inside the while loop, we need to create a new brick sprite and add it.

First, we calculate the new sprite's position. The line at ❷ determines the new brick sprite's x-position by adding one full brick's width to the current farthest-right position, plus an extra one-point gap. This extra one-point gap will leave a tiny space between each brick, which makes the movement of the bricks easier to see. (Later, try seeing how the sidewalk looks without the + 1.0 gap.) The line at ❸ calculates the new brick sprite's y-position by dividing the brick's height in half. This will place the brick at the bottom edge of the screen. Later on, we'll vary this y-position so the player has to jump up to reach higher sidewalks. For now, we're just going to place all the bricks on the bottom edge, like a normal sidewalk.

LEAVING GAPS TO JUMP

While we're positioning the bricks, let's make the game more fun for the player. The next bit of code adds some random gaps in the sidewalk that the player will have to jump over. Add this code inside the while loop, below the let brickY line:

GameScene.swift

```
    let brickY = brickSize.height / 2.0

    // Every now and then, leave a gap the player must jump over
❶   let randomNumber = arc4random_uniform(99)

❷   if randomNumber < 5 {

        // There is a 5 percent chance that we will
        // leave a gap between bricks
❸       let gap = 20.0 * scrollSpeed
❹       brickX += gap
    }

    // Spawn a new brick and update the rightmost brick
❺   let newBrick = spawnBrick(atPosition: CGPoint(x: brickX, y: brickY))
❻   farthestRightBrickX = newBrick.position.x
    }
}
```

Adding random elements to games is important to keep the gameplay from being predictable. We achieve randomness by asking the computer to generate a random number, which is like rolling a die. The function arc4random_uniform() is a good way to create random integers by simply passing in an integer representing the maximum value for your random number. The line at ❶ creates a random integer between 0 and 99 using this function. This is like rolling a 100-sided die because there are 100 possible numbers between 0 and 99. Next we use an if statement at ❷ to check if this number is less than 5. This means the code inside the if statement will have a 5 percent chance of executing.

The line at ❸ calculates how large of a gap to create. As the skater's speed increases, we want the gaps to get bigger and bigger, so this gap amount is set to 20.0 times the scroll speed. As the speed increases, the gaps will get larger. Finally, the line at ❹ adds this gap to our brickX variable. Now when we set the brick's position, instead of being right next to the previous brick, it will be placed a good amount farther to the right, creating a gap.

After determining the x- and y-positions of the new brick, we spawn a new brick at ❺. Since we've added this new brick to the right of any existing bricks, we set farthestRightBrickX at ❻ to this new brick's x-position. This will create our exit condition for the while loop. Figure 15-4 shows how the while loop works.

Figure 15-4: The while loop keeps adding bricks until the width of the screen is filled.

Once enough bricks have been added and the farthestRightBrickX is greater than or equal to the scene's width, the while loop will stop executing.

THE GAME LOOP

It's time to bring it all together by writing the main game loop. The game loop is a block of code that the game engine (SpriteKit) will execute over and over whenever the game is running. It's where we'll update all of our sprite's positions, creating the actual animation in our game. All SpriteKit scenes have a method called update(_:), which we must override to update our sprite positions.

TRACKING THE UPDATE TIME

Before we write the main game loop code, however, we need to add a class property to keep track of when the last update happened. Add an optional lastUpdateTime property to GameScene, right below scrollSpeed:

GameScene.swift

```
var scrollSpeed: CGFloat = 5.0

// The timestamp of the last update method call
var lastUpdateTime: TimeInterval?

// The hero of the game, the skater, is created here
```

Our update(_:) method will be called very often, about 30 times per second. Notice I didn't say *exactly* 30 times per second. The game engine will attempt to call the update(_:) method 30 times per second, but it's not guaranteed to run exactly that number of times. And on some devices it will actually be targeting 60 times per second. So we need to keep track of how much time has *actually* passed between each update in order to make sure everything animates smoothly. We don't want our skater to look like she's constantly speeding up and slowing down just because this method isn't called at an exact time interval. By keeping track of how much time has passed, we can adjust how much we move our sprites in each update and keep them moving smoothly.

CALCULATING ELAPSED TIME FOR EACH UPDATE

When we first created this project using the Game template, an empty update(_:) method was added automatically. Inside this method, add the following code to calculate how much time has passed since the last update:

GameScene.swift

```
override func update(_ currentTime: TimeInterval) {

    // Determine the elapsed time since the last update call
❶   var elapsedTime: TimeInterval = 0.0
```

```
❷ if let lastTimeStamp = lastUpdateTime {
    ❸ elapsedTime = currentTime - lastTimeStamp
  }
}
```

The line at ❶ creates an elapsedTime variable of the TimeInterval data type. TimeInterval is a Double data type used to track time intervals in seconds. Just like when we create a CGFloat, we need to specify that this is a TimeInterval, or Xcode will use type inference to assume this is a plain Double. The line at ❷ unwraps the lastUpdateTime, if it exists. It is an optional because at the start of the game there will be no last update. So, the first time the update(_:) method is called, lastUpdateTime will be nil. If we're able to unwrap it, then the line at ❸ calculates the elapsedTime, which is how much time has passed since the last update call.

Now add the following line to the update(_:) method, to set lastUpdateTime equal to the currentTime:

```
override func update(_ currentTime: TimeInterval) {
    --snip--
        elapsedTime = currentTime - lastTimeStamp
    }

    lastUpdateTime = currentTime
}
```

This ensures that the next time the update(_:) method is called, our lastUpdateTime variable will be accurate.

ADJUSTING SCROLL SPEED USING THE ELAPSED TIME

Next, we will calculate our scroll speed. Add the following to your update(_:) method:

GameScene.swift

```
override func update(_ currentTime: TimeInterval) {
    --snip--
    lastUpdateTime = currentTime

❶  let expectedElapsedTime: TimeInterval = 1.0 / 60.0

    // Here we calculate how far everything should move in this update
❷  let scrollAdjustment = CGFloat(elapsedTime / expectedElapsedTime)
❸  let currentScrollAmount = scrollSpeed * scrollAdjustment
}
```

The line at ❶ calculates the expected time lapse. About 1/60 of a second should pass between each call to update(_:) since the app will probably run at 60 frames per second on an actual iOS device (though it will probably run at less than 60 frames per second in the iOS simulator). The code we're adding here will ensure that the skater appears to move at the same speed, regardless of which device (or simulator) is used.

The line at ❷ calculates a scroll adjustment factor by dividing the actual elapsed time by the expected elapsed time. If more time has passed than expected (greater than 1/60 of a second), this factor will be greater than 1.0. If less time has passed than expected, this factor will be less than 1.0. The line at ❸ determines what our scroll speed should be for this update by multiplying scrollSpeed by this adjustment factor.

UPDATING THE BRICKS

Add the following line of code to finish the update(_:) method:

GameScene.swift

```
override func update(_ currentTime: TimeInterval) {
    --snip--
    let currentScrollAmount = scrollSpeed * scrollAdjustment

    updateBricks(withScrollAmount: currentScrollAmount)
}
```

Now that we've calculated the correct scroll amount for this update, we call our udpateBricks(_:) method and pass in the calculated scroll amount.

We've now reached a good time to test out the app. Press ⌘-R to run the app and see what happens! Your screen should look something like Figure 15-5.

Figure 15-5: Our skater is now skating along the sidewalk!

It should now look like the skater is skating along the sidewalk. You can see the sidewalk bricks moving from right to left, and every now and then (a 5 percent chance every time a brick is spawned) a gap appears. Notice that the count of nodes in the lower right should stay fairly consistent. This tells us that we are properly removing the bricks that went offscreen. If this number kept going up, we'd know that we forgot to remove them. It's starting to look more like a game, but the skater just slides right over the gaps. Let's give her the ability to jump.

UP, UP, AND AWAY— MAKING THE SKATER JUMP

We're going to add code so that when the player taps on the screen, the skater jumps. To know when the player taps, we'll use a *tap gesture recognizer*. Table 15-1 shows some common types of gesture recognizers you can use to know when the user has performed certain actions.

Table 15-1: Common Gesture Recognizers

Gesture	Gesture recognizer	What it detects
Tap	UITapGestureRecognizer	One or more fingers tapping on the screen one or more times
Pinch	UIPinchGestureRecognizer	Pinches with two fingers, typically used for zooming in or out
Swipe	UISwipeGestureRecognizer	Swipes across the screen with one or more fingers
Pan	UIPanGestureRecognizer	One or more fingers moving across the screen in any direction
Long press	UILongPressGestureRecognizer	One or more fingers being held down on the screen for a certain amount of time

We want to know about taps, so we'll use the UITapGestureRecognizer. The tap gesture recognizer will call a method of our choosing any time the user taps a finger anywhere on the screen.

USING A TAP GESTURE RECOGNIZER

To use a gesture recognizer, you simply create it and then add it to the view. Add this code at the bottom of the didMove(to:) method to create and add the tap gesture recognizer:

GameScene.swift

```
override func didMove(to view: SKView) {
    --snip--
    addChild(skater)

    // Add a tap gesture recognizer to know when the user tapped the screen
❶ let tapMethod = #selector(GameScene.handleTap(tapGesture:))
❷ let tapGesture = UITapGestureRecognizer(target: self, action: tapMethod)
❸ view.addGestureRecognizer(tapGesture)
}
```

With this code, any time the user taps on the screen, the `handleTap(_:)` method will be called on our game scene. First, we create a *selector* called `tapMethod` ❶. A selector is a reference to the name of a method. Soon we're going to add a new method called `handleTap(_:)`, and this constant, `tapMethod`, is just a reference to that method. This will allow us to tell the tap gesture recognizer which method it should call when the user taps on the screen.

At ❷, we create the tap gesture recognizer. Its initializer takes a target and a selector. The target tells the gesture recognizer what class the selector will be in, and the selector is the method to call. Since we're going to add the `handleTap(_:)` method to the `GameScene` class that we're already in, we use `self` to refer to this class.

Finally, the line at ❸ adds the new gesture recognizer to the scene's view. A gesture recognizer must be added to the view, or it won't do anything. We put this code inside the `didMove(to:)` method because a gesture recognizer only needs to be added to a view once and it will keep handling gestures until you remove it.

Now we just have to add this `handleTap(_:)` method! Add this new method just below the existing `update(_:)` method:

```
override func update(_ currentTime: TimeInterval) {
    --snip--
}

❶ @objc func handleTap(tapGesture: UITapGestureRecognizer) {
      // Make the skater jump if player taps while the skater is on the ground
   ❷ if skater.isOnGround {
         // Set the skater's y-velocity to the skater's initial jump speed
      ❸ skater.velocity = CGPoint(x: 0.0, y: skater.jumpSpeed)
         // Keep track of the fact that the skater is no longer on the ground
      ❹ skater.isOnGround = false
      }
}
```

At ❶, we're using an `@objc` tag, which we need on any method called by a selector, because selectors are part of the old language used for iOS development, Objective-C. Swift can't reference methods by name, so we borrow selectors from Objective-C.

When the user taps on the screen, we need to make sure the skater is on the ground, so we check for this using an `if` statement at ❷. If the skater is already in the air, she can't jump again (without a jetpack, anyway). The line at ❸ sets the `velocity` of the skater sprite so that the x velocity is still `0.0` and the y velocity is equal to the sprite's `jumpSpeed` (which we defined in the `Skater` class). This allows us to make the skater jump straight up. Next, we set the skater sprite's `isOnGround` property to `false` at ❹ because once she starts a jump, she is no longer on the ground and shouldn't be allowed to jump again until she lands.

SIMULATING GRAVITY IN A SIMPLE WAY

Setting the skater's velocity doesn't make her jump, though. We need to use this velocity, in the `update(_:)` method, to update the skater's y-position.

First, we need to add one more class property, gravitySpeed, right under the declaration of var scrollSpeed at the top of the class, as follows.

GameScene.swift

```
var scrollSpeed: CGFloat = 5.0

// A constant for gravity, or how fast objects will fall to Earth
let gravitySpeed: CGFloat = 1.5

// The timestamp of the last update method call
```

We'll use this constant to determine how fast the skater should come back down when jumping. Now add the following method declaration just below the updateBricks(_:) method:

```
func updateSkater() {

}
```

We'll use this method to update the skater's position when she jumps. Add the following code inside this method:

```
func updateSkater() {
❶   if !skater.isOnGround {

        // Set the skater's new velocity as it is affected by "gravity"
❷       let velocityY = skater.velocity.y - gravitySpeed
❸       skater.velocity = CGPoint(x: skater.velocity.x, y: velocityY)

        // Set the skater's new y-position based on her velocity
❹       let newSkaterY: CGFloat = skater.position.y + skater.velocity.y
❺       skater.position = CGPoint(x: skater.position.x, y: newSkaterY)

    }
}
```

First, at ❶, we use an if statement to make sure we're moving the skater up or down only if she's not already on the ground. If she's not on the ground, then she must be jumping. So we need to move her up (if she's jumping up) or down (if gravity is pulling her back down).

The line at ❷ calculates a new y velocity by subtracting gravitySpeed from the current y velocity. When she jumps, she'll start at a fast, positive velocity. Then gravity will slowly decrease that velocity until she reaches the peak of her jump. After that, the velocity will become negative as she falls back to Earth. Picture throwing a ball straight up into the air: it will have a positive speed as it rises, slowing down until it

comes to a complete standstill, for an instant, at the top of its arc. Then it will fall back to you, gaining speed until you catch it or it hits the ground. This one line of code simulates that effect of gravity.

Next, the line at ❸ updates the skater's velocity with this new value (but keeps her x velocity unchanged, as this sprite doesn't actually move left or right). Now that we have the skater's velocity updated, we can calculate her new y-position by using this velocity ❹. We add the skater's velocity to her current y-position, and this gives us what her new y-position should be. The line at ❺ sets the skater's new position.

CHECKING FOR LANDINGS

The last thing we need to do in the updateSkater() method is to check if the skater has landed. Add the following code to the end of the method:

GameScene.swift

```
func updateSkater() {
    --snip--
        skater.position = CGPoint(x: skater.position.x, y: newSkaterY)

        // Check if the skater has landed
❶   if skater.position.y < skater.minimumY {

❷       skater.position.y = skater.minimumY
❸       skater.velocity = CGPoint.zero
❹       skater.isOnGround = true
    }
    }
}
```

The line at ❶ checks if the skater's y-position is less than her minimumY, which we already gave a value for in the resetSkater() method. If it is true, then she is on the ground (or below it).

Whenever the skater lands back on the ground, we need to do three things. At ❷, we set her y-position equal to her minimumY position to make sure she doesn't fall through the sidewalk. At ❸, we set her velocity to zero since the ground should stop her from falling any farther. Finally, at ❹, we set her isOnGround property to true so she can jump again.

Now, all we have to do is add a method call for our new updateSkater() method. Inside the update(_:) method, at the very end, add this code:

```
    updateBricks(withScrollAmount: currentScrollAmount)

    updateSkater()
}
```

Once again, run your game by pressing ⌘-R, and try tapping the screen to jump (when using the iOS simulator, clicking the mouse on the screen is the same as tapping). Your skater will jump, as shown in Figure 15-6.

Figure 15-6: Like any self-respecting skateboarder, our hero can finally ollie!

Now when you tap on the screen, the skater jumps! Tapping the screen triggers a call to handleTap(_:), thanks to our tap gesture recognizer. In that method, we set a positive y-velocity. Then in the ensuing calls to our game loop, or update(_:) method, the skater sprite's velocity is used to update her y-position until gravity pulls her back to Earth.

WHAT YOU LEARNED

In this chapter, you made the Schoolhouse Skateboarder app feel more like a game. You created a subclass of SKSpriteNode so that it could be a specialized Skater sprite, and then you added a skater to the game scene. Next, you added a whole bunch of sidewalk bricks and had them spawn, move, and then go away, all to give the appearance that our skater is skating along the sidewalk. Finally, you learned how to use velocity and position updates to make the skater jump.

You may have noticed that when the skater gets to a gap in the bricks, she just glides right over them. To make her fall in the gap, we would have to detect when the skater is moving over it and adjust her y-position accordingly. This approach can start to get complicated, but there's a better way: SpriteKit comes with a built-in physics engine that can do the hard work of velocity and position updates for you. In Chapter 16, we'll use SpriteKit's physics engine to bring the Schoolhouse Skateboarder game to life.

16

USING THE SPRITEKIT
PHYSICS ENGINE

In this chapter, we'll use SpriteKit's physics engine in our skateboarder game. A *physics engine* handles physical actions in games, such as how gravity works, objects' speeds, how things bounce off one another, and more so that you can make more complex games with less code. When coding a game, you define how the game elements (the skater, the bricks, the gems) should behave, and then the physics engine takes care of moving everything around.

For example, rather than changing the skater's velocity when she jumps, we'll simply tell the computer how heavy she is and then apply an upward force. This tells the physics engine to push the skater upward and lets gravity pull her back down. We don't have to do anything else. The physics engine takes care of changing the skater's velocity and position as she jumps, and it makes sure her wheels collide with the sidewalk bricks when she comes back down to land.

But first, the physics engine needs you to tell it a few things about the game's *physics world*. For example, if your game takes place in outer space, you'd tell it there is no gravity. For a game on Earth, you'd tell it to use a downward gravity. You also need to define *physics bodies* for each sprite or node in your world. This helps the computer determine how each item should behave based on its weight, whether it's affected by gravity, and its bounciness. Once you've done that, the sprites will automatically move around and behave like real-world objects when you run your game.

Now that you understand what the physics engine does, let's see it in action. We'll set up our physics world, create physics bodies for our sprites, apply forces, and check for collisions.

SETTING UP THE PHYSICS WORLD

Every SKScene comes with an SKPhysicsWorld property called physicsWorld. This is where we set global properties that apply to everything in this scene, such as gravity. Add the following line to the top of your didMove(to:) method inside the GameScene class:

GameScene.swift

```
override func didMove(to view: SKView) {

    physicsWorld.gravity = CGVector(dx: 0.0, dy: -6.0)

    anchorPoint = CGPoint.zero
    --snip--
}
```

This sets the gravity of the world using a CGVector, a data type that holds an x and a y value. It's just like a CGPoint, except that these values represent the components of a vector instead of the coordinates of a point. A *vector* is a speed combined with a direction that is determined by horizontal (x) and vertical (y) components. In other words, when we set the x and y values, we're setting the speed in the x-direction and the speed in the y-direction, which are then combined to make a vector. In our game, we set an x value of 0.0 and a y value of -6.0. This means there's no gravity in the horizontal direction and moderate gravity in the down direction. Normal Earth gravity has a y value of -9.8, so our value of -6.0 should make for a lighter, cartoony world. If we wanted gravity to pull everything upward, we could set a positive y value for the gravity.

The other physicsWorld property we can set is speed, which tells the physics engine how fast everything should run. The default value is 1.0, which means everything runs at normal speed. Setting a speed of 2.0 would make the entire physics simulation run twice as fast. This property can be useful for special effects in your game, such as slow motion or fast forward. For Schoolhouse Skateboarder, we'll leave the speed at the default value.

PHYSICS BODIES

When you add a sprite (like your skater) to a scene, the computer knows what that sprite should look like, but that's about it. It doesn't know if the sprite is light or heavy, rough or smooth, and whether it should bounce off other objects. SpriteKit has a class called SKPhysicsBody that we add to sprites to give them physics bodies.

GIVING SHAPE TO THE PHYSICS BODIES

All sprites are rectangles. An image file of a baseball, for example, is a rectangular image with a baseball drawn in the middle. When you create a sprite using that baseball image, the computer won't know it's round unless you tell it that information. If you want that sprite to bounce around like a real baseball, you need to add a *circular* physics body to the sprite.

Before you can apply a physics body to a sprite, you need to create one using the SKPhysicsBody class. This example code shows three different ways of creating physics bodies:

```
❶ let ballBody = SKPhysicsBody(circleOfRadius: 30.0)
❷ let boxBody = SKPhysicsBody(rectangleOf: box.size)
❸ let skaterBody = SKPhysicsBody(texture: skaterTexture, size: skater.size)
```

The first example creates a circular physics body with a radius of 30.0 points ❶. This would be perfect for a ball. The second example creates a rectangular body for a box-shaped sprite ❷. If you have a sprite you've already created, you can just use the size of the sprite for the physics body's size. In this case, we have a hypothetical box sprite that we use to set the size.

The final example creates a physics body by supplying a *texture* ❸, an image format commonly used in game development. Every SKSpriteNode you create has a property, texture, that you can use to access the sprite's texture, no matter which file type was used to create the sprite (PNG, JPEG, and so on). When you use a sprite's texture to create its physics body, SpriteKit automatically inspects the texture and creates a physics body that approximates the image's actual shape by finding any edges and ignoring the transparent parts of the image. In this case, we're using the texture skaterTexture, which we would have defined earlier in the code (you'll learn how to access the texture of a sprite in "Giving the skater Sprite a Physics Body" on page 244; don't worry about it for now). A texture doesn't define the size of a physics body, so we've also set the body's size to the skater sprite's size.

A sprite's texture is what gets displayed on the screen, and the physics body defines how that sprite will behave. The two don't need to line up exactly. You could use a circular physics body for a skater sprite, and that sprite would look like a skater but would roll around like a ball. While that would be funny to see, it's usually best to create a physics body that most closely matches the look of the sprite.

Figure 16-1 shows a skater sprite with different physics bodies applied. The figure shows the physics bodies in gray, but you won't actually see them on your screen. They are completely invisible and are only used by the computer to determine how that sprite should behave.

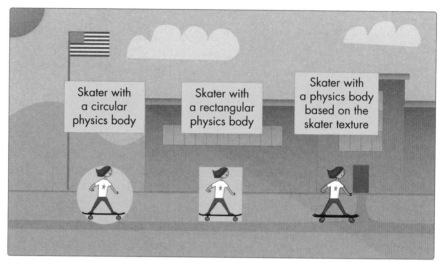

Figure 16-1: Various physics bodies applied to a skater sprite

The skater with the circular physics body would roll around like a ball. The one with the rectangular body would behave like a box. And the third one, with a physics body based on the actual texture, would behave much more like we would expect a real-world skater to behave. If the tip of her hand hits something, it will look like that's exactly what happened.

SETTING PROPERTIES OF PHYSICS BODIES

You set properties on physics bodies in order to describe them to the computer. A cloud would have a very low mass, meaning it's lightweight and wouldn't be affected by gravity. A bowling ball would be heavy and have a high mass, and it would definitely be affected by gravity. Table 16-1 lists some common properties of physics bodies.

Table 16-1: Common Properties of SKPhysicsBody

Property	Description
mass	Defines how heavy something is. You can use any valid CGFloat value for this. The actual values used are not important as long as you are consistent throughout your app.
friction	Defines how rough the surface is. For example, ice would have low friction, and objects touching it would tend to keep sliding. Values range from 0.0 to 1.0.
restitution	Defines the bounciness of an object. It's used when objects collide with each other. Values range from 0.0 to 1.0, where higher values mean bouncier.
affectedByGravity	Defines whether this object should be affected by gravity.
allowsRotation	Defines whether something should be allowed to rotate.

Let's see how we would use these properties. Since we won't actually use these examples for our game, you don't need to enter this code. Here are some examples:

```
  let bowlingBall = SKPhysicsBody(circleOfRadius: 10.0)
❶ bowlingBall.mass = 100.0
❷ bowlingBall.friction = 0.3
❸ bowlingBall.restitution = 0.1
❹ bowlingBall.affectedByGravity = true
❺ bowlingBall.allowsRotation = true

  let basketball = SKPhysicsBody(circleOfRadius: 10.0)
  basketball.mass = 12.0
  basketball.friction = 0.5
  basketball.restitution = 0.7
  basketball.affectedByGravity = true
  basketball.allowsRotation = true

  let iceCube = SKPhysicsBody(rectangleOf: CGSize(width: 1.0, height: 1.0))
  iceCube.mass = 7.0
  iceCube.friction = 0.1
  iceCube.restitution = 0.2
  iceCube.affectedByGravity = true
  iceCube.allowsRotation = false

  let cloud = SKPhysicsBody(texture: cloudTexture, size: cloudSize)
  cloud.mass = 1.0
  cloud.friction = 0.0
  cloud.restitution = 0.0
❻ cloud.affectedByGravity = false
  cloud.allowsRotation = false
```

In these examples, the bowling ball is heavy ❶, has low friction ❷, and has low restitution (bounciness) ❸. The basketball's code is the same, but its values are set so that it is light, has moderate friction, and is very bouncy. The ice cube is light, has low friction, and isn't very bouncy. And the cloud is very light, has no friction, and has no bounciness. All of the physics bodies are set to be affected by gravity ❹ except the cloud ❻ (since we don't want it to fall to Earth). Also, the bowling ball and basketball physics bodies are set to allow rotation of the object ❺, while the ice cube and the cloud are not.

When you're setting up physics bodies for your game sprites, it will take some trial and error to find the right values that make your objects behave the way you want.

GIVING THE SKATER SPRITE A PHYSICS BODY

Earlier, we talked about the various ways to assign a shape to a physics body. For our skater sprite, we're going to use the sprite's texture so that the physics body is shaped exactly like our skater. Switch to the *Skater.swift* file and add the following method to the Skater class:

Skater.swift

```
class Skater: SKSpriteNode {
    --snip--
    var isOnGround = true

    func setupPhysicsBody() {

❶      if let skaterTexture = texture {
❷          physicsBody = SKPhysicsBody(texture: skaterTexture, size: size)

❸          physicsBody?.isDynamic = true
❹          physicsBody?.density = 6.0
❺          physicsBody?.allowsRotation = true
❻          physicsBody?.angularDamping = 1.0
        }
    }
}
```

In order to create a physics body based on the skater sprite's texture, we first need to check that the texture exists, since texture is an optional property of SKSpriteNode. The line at ❶ unwraps the texture as skaterTexture. The line at ❷ sets the skater's physicsBody to a new SKPhysicsBody created using the texture and size of the skater sprite.

Next, we set some properties of the physics body in order to get it to behave the way we want. Setting the body's isDynamic property to true ❸ indicates that we want this object to be moved by the physics engine. Sometimes you want an object to be part of the physics simulation so that you can know when it contacts something, but you don't want the object to be moved around by the physics engine's forces, gravity, or collisions. In that case, you would set isDynamic to false.

At ❹, we set the density property of the skater sprite's physics body to 6.0. Density is how heavy something is for its size. A bowling ball is much more dense than a volleyball—in other words, it's the same size but much heavier. Setting the density tells the physics engine how this object should behave when it bumps into other objects or when forces are applied to it. If a bowling ball bumps into another object, it's more likely to push the other object away than a volleyball would be, because of the bowling ball's high density.

Setting the allowsRotation property to true ❺ tells the physics engine that this physics body may rotate, or spin. If we wanted the skater to never tip over, we could set this to false.

Finally, we set an angularDamping value ❻. *Angular damping* is how much a physics body resists rotating. A lower value allows the object to spin more freely, while a higher value means the object is less likely to tip over. Right now we'll set angularDamping to a value of 1.0, but later we may discover that the skater tips over too easily or not easily enough, and we may come back to change this value.

Now that we have a method on the Skater class to set up the skater sprite's physics body, we just need to call this method after the skater is created. Switch back to *GameScene.swift* and add this line inside the didMove(to:) method:

GameScene.swift

```
override func didMove(to view: SKView) {
    --snip--
    addChild(background)

    // Set up the skater and add her to the scene
    skater.setupPhysicsBody()
    resetSkater()
```

Since our skater sprite is created as a property of the GameScene class, it will already exist when didMove(to:) is called on the scene, so this is a good spot to set up the skater's physics body.

Next, we'll set up physics bodies for the sidewalk bricks as well so that the skater will be able to bump into them.

ADDING PHYSICS BODIES TO BRICKS

We need to add physics bodies to the bricks where they're created. Inside the spawnBrick(_:) method, add the following to the end of the method but before the last line, return brick:

GameScene.swift

```
func spawnBrick(atPosition position: CGPoint) -> SKSpriteNode {
    --snip--
    bricks.append(brick)

    // Set up the brick's physics body
❶  let center = brick.centerRect.origin
❷  brick.physicsBody = SKPhysicsBody(rectangleOf: brick.size, center: center)
❸  brick.physicsBody?.affectedByGravity = false

    // Return this new brick to the caller
```

For the bricks, we want to specify the physics body as a simple rectangle. Therefore, we'll need to know the size and the center point to place the rectangular body. The line at ❶ finds the center point of the newly created brick. The line at ❷ creates and assigns the brick sprite's physics body by specifying a rectangle the same size as the brick and placing it at the brick's center. Now that this physics body is set, it's attached directly on top of the brick sprite. The line at ❸ tells the brick sprite's physics body that it shouldn't be affected by gravity. We don't want the sidewalk to fall through the bottom of the screen.

CONTACTS AND COLLISIONS

The next thing the computer needs to know about your physics bodies is which ones should *collide* with each other. For example, we want the skater to collide with the sidewalk bricks so she won't pass through them. Some objects shouldn't collide, though. Later we'll add gems for our skater to collect. We *don't* want her to bounce off of the gems, so we'll tell the computer that the skater and gems do not have collisions. We'll want to know when the skater touches a gem, however. This is called *contact*. When any two objects contact each other, a special SpriteKit method is called to let us know so we can handle it. When the skater makes contact with a gem, we'll want to remove the gem so it looks like she collected it.

HANDLING CONTACTS AND COLLISIONS

Now that we've set up the world's gravity and given physics bodies to some sprites, try running the game and see what happens. Pay close attention when the app first starts or you'll miss it. You should see something like Figure 16-2, but the skater will disappear quickly.

Figure 16-2: She looks a little too happy for what's happening.

What's going on here? The skater and the bricks are all part of the physics simulation now, so the skater falls due to gravity, and we're moving the bricks to the left, so they bump into her. To fix this, we need to tell SpriteKit which objects should collide with one another and which ones shouldn't. In order to do that, we need a way to classify each object as a skater, a brick, or a gem (we won't add gems until later, but we'll create a category for them now).

In *GameScene.swift*, add the following struct at the top of the file after the import statement but before the GameScene's class definition:

GameScene.swift

```
import SpriteKit

/// This struct holds various physics categories, so we can define
/// which object types collide or have contact with each other
struct PhysicsCategory {
    static let skater: UInt32 = 0x1 << 0
    static let brick: UInt32 = 0x1 << 1
    static let gem: UInt32 = 0x1 << 2
}

class GameScene: SKScene {
```

This PhysicsCategory struct defines a few different categories to which physics bodies can belong. The values must be of type UInt32, a special type of unsigned 32-bit integer SpriteKit uses for physics categories. *Unsigned* means that the integer has no positive or negative sign. Unsigned integers must always be zero or positive, never negative. A 32-bit integer is a type of integer that can hold a very large number. Integers may be specified as 8-bit, 16-bit, 32-bit, or 64-bit. In Swift, we normally don't have to specify how many bits to use for an integer because the Swift type Int automates this. But since SpriteKit physics categories specifically require a UInt32, we need to specify this type or we'll get an error later when we assign these physics categories to our physics bodies.

We assign these PhysicsCategory values using a bitmask (0x1 << 0). It's not necessary at this point to understand what a bitmask is. It's enough to know that each physics category needs a unique bitmask number that distinguishes it from other categories. Each new category you add should have a value after the << that is 1 higher than the previous one—but all the values must be less than 32. Now that we've defined this struct, we can put each physics body into the appropriate category.

For the bricks, add the following code inside the spawnBrick(atPosition:) method, just after the line of code that sets the affectedByGravity property:

```
func spawnBrick(atPosition position: CGPoint) -> SKSpriteNode {
    --snip--
    brick.physicsBody?.affectedByGravity = false
```

```
❶ brick.physicsBody?.categoryBitMask = PhysicsCategory.brick
❷ brick.physicsBody?.collisionBitMask = 0

    // Return this new brick to the caller
```

The line at ❶ sets the physics body's `categoryBitMask` to the brick category we created. This tells SpriteKit what type of object this body is. Next, we set the physics body's `collisionBitMask` to 0 ❷. Setting one of the physics body's bitmasks to 0 means it should not be assigned to any categories for that bitmask property. So setting the `collisionBitMask` to 0 tells SpriteKit that bricks shouldn't collide with anything. In SpriteKit, when a physics body hits and bounces off another physics body, that's called a collision. When we want something to collide with other physics bodies, we define `collisionBitMask`. But since we don't want the bricks to ever bounce off anything, including the skater, we don't want them to collide with anything. They should stay where they are. The `collisionBitMask` tells SpriteKit only how the current object should behave for collisions. It doesn't tell *other* objects how they should behave when hitting the bricks—that's up to the other objects' physics bodies.

For the skater, open *Skater.swift* and add the following code inside `setupPhysicsBody()` at the end of the method:

Skater.swift

```
func setupPhysicsBody() {
    --snip--
        physicsBody?.angularDamping = 1.0

  ❶    physicsBody?.categoryBitMask = PhysicsCategory.skater
  ❷    physicsBody?.collisionBitMask = PhysicsCategory.brick
  ❸    physicsBody?.contactTestBitMask = PhysicsCategory.brick | ↵
            PhysicsCategory.gem
    }
}
```

First, we set the category of the skater equal to the skater physics category we created ❶. Next, we set the `collisionBitMask` equal to the brick category ❷. This tells SpriteKit that we want the skater to be affected by collisions with bricks—she should bounce off the bricks.

Finally, we set the `contactTestBitMask` to be both the brick and the gem categories ❸. This tells SpriteKit that we want to know when the skater has contacted, or touched, either of these types of objects. The vertical line (|), or pipe character, is a way of specifying multiple bitmask values for a property. Since we defined the PhysicsCategory struct using a bitmask, we can set one or more values for any of the physics category properties using

this pipe character to separate the values. We could string together as many different categories as we wanted here using pipes. Setting the contactTestBitMask doesn't affect how the objects behave in the physics simulation. It simply means we'll be notified when these objects touch. We want to know when the skater touches a brick because that tells us whether she is on the ground. We also want to know when she touches a gem so that she can collect the gem and get points for it.

If you run the project now, you should see the skater skating along the top of the bricks. If you watch closely, you should also see that she dips into the gaps in the bricks, thanks to the physics engine. If you make the skater jump a bunch of times, you may even be able to get her to tip over.

RESPONDING TO CONTACTS

Now that we've set the categories of the physics bodies, and set a contact bitmask for the skater's physics body, we can have the physics engine tell us when the skater touches a brick. We'll use this information to know when the skater sprite is on the ground. If she's touching any brick objects, then she is on the ground. The physics engine reports contacts to us through a protocol called SKPhysicsContactDelegate. Let's make our GameScene class implement this protocol.

First, in *GameScene.swift*, add the protocol to the class definition by typing a comma followed by the protocol name, like this:

GameScene.swift

```
class GameScene: SKScene, SKPhysicsContactDelegate {
```

Next, we have to set our GameScene as the contact delegate of the physics world. This means that our GameScene class is where contacts will be reported. Inside the didMove(to:) method, add this line just below the existing line where we set the gravity of the physics world:

```
override func didMove(to view: SKView) {

    physicsWorld.gravity = CGVector(dx: 0.0, dy: -6.0)
    physicsWorld.contactDelegate = self

    anchorPoint = CGPoint.zero
```

Finally, we have to add the method that will be called whenever two physics bodies come into contact with each other. SKPhysicsContactDelegate defines a method called didBegin(_:) to do this. Add this method inside *GameScene.swift* at the bottom of the GameScene class:

```
@objc func handleTap(tapGesture: UITapGestureRecognizer) {
    --snip--
}

// MARK:- SKPhysicsContactDelegate Methods
❶ func didBegin(_ contact: SKPhysicsContact) {
```

```
    // Check if the contact is between the skater and a brick
❷ if contact.bodyA.categoryBitMask == PhysicsCategory.skater && ↵
        contact.bodyB.categoryBitMask == PhysicsCategory.brick {

    ❸ skater.isOnGround = true
    }
}
```

You may have noticed that when you start typing func didBegin ❶, Xcode autocomplete suggests this method declaration. Xcode is expecting you to add this method since you added the SKPhysicsContactDelegate protocol to the class definition. The contact object passed in to this method has two physics bodies as properties called bodyA and bodyB. By checking the categories of the bodies ❷, we can test if this contact occurred between the skater and a brick. If so, at ❸ we set the skater sprite's isOnGround property to true because we know the skater is on the ground. We'll add code to handle gem contacts in Chapter 17.

APPLYING FORCES TO PHYSICS BODIES

To make objects move around, we can apply forces to them. Earlier, we used the example of applying an upward force to the skater to make her jump, but forces can be applied in any direction. Think of a force as an unseen hand pushing on something in our game. Forces can also be applied as a *continuous* force or as an *impulse*. A continuous force is one that keeps pushing on something, like the thrust of a rocket.

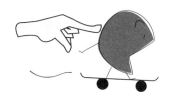

An impulse is a one-time force that is applied instantaneously to an object, such as kicking a soccer ball. There are two different functions we could use on a physics body to apply an upward force: applyForce(_:) for continuous forces, and applyImpulse(_:) for impulses.

Before implementing the physics engine, we handled jumping by setting a velocity on the skater when the player tapped on the screen. But now that we have physics bodies, we want to make her jump by applying a one-time force. To make our skater jump, we'll apply an impulse by calling applyImpulse(_:).

Remove the existing code from the handleTap(_:) method, and add the following code so that the entire method looks like this:

GameScene.swift

```
@objc func handleTap(tapGesture: UITapGestureRecognizer) {

    // Make the skater jump if player taps while she is on the ground
    if skater.isOnGround {

    ❶ skater.physicsBody?.applyImpulse(CGVector(dx: 0.0, dy: 260.0))
    }
}
```

Now, we apply an impulse force to the skater sprite's physics body ❶. When you apply a force to a physics body, you have to supply a CGVector to determine how much that force pushes in the x-direction (dx) and how much it pushes in the y-direction (dy). We want this jump to go straight up, so we give it a positive y value only. Through trial and error, we already found a value that works—260.0, the second parameter. You can try other values and see how they affect the jump. In fact, run the game now and test it out!

Notice that we are no longer setting skater.isOnGround = false in this handleTap(_:) method. Now that we're using the physics engine to make the skater jump, applying an upward force doesn't necessarily mean she'll be off the ground. For example, what if there are bricks just above her head that block her from jumping up? Even though an upward force was applied, she wouldn't leave the ground. For this reason, it's not always right to set skater.isOnGround = false after applying an upward force to the skater sprite. Instead, we will inspect her velocity in the updateSkater() method to determine whether she's on the ground. We'll update that method in "Ending the Game" on page 254.

STARTING AND ENDING THE GAME

Now that we have the SpriteKit physics engine working in our game, we can use it to determine when the game is over. For example, when the skater tips over, the game should end. But before we end the game, we need a way to start a new game. Currently, when you run the app, the game starts because the code we put into the didMove(to:) function is called. But we don't have a way to make the game end and start over. We need to arrange our code so the work done in didMove(to:) is everything that we want to happen only once (like adding the skater sprite to the scene). Also, we'll need to create a startGame() method that does the work that should be done at the start of every game (like moving the skater sprite into her starting position).

STARTING THE GAME

In this game, the skater will go faster and faster as the game goes on. But when the game starts over again, she needs to go back to her slower starting speed. So the first thing we need to do is create a class property to store her starting speed. Near the top of your GameScene class, next to the line where we declared the scrollSpeed class property, add the following line:

GameScene.swift

```
var scrollSpeed: CGFloat = 5.0
let startingScrollSpeed: CGFloat = 5.0

// A constant for gravity, or how fast objects will fall to Earth
```

Now as we increase the scrollSpeed, we'll always know what the starting speed should be when the game starts over.

Next, after the existing resetSkater() method, add the following new method:

```
func resetSkater() {
    --snip--
}

func startGame() {

    // When a new game is started, reset to starting conditions

❶  resetSkater()

❷  scrollSpeed = startingScrollSpeed
❸  lastUpdateTime = nil

❹  for brick in bricks {
        brick.removeFromParent()
    }

❺  bricks.removeAll(keepingCapacity: true)
}
```

This method's job is to reset the game so that everything is back to how it should be at the start of a new game. First, we call the method to reset the skater ❶. This will move her back into the starting position. Then we reset a few class variables. The scrollSpeed is set to the starting speed ❷, and the lastUpdateTime is set back to nil ❸.

Finally, we need to remove all the brick sprites from the scene. At the end of a game, the bricks could be all over the place (especially later when we add higher bricks that the skater needs to jump to reach), so it's best to just remove them all and let the updateBricks(withScrollAmount:) method take care of adding them back in at the right place. At ❹, we loop through all the brick sprites in our bricks array and remove each one from the scene by calling removeFromParent(). Then we have to remove the brick sprites from the bricks array. The easiest way to do this is to call removeAll(_:) on the bricks array ❺.

Now that we have a startGame() method, we need to call it when the scene first appears. Add the following line to the end of the didMove(to:) method:

```
override func didMove(to view: SKView) {
    --snip--
    view.addGestureRecognizer(tapGesture)

    startGame()
}
```

Since the startGame() method now calls resetSkater(), we no longer need to call it in didMove(to:). Remove the following line from the didMove(to:) method.

```
// Set up the skater and add her to the scene
skater.setupPhysicsBody()
resetSkater() // ← Remove this line of code
addChild(skater)
```

Your `didMove(to:)` method should now look like this:

```
override func didMove(to view: SKView) {

    physicsWorld.gravity = CGVector(dx: 0.0, dy: -6.0)
    physicsWorld.contactDelegate = self

    anchorPoint = CGPoint.zero

    let background = SKSpriteNode(imageNamed: "background")
    let xMid = frame.midX
    let yMid = frame.midY
    background.position = CGPoint(x: xMid, y: yMid)
    addChild(background)

    // Set up the skater and add her to the scene
    skater.setupPhysicsBody()
    addChild(skater)

    // Add a tap gesture recognizer to know when the user tapped the screen
    let tapMethod = #selector(GameScene.handleTap(tapGesture:))
    let tapGesture = UITapGestureRecognizer(target: self, action: tapMethod)
    view.addGestureRecognizer(tapGesture)

    startGame()
}
```

The last thing we need to take care of when starting a new game is to reset some extra properties of the skater sprite that may have changed because of the physics simulation. Add the following code to the end of your resetSkater() method:

```
func resetSkater() {
    --snip--
    skater.minimumY = skaterY

  ❶ skater.zRotation = 0.0
  ❷ skater.physicsBody?.velocity = CGVector(dx: 0.0, dy: 0.0)
  ❸ skater.physicsBody?.angularVelocity = 0.0
}
```

The line at ❶ sets the skater sprite's zRotation back to 0.0. The zRotation is how far the sprite is rotated to the right or left. Setting this to 0.0 will make the skater stand up straight in case she tipped over. The line at ❷ sets the velocity of her physics body to 0.0. If she was jumping or falling, this will make her stand still again. The line at ❸ sets her angularVelocity, or rotational speed, back to 0.0. It's one thing to set the sprite's zRotation to 0.0 so she appears to be standing up straight, but the physics body may still be rotating, so we need to zero that out as well.

ENDING THE GAME

If you run the game now and don't make the skater jump at all, you should see that she just tips over and then slides along like that or falls down a hole, but nothing else happens. Let's add some code to detect if she tipped over and end the game when she does. Add the following method after the existing startGame() method:

GameScene.swift

```
func gameOver() {

    startGame()
}
```

When the game ends, we can call the gameOver() method now, and it will start a new game. Next, replace the entire contents of the updateSkater() method to look like the following code:

```
func updateSkater() {

    // Determine if the skater is currently on the ground
❶  if let velocityY = skater.physicsBody?.velocity.dy {

❷      if velocityY < -100.0 || velocityY > 100.0 {
            skater.isOnGround = false
        }
    }

    // Check if the game should end
❸  let isOffScreen = skater.position.y < 0.0 || skater.position.x < 0.0

❹  let maxRotation = CGFloat(GLKMathDegreesToRadians(85.0))
❺  let isTippedOver = skater.zRotation > maxRotation || ↵
        skater.zRotation < -maxRotation

❻  if isOffScreen || isTippedOver {
        gameOver()
    }
}
```

The updateSkater() method needs to do two things. First, it needs to check if the skater is jumping, because she can't jump while she's already in the air. Second, it needs to see if she has tipped over or has been pushed off the screen. If so, then the game should be over.

To check if the skater is on the ground, we will inspect her y velocity. In order to use the y velocity, we need to unwrap it, which we do at ❶. When the skater is jumping or falling, her physics body will have a large velocity—it will be positive if she's jumping up and negative if she's falling down. In either case, she should not be allowed to jump again. So the line at ❷ checks if her physics body's y velocity is either less than -100.0 or greater than 100.0. If so, the skater sprite's isOnGround property is set to false.

If the skater falls off the bottom of the screen, her y-position will be less than zero, and if she gets pushed off the left side of the screen, her x-position will be less than zero. The line at ❸ sets a Bool called isOffScreen to true if either of these conditions is true.

To figure out whether the skater tipped over, we need to check her sprite's zRotation. If it's greater than 85 degrees or less than -85 degrees, we'll say she has tipped over, since she'd be flat on her side at 90 degrees. Using 85 degrees as the check instead of 90 gives a little buffer in case she hasn't quite tipped all the way over but has tipped far enough that she's not getting back up. The zRotation property is measured in *radians*, which are another way of measuring angles. Since it's easier to think about angles in degrees, we use a math function to create a maxRotation constant in radians that is equal to 85 degrees ❹. The line at ❺ sets a Bool called isTippedOver to true if the skater's rotation is greater than 85 degrees or less than -85 degrees.

Now that we have these Bool variables representing the game-over conditions, we simply check if either is true ❻, and if so, we call the gameOver() function. That's it! Now every update frame we'll check if the skater has gone off the screen or tipped over, and the game will end if she has. Right now, ending the game will automatically start a new game. In Chapter 18, we'll add a simple "game over" screen where the player has to tap to start a new game.

WHAT YOU LEARNED

In this chapter, you learned how to use SpriteKit's physics engine to do some of the heavy lifting for game development. You did this by setting up physics bodies for your sprites to define how each sprite should behave in the physics simulation. You learned how to make sprites collide with each other, how to detect contact between two sprites, and how to apply a force to a sprite to make it move. Finally, you learned how to cleanly start and stop your game by making separate methods for each process.

17

ADJUSTING DIFFICULTY, COLLECTING GEMS, AND KEEPING SCORE

In this chapter, we'll add a whole bunch of game elements to make Schoolhouse Skateboarder more challenging and fun. We'll speed the game up and add multilevel platforms, gems to collect, and a scoring system.

SPEEDING THINGS UP

We don't want our game to be too easy, or the player will get bored. One way to ramp up the difficulty is to have the game speed up. (Also, when you're playing on your iPhone or iPad, a game that lasts a couple of minutes is more practical than a game that lasts an hour.) We can speed up the game by increasing the scrollSpeed variable by a little bit in our game loop method. Add the following code to the update(_:) method in the GameScene class.

GameScene.swift

```
override func update(_ currentTime: TimeInterval) {

    // Slowly increase the scrollSpeed as the game progresses
    scrollSpeed += 0.01

    // Determine the elapsed time since the last update call
```

This line increases the scrollSpeed by 0.01 every time update(_:) is called. Now the further the player makes it in the game, the faster it'll go, making things more challenging.

ADDING MULTILEVEL PLATFORMS

Another way we can increase the game's difficulty is by varying the y-position of the sidewalk bricks. We'll make some sections of brick higher so that the player will have to jump up to reach them, as shown in Figure 17-1.

Figure 17-1: Multilevel sidewalk platforms

In order to do this, we'll have two categories of bricks: low and high. The bricks at the usual y-position, like those on the left side of Figure 17-1, are the low bricks, and the raised bricks, like those on the right side of the figure, are the high bricks. We'll need to assign each brick one of these categories as well as a y-position based on the category it's in. We could make CGFloat variables with the y-positions and assign them to the bricks, but using CGFloat variables in that way might become confusing. If we had a lot of other variables, it would be harder for us to read the code and find those CGFloat variables if we needed to change them. So instead of using regular variables, we'll use something new called an enumeration to make our brick categories.

An *enumeration*, often called an *enum* for short, is a way to make a new data type that groups related values. Once you define an enum, you can use it just as you would any other data type when defining new variables, constants, and functions. By making an enum for the brick level, we can create a new data type that stores all the brick levels together so that our code will be easier to read.

DEFINING MULTIPLE BRICK LEVELS

We're going to create an enum to describe two different brick levels. Each value in an enum is called a *case*, which is what our low and high brick levels will be. We'll assign each brick an enum case, and then we'll set the y-position of each brick to be the same as its enum case value. In order to do this, we need the enum to be a CGFloat to match the y-position's data type.

To make the enum, add the following code inside the GameScene class declaration at the top of the class:

GameScene.swift

```
class GameScene: SKScene, SKPhysicsContactDelegate {

    // Enum for y-position spawn points for bricks
    // Ground bricks are low and upper platform bricks are high
❶ enum BrickLevel: ❷CGFloat {
    ❸ case low = 0.0
    ❹ case high = 100.0
    }

    // An array that holds all the current sidewalk bricks
```

We start by defining the enum. An enum definition is similar to a class or struct definition. The line at ❶ starts with the keyword enum, followed by the enumeration name. Like a class or struct, the enum name should always start with an uppercase letter. We'll call this enum BrickLevel because it describes the two different types of brick levels we'll have in our game.

At ❷, we add a colon (:) after the enum name, followed by the data type CGFloat, which makes the enum the same data type as the y-position of the bricks. When you define an enum, you can give it a *raw value* (as we'll do next), but enums don't have to have raw values. The raw value can be of any data type, but that data type must be the same for all of the enum cases. We defined the enum to be a CGFloat, so all the enums' raw values will be CGFloats. We'll access the values later using the enum's rawValue property.

The enum definition sits inside a pair of braces where you define the cases of the enumeration. For BrickLevel, we have just two cases, low and high, but an enum can have an unlimited number of cases. Our normal sidewalk will be made of low bricks that spawn with a y value of 0.0, so at ❸ we define our `low` case and set its raw value to 0.0. Our upper platform will be made up of `high` bricks that spawn with a y value of 100.0, so at ❹ we create a `high` case with a raw value of 100.0.

Next, we'll access the value of an enum by creating a property to hold the current brick level. Add this to the `GameScene`:

```
var brickSize = CGSize.zero

// The current brick level determines the y-position of new bricks
var brickLevel = BrickLevel.low

// Setting for how fast the game is scrolling to the right
```

Here we create a variable called `brickLevel` and set it to `BrickLevel.low`. The `brickLevel` property will track the current state of our sidewalk as it changes from `low` to `high` and back. We want to always start with `low` bricks, so we give `brickLevel` a starting value of `low`. You can access an enum's case using dot notation by writing the enum name, followed by a period, followed by the case.

There's one other spot where we need to set the `brickLevel` before we can start using it. Add this line of code to the method `startGame()`:

```
func startGame() {
    --snip--
    scrollSpeed = startingScrollSpeed
    brickLevel = .low
    lastUpdateTime = nil
    --snip--
}
```

Now whenever the game starts over, the `brickLevel` will reset to `low`. You may have noticed here that we left off the `BrickLevel` part before `.low`. What gives? When we created the `brickLevel` property, Swift used type inference to figure out that `brickLevel` must be of type `BrickLevel`. When we use `brickLevel` here, Swift knows what data type it is, so we don't need to write out `BrickLevel`. We can access the case by just typing a period followed by `low`. Swifty!

CHANGING HOW BRICKS SPAWN

Now that we've established a way to track the brick level, let's use it to determine the y-position where each brick will be spawned. Find the `updateBricks(withScrollAmount:)` method, and change the line of code for `brickY` to this:

GameScene.swift

```
while farthestRightBrickX < frame.width {

    var brickX = farthestRightBrickX + brickSize.width + 1.0
    let brickY = (brickSize.height / 2.0) + brickLevel.rawValue
```

Now when new sidewalk bricks are spawned, the y-position will be adjusted by the CGFloat raw values we set up in the BrickLevel enum, depending on what the current brickLevel is. Notice how easy it is to access the raw value of an enum. It's contained in the property called rawValue, so you just put a period after the enum variable, followed by rawValue. When brickLevel is .low, this will be 0.0. When brickLevel is .high, it will be 100.0.

Lastly, we need brickLevel to change every now and then. We could randomly change brickLevel every time a new brick spawns, but that would look a bit odd, as Figure 17-2 shows.

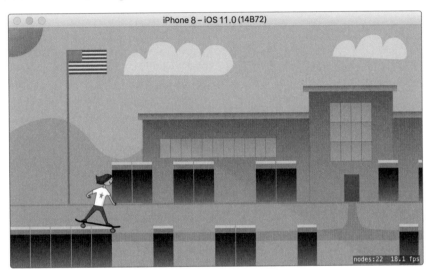

Figure 17-2: How it would look to randomly spawn low and high bricks

As you can see, that setup might be a little *too* hard for the player. It's not going to work if we randomly switch back and forth between low and high bricks. We do want to introduce a bit of randomness here, but we need to be smarter about how we do it. What we'll do is add a 5 percent chance that brickLevel will change every time a brick spawns. Once brickLevel changes, it'll stay in the new position until that 5 percent chance is encountered again. This means the sidewalk will stay at the low level for a while, then at the high level for a while, then go back to the low level, and so on, without so many jumps. Add the following else-if block to the updateBricks(withScrollAmount:) method, incorporating the randomNumber constant that we generated there earlier:

```
func updateBricks(withScrollAmount currentScrollAmount: CGFloat) {
    --snip--
    if randomNumber < 5 {
        --snip--
    }
❶ else if randomNumber < 10 {
```

```
    // There is a 5 percent chance that the brick level will change
    if brickLevel == .high {
        brickLevel = .low
    }
    else if brickLevel == .low {
        brickLevel = .high
    }
}

// Spawn a new brick and update the rightmost brick
```

Now, every time a new brick spawns, there is a small chance that the sidewalk level will switch from low to high or high to low. You may be wondering why the line at ❶, which checks if randomNumber is less than 10, results in a 5 percent chance of a brick level change. The randomNumber constant was created to be a random number between 0 and 99, so there are 100 possible values. On the first line of the if statement that we added previously, the code checks if randomNumber is less than 5, so there are 5 possible values out of 100 that will create a gap in the bricks. The else-if condition that we added at ❶ will only be checked if randomNumber was not less than 5. This means the code in the else-if block will be run only if randomNumber is between 5 and 9, or 5 values out of the possible 100, which results in a 5 percent chance of a brick level change. Run the game now and try it out, and then read on to learn about another way to increase the game's difficulty!

ADDING GEMS TO COLLECT

Adding a collectable item to a game can also give the player more of a challenge. Let's add some gems for the player to collect. Instead of just jumping over the gaps in the sidewalk, the player also will have to decide when it's worth the risk to try to grab a gem. We'll start by adding an array to hold the gem sprites, and then we'll write some code to spawn, move, and remove gems.

SPAWNING AND TRACKING THE GEMS

As we spawn the gems, we'll need an array to keep track of each gem that's currently on the screen. Add this gems array declaration to the GameScene class, as shown here:

GameScene.swift

```
var bricks = [SKSpriteNode]()

// An array that holds all the current gems
var gems = [SKSpriteNode]()

// The size of the sidewalk brick graphics used
```

Each gem will be a sprite, so gems is an array of SKSpriteNode elements. Now that we have an array to hold gems, we can create our method to spawn new gems. Add this method after the existing spawnBrick(atPosition:) method:

```
func spawnBrick(atPosition position: CGPoint) -> SKSpriteNode {
    --snip--
}

❶ func spawnGem(atPosition position: CGPoint) {

    // Create a gem sprite and add it to the scene
❷   let gem = SKSpriteNode(imageNamed: "gem")
    gem.position = position
    gem.zPosition = 9
    addChild(gem)

❸   gem.physicsBody = SKPhysicsBody(rectangleOf: gem.size, ↵
        center: gem.centerRect.origin)
❹   gem.physicsBody?.categoryBitMask = PhysicsCategory.gem
❺   gem.physicsBody?.affectedByGravity = false

    // Add the new gem to the array of gems
❻   gems.append(gem)
}
```

The line at ❶ defines the method to spawn gems, which is very similar to the method to spawn bricks. It has a CGPoint passed in for position so that the gem can be placed there. Just like most of our other sprites, we create the gem sprite using the SKSpriteNode(imageNamed:) initializer ❷. The image name, *gem*, matches the name of the graphic file (*gem.png*) we added to the asset catalog in "Adding Images" on page 206. Once the gem sprite is created, we set its position equal to the position that was passed in to the method. Then we set a zPosition of 9, so it'll be behind the skater but in front of the bricks. Next, we add the gem sprite as a child of the scene so it'll show up on the screen.

The player collects gems by touching them, so each gem sprite needs to be added to the physics simulation so we'll know when the skater has made contact with a gem. To do this, we set the gem sprite's physicsBody equal to a new SKPhysicsBody ❸, which we create using a rectangle equal to the size of the gem sprite, positioned at its center. Then at ❹, we set the categoryBitMask for the gem sprite's physics body equal to the .gem value that we defined in the PhysicsCategory struct. This way we can tell when the skater contacts a gem by inspecting the categoryBitMask of the bodies in the didBegin(_:) method. The last thing we need to do for the physics body is make sure it won't be affected by gravity ❺, since we want the gems to float in the air.

Now that the gem sprite is all set up, we simply add it to our gems array ❻ that keeps track of all the gems currently being displayed. This method is now ready to be called any time we want to spawn a new gem.

DECIDING WHEN TO SPAWN A GEM

Inside the updateBricks(withScrollAmount:) method, just below the code that adjusts the brickX to add gaps, add this code:

GameScene.swift

```
func updateBricks(withScrollAmount currentScrollAmount: CGFloat) {
    --snip--
❶  if randomNumber < 5 {

        // There is a 5 percent chance that we will leave a gap between bricks
        let gap = 20.0 * scrollSpeed
        brickX += gap

        // At each gap, add a gem
❷      let randomGemYAmount = CGFloat(arc4random_uniform(150))
❸      let newGemY = brickY + skater.size.height + randomGemYAmount
❹      let newGemX = brickX - gap / 2.0

❺      spawnGem(atPosition: CGPoint(x: newGemX, y: newGemY))

    }
```

The method that updates the bricks already has code for determining when to make a gap in the bricks that the skater has to jump over. We're going to use this code to spawn a gem every time there's a gap in the bricks. Since the player is already jumping over the gap, this is a natural spot to put a gem. We do this inside the if statement ❶ that includes our code to create a 5 percent chance of something happening. At ❷, we calculate a randomized y-position for the new gem by generating a random number between 0 and 150 and converting it to a CGFloat. Then at ❸, we add the brickY and the skater sprite's height to that random amount. This will give us a y-position for the gem that is up above where the skater is so that the player has to jump to reach it.

Next, we calculate an x-position, newGemX, that places the gem in the middle of the sidewalk gap ❹. Then at ❺, we call the spawnGem(atPosition:) method, passing in the newGemX and newGemY values we just calculated. Now that we're creating gems, let's add a way to remove them when needed.

REMOVING GEMS

When a gem goes off the screen or is collected by the skater, we'll need to remove the gem sprite from the screen and also from our gems array. Add the following method right after the spawnGem(atPosition:) method you just added.

```
func spawnGem(atPosition position: CGPoint) {
    --snip--
}

func removeGem(_ gem: SKSpriteNode) {

  ❶ gem.removeFromParent()

  ❷ if let gemIndex = gems.index(of: gem) {
      ❸ gems.remove(at: gemIndex)
      }
}
```

This method allows you to pass in the gem sprite that should be removed. At ❶, we call removeFromParent() on the gem sprite to remove it from the scene we previously added it to as a child when it spawned. This makes it disappear from the screen, but it's still taking up space in our gems array. In order to remove it from the array, we need to find its position in the array.

At ❷, we use an if-let statement to create the gemIndex constant. If the gem sprite is found in the array with the array's index(of:) method, then the if-let statement will assign gemIndex the index of the gem sprite. An if-let statement must be used here because the index(of:) method returns an optional index—it's possible the item we're looking for in the array won't be found there. In our case, we're sure the gem sprite is in the array, but Swift requires you to check first, just to be safe. If the gem sprite isn't found in the array, then the gemIndex will be nil, and the code inside the braces of the if-let statement won't be called. If the index is found, then the array's remove(at:) method is called with the gemIndex we just discovered as an argument ❸. This method removes the gem sprite from the gems array at the index it's given.

Now that we have an easy way to remove gems, we should add some code to remove all the gems whenever a new game starts so that gems from the previous game don't stick around. Add this code to the startGame() method:

```
func startGame() {
    --snip--
    bricks.removeAll(keepingCapacity: true)

    for gem in gems {
        removeGem(gem)
    }
}
```

This for-in loop simply loops through all the gem sprites (if there are any) in the gems array and calls our handy removeGem(_:) method on each gem.

UPDATING GEMS

Now that we can spawn and remove gems, we need a method to handle updating their position so they move to the left and match the speed of the bricks. We'll also need to remove any gems that move off the left edge of the screen. Add this method just after the updateBricks(withScrollAmount:) method:

GameScene.swift

```
func updateBricks(withScrollAmount currentScrollAmount: CGFloat) {
    --snip--
}

❶ func updateGems(withScrollAmount currentScrollAmount: CGFloat) {

    for gem in gems {

        // Update each gem's position
❷        let thisGemX = gem.position.x - currentScrollAmount
❸        gem.position = CGPoint(x: thisGemX, y: gem.position.y)

        // Remove any gems that have moved offscreen
❹        if gem.position.x < 0.0 {

            removeGem(gem)
        }
    }
}
```

The updateGems method ❶ takes the currentScrollAmount as an input parameter so we know how much to move each gem. We loop through the gems array and do some work for each gem. At ❷, we calculate a new x-position, thisGemX, by subtracting the scroll amount from the gem's current x-position. Then, at ❸ we set a new position on the gem using this newly calculated x-position, but we keep the same y-position. This will make the gem sprite move to the left at the same speed as the bricks.

Next, at ❹, we check if this new x-position is less than 0.0. If so, it has moved too far to the left and is about to go offscreen, so we remove the gem by calling our removeGem(_:) method. Now that we have the code to update the gems, we need to use it by calling updateGems(withScrollAmount:) from our main game loop, which is the update(_:) method.

Add the following line of code to the existing update(_:) method:

```
override func update(_ currentTime: TimeInterval) {
    --snip--
    updateBricks(withScrollAmount: currentScrollAmount)
    updateSkater()
    updateGems(withScrollAmount: currentScrollAmount)

}
```

Now, every time our update(_:) method is called, the gems will move just like the bricks. Try running the game now, and you should see the gems appearing over sidewalk gaps, as shown in Figure 17-3.

Figure 17-3: Gems now appear over the sidewalk gaps.

If you make the skater jump and hit any of the gems, you'll notice they just get pushed around. That's not quite right—we want the gems to disappear when the skater touches them so it'll look like she collected them.

COLLECTING GEMS

Writing the code to collect the gems is simple because we already added them to the physics simulation, and we already added a method to remove them. Inside the existing method didBegin(_:), add the following code to collect gems that are touched:

GameScene.swift

```
func didBegin(_ contact: SKPhysicsContact) {

    // Check if the contact is between the skater and a brick
    if contact.bodyA.categoryBitMask == PhysicsCategory.skater && ↵
        contact.bodyB.categoryBitMask == PhysicsCategory.brick {
    --snip--
    }
❶ else if contact.bodyA.categoryBitMask == PhysicsCategory.skater && ↵
        contact.bodyB.categoryBitMask == PhysicsCategory.gem {

        // Skater touched a gem, so remove it
      ❷ if let gem = contact.bodyB.node as? SKSpriteNode {
            removeGem(gem)
        }
    }
}
```

When two physics bodies touch each other, this method gets called. So all we have to do is have the method check if the physics bodies that touched are the skater and a gem. Line ❶ adds an else-if to our existing if statement and checks if bodyA is a skater and bodyB is a gem by comparing their categoryBitMask properties.

In order to remove the gem, we need to get a reference to the actual gem sprite. The contact object in this method has a reference to the two physics bodies, bodyA and bodyB. We already know that bodyB is our gem's physics body and that the sprite is attached to it, so we can get the physics body's sprite reference via the physics body's node property. The node is an SKNode object, which is the superclass of SKSpriteNode. The if-let statement at ❷ gives us the reference to the gem sprite by downcasting the node to an SKSpriteNode. Now we can pass this gem into our removeGem(_:) method and it'll disappear.

If you run the game again now, you should find that when the skater jumps into a gem, it disappears!

ADDING SCORING AND LABELS

What's even better than collecting gems for fun? Collecting gems for a high score! It's fun to see if you can beat your high score or your friends' scores. Adding a score-keeping mechanism will make players want to play your game again and again. In this section, we'll add a simple scoring system and labels to display the player's current score and all-time high score.

CREATING LABELS

Before we start keeping track of the player's score, we need to add some labels to display the current score and the high score on the screen. We'll add four labels, as shown in Figure 17-4.

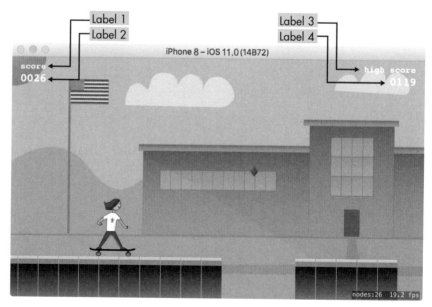

Figure 17-4: The four scoring labels

The player's current score will be at the top left of the screen, and the high score will be at the top right. We'll use two labels for each score. Label 1 is the string "score" and will never change. Label 2 is the actual score for the current game. This label will keep changing to reflect the player's score. Label 3 is the string "high score" and will never change. And finally, label 4 displays the player's high score. At the end of each game, that label should be updated if the player got a new high score.

To create these labels, we'll add a method, setupLabels(), just after the resetSkater() method. We'll only need to call this method once, when the game is first run. It will create the four labels, set them up properly, and add them as children of the scene. Let's start by creating the first label. Add the following code now:

GameScene.swift

```
func resetSkater() {
    --snip--
}

func setupLabels() {

    // Label that says "score" in the upper left

❶  let scoreTextLabel: SKLabelNode = SKLabelNode(text: "score")
❷  scoreTextLabel.position = CGPoint(x: 14.0, y: frame.size.height - 20.0)
❸  scoreTextLabel.horizontalAlignmentMode = .left

}
```

Let's go over everything that's new here. First, we're creating an SKLabelNode, which is the label class in SpriteKit. It's similar to a UILabel, but it's a type of SpriteKit node, so it can be used in SpriteKit scenes with animations and physics. We won't be animating these particular labels or adding them to the physics simulation. They're just going to hang there in the sky. At ❶, we use the initializer SKLabelNode(text:), which creates the label and gives it a starting text string. This is the string that the label will display on the screen. Since we decided this label would always just display the word score, we'll never have to change this text again.

At ❷, we set the position of the label by creating a CGPoint with an x-position of 14.0 and a y-position of the scene's height minus 20.0. This will position the label in the upper left of the screen. If we set the y-position equal to the height of the scene's frame, then the label would be just off the top of the screen. Subtracting 20.0 from the height positions it near the top of the scene instead. At ❸, we set the label's horizontalAlignmentMode to .left. This makes the label's text hug the left side, so it will always be lined up properly. See Figure 17-5 for examples of left and right text alignment.

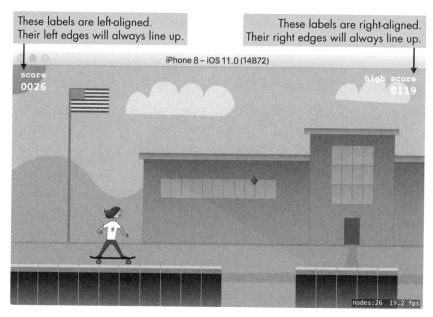

These labels are left-aligned. Their left edges will always line up.

These labels are right-aligned. Their right edges will always line up.

Figure 17-5: Labels that are left-aligned and right-aligned

Now add the following code to finish setting up this first label:

```
func setupLabels() {
    --snip--
    scoreTextLabel.horizontalAlignmentMode = .left
❶  scoreTextLabel.fontName = "Courier-Bold"
❷  scoreTextLabel.fontSize = 14.0
❸  scoreTextLabel.zPosition = 20
    addChild(scoreTextLabel)
}
```

At ❶, we set up the font for the label. You've got a lot of choices with iOS, but we picked Courier Bold. To see the full list of available fonts, visit *http://www.iosfonts.com/*. At ❷, we set the font size to 14.0. This makes the label pretty small but still easily readable, which is what we want. It's not recommended to use font sizes any smaller than about 10.0, or the label may be too hard to read.

Notice that we never set a frame for the label. We didn't set a width and height, just a position. An SKLabelNode is sized automatically based on the font size you pick and the text you need to display, which in this case is score.

At ❸, we set a zPosition of 20 so that the label will always be on top of everything else we've added in the game scene. And finally, don't forget to add the label as a child of the scene, or it won't show up on the screen.

The other three labels are created and set up in a very similar way to the first one, so we won't walk you through each line of this code. For the other three labels, add this code:

```
func setupLabels() {
    --snip--
    addChild(scoreTextLabel)

    // Label that shows the player's actual score

❶  let scoreLabel: SKLabelNode = SKLabelNode(text: "0")
❷  scoreLabel.position = CGPoint(x: 14.0, y: frame.size.height - 40.0)
❸  scoreLabel.horizontalAlignmentMode = .left
    scoreLabel.fontName = "Courier-Bold"
    scoreLabel.fontSize = 18.0
❹  scoreLabel.name = "scoreLabel"
    scoreLabel.zPosition = 20
    addChild(scoreLabel)

    // Label that says "high score" in the upper right

    let highScoreTextLabel: SKLabelNode = SKLabelNode(text: "high score")
    highScoreTextLabel.position = CGPoint(x: frame.size.width - 14.0, ↵
        y: frame.size.height - 20.0)
❺  highScoreTextLabel.horizontalAlignmentMode = .right
    highScoreTextLabel.fontName = "Courier-Bold"
    highScoreTextLabel.fontSize = 14.0
    highScoreTextLabel.zPosition = 20
    addChild(highScoreTextLabel)

    // Label that shows the player's actual highest score

    let highScoreLabel: SKLabelNode = SKLabelNode(text: "0")
    highScoreLabel.position = CGPoint(x: frame.size.width - 14.0, ↵
        y: frame.size.height - 40.0)
    highScoreLabel.horizontalAlignmentMode = .right
    highScoreLabel.fontName = "Courier-Bold"
    highScoreLabel.fontSize = 18.0
❻  highScoreLabel.name = "highScoreLabel"
    highScoreLabel.zPosition = 20
    addChild(highScoreLabel)
}
```

Each label is initialized with a different text string ❶ and given a different position ❷. Notice that the labels we placed on the left side of the screen have a horizontalAlignmentMode of .left ❸ while the labels we placed on the right have .right ❺.

There's one new step: we set a name property on the scoreLabel ❹ and highScoreLabel ❻. Giving a label a name doesn't change anything about how the label is displayed. It simply gives you, the programmer, an easy way to get a reference to that particular label later in the code. Any object in your scene that is a type of SpriteKit node, such as an SKSpriteNode or SKLabelNode, can be given a name. Instead of keeping a class property for every node in your scene, you can assign names to the nodes and then get references to them later by using their name properties. You'll see how this works in the next section, when we update the text of these labels.

Now that we have a method to create and set up the four labels, we just need to call this method within our didMove(to:) method. Add this line:

```
override func didMove(to view: SKView) {
    --snip--
    addChild(background)

    setupLabels()

    // Set up the skater and add her to the scene
    --snip--
}
```

Now when the game first starts, the labels will be created and added to the scene. Run the game now to make sure they show up.

TRACKING THE SCORE

As the player's score changes, we'll need a way to update the labels to reflect the new score. First, let's add some new class properties to keep track of the score. Add the following code near the top of the GameScene class:

GameScene.swift

```
let gravitySpeed: CGFloat = 1.5

// Properties for score-tracking
❶ var score: Int = 0
❷ var highScore: Int = 0
❸ var lastScoreUpdateTime: TimeInterval = 0.0

// The timestamp of the last update method call
```

This creates a score integer we'll use to track the current score ❶, a highScore integer we'll use to track the player's highest score ❷, and a TimeInterval called lastScoreUpdateTime ❸. A TimeInterval is a type of Double used to track how much time has passed in seconds. Inside our game loop, we'll be updating the score label, but we don't want to update the label every single time our game loop runs (remember, that's usually 30 or 60 times per second). Instead, we'll update the label once a second using this TimeInterval to track the elapsed time between updates.

UPDATING LABELS

Since we'll be using the score variable to update the score label's text, let's write a quick method to do that update. Add the following new method just after the existing setupLabels() method:

GameScene.swift

```
func setupLabels() {
    --snip--
}

func updateScoreLabelText() {
❶  if let scoreLabel = childNode(withName: "scoreLabel") as? SKLabelNode {
❷      scoreLabel.text = String(format: "%04d", score)
    }
}
```

The line at ❶ finds a child node of the scene that has the name "scoreLabel". When we created the score label, we set its name property to "scoreLabel". Then, as with the other labels, we added the label as a child of the scene. We can call the childNode(withName:) method on any node (whether it's a scene, sprite, or label) to find a child node that has a particular name. Doing this means we didn't have to create a class property to keep track of this label. We simply look it up by name when we need to use it. It's good practice to keep the number of class properties you create to a minimum, and using this technique for nodes that we won't need to refer to very often does just that.

The line at ❷ sets the text of the scoreLabel to a new string that we create using our score variable. The String initializer, String(format:), creates a new string using a string format specifier to display variables in a specific way. In this case, we want to display the score always as four digits, adding zeros to the front of the string when needed, such as 0230 instead of 230 when the player has 230 points. In the format string %04d, the % specifies that we'll be inserting a variable here, the 04 specifies that we want the string to always be four digits long with zeros in front, and the d specifies that the variable we're inserting is an integer.

Table 17-1 lists some examples of common string format specifiers.

Table 17-1: Common String Format Specifiers

Specifier	Description
%d	Used to insert an Integer
%f	Used to insert a Double, Float, or CGFloat
%@	Used to insert a String or other object
%%	Used to insert a percent sign into the string

Table 17-2 lists a few examples of string format specifiers used to get different number formats.

Table 17-2: String Format Specifiers in Action

Specifier	Input	Output
%05d	123	00123
%.2f	1.0	1.00
%.3f	33.0	33.000

Using the String(format:) method is a handy way to get labels to look the way you want them to. Forcing our score label to always show four digits ensures that it will look consistent as the score changes.

UPDATING THE PLAYER'S SCORE

First things first: whenever a new game starts, the score should be 0. Add this line to the startGame() method:

GameScene.swift

```
func startGame() {

    // When a new game is started, reset to starting conditions
    resetSkater()

    score = 0

    scrollSpeed = startingScrollSpeed
```

Next let's create a method that can add some points to the player's score based on how long they've survived. Add the following method after the updateSkater() method:

```
func updateScore(withCurrentTime currentTime: TimeInterval) {

    // The player's score increases the longer they survive
    // Only update score every 1 second

❶   let elapsedTime = currentTime - lastScoreUpdateTime

    if elapsedTime > 1.0 {

        // Increase the score
❷       score += Int(scrollSpeed)

        // Reset the lastScoreUpdateTime to the current time
❸       lastScoreUpdateTime = currentTime

        updateScoreLabelText()
    }
}
```

Since we only want to update the score label once per second, we've declared this method to take a parameter of the currentTime. The currentTime is passed automatically by SpriteKit into the update(_:) method, so we'll just pass that currentTime into this scoring method when we call it. We use the currentTime to calculate how much time has elapsed since the last time we updated the score label ❶. If more than one second has elapsed, then we increase the player's score by adding the scrollSpeed ❷. We could just add an amount like 10 to the score, but using the scrollSpeed makes the player's score go up faster as they get further into the game, because the scrollSpeed keeps increasing.

Then at ❸, we set our lastScoreUpdateTime tracker equal to the current time. This way, next time we calculate the elapsed time, we'll be able to check if one second has passed since the current time. Finally, we make a call to our updateScoreLabelText() method, which will make the score label display the new score.

Now all we have to do is call the updateScore(withCurrentTime) method from within our main game loop, or update(_:) method. Add this line of code into the update(_:) method:

```
override func update(_ currentTime: TimeInterval) {
    --snip--
    updateGems(withScrollAmount: currentScrollAmount)
    updateScore(withCurrentTime: currentTime)
}
```

This will call the new method to update the score every time update(_:) is called. Run the game now, and watch the score go up! You may notice that collecting gems doesn't increase the score. Let's fix that!

MAKING THE GEMS VALUABLE

Now that all of our score tracking and updating is set up, adding new scoring elements is simple. We already know when the player collects a gem because of the work we did in the didBegin(_:) method. Add this code to the didBegin(_:) method:

GameScene.swift

```
func didBegin(_ contact: SKPhysicsContact) {
    --snip--
        // Skater touched a gem, so remove it
        if let gem = contact.bodyB.node as? SKSpriteNode {
            removeGem(gem)

            // Give the player 50 points for getting a gem
            score += 50
            updateScoreLabelText()
        }
    }
}
```

Simple, right? At the point in the code where we know the player got a gem, we just add 50 to the score variable and call our updateScoreLabelText() method. Now collecting gems pays.

One final thing you may have noticed is that our high score just sits there at 0. Let's fix that now.

TRACKING THE HIGH SCORE

To update the high score label, add the following method just after the updateScoreLabelText() method:

GameScene.swift

```
func updateScoreLabelText() {
    --snip--
}

func updateHighScoreLabelText() {
    if let highScoreLabel = childNode(withName: "highScoreLabel") ↵
        as? SKLabelNode {
        highScoreLabel.text = String(format: "%04d", highScore)
    }
}
```

This method is exactly the same as the updateScoreLabelText() method you added before, but it handles the high score. We only need to check if the player got a new high score at the end of every game. The gameOver() method we created is perfect for that. Add this code to it:

```
func gameOver() {

    // When the game ends, see if the player got a new high score

    if score > highScore {
        highScore = score

        updateHighScoreLabelText()
    }

    startGame()
}
```

This code is pretty straightforward. When the game is over, we check if score is higher than the current highScore. If it is, then we set the highScore equal to the new score, and we update the high score label text. Try playing the game a few times now, and you should see the high score being tracked and displayed.

TWEAKING THE GAMEPLAY

Right now the game is pretty difficult. What if we wanted to make it easier? It's our game, and we can change whatever we want, so let's do it! The first thing we need to address is that when you start a game, there are sometimes gaps and multilevel platforms right away, so it's impossible to survive more than a few seconds in the game.

Let's change our code that determines when to add a gap in the sidewalk so that there will be no gaps during the start of the game. The player's score starts at 0, so we can add a check for the player's score being greater than 10 before we start adding gaps. Let's also make it so the player's score has to be greater than 20 before we start changing the platform level. And while we're changing that code, we'll also decrease the 5 percent chance for the gaps and the level changes to a 2 percent chance. Modify the `updateBricks(withScrollAmount:)` method to look like this:

GameScene.swift

```
func updateBricks(withScrollAmount currentScrollAmount: CGFloat) {
    --snip--
        let randomNumber = arc4random_uniform(99)

        if randomNumber < 2 && score > 10 {
            // There is a 2 percent chance that we will leave a gap between
            // bricks after the player has reached a score of 10
            let gap = 20.0 * scrollSpeed
            brickX += gap
            --snip--
        }
        else if randomNumber < 4 && score > 20 {
            // There is a 2 percent chance that the brick Y level will change
            // after the player has reached a score of 20
            if brickLevel == .high {
                brickLevel = .low
            }
        --snip--
}
```

Now there will be fewer gaps and level changes, and they won't show up right at the start of the game anymore. Run the game and see if it's easier.

Another quick change that will make the gameplay even easier is keeping the skater from being able to tip over. In the *Skater.swift* file, change the `allowsRotation` property of the physics body to `false`:

Skater.swift

```
physicsBody?.density = 6.0
physicsBody?.allowsRotation = false
physicsBody?.angularDamping = 1.0
```

If you run the game now, you will probably survive a lot longer and get a higher score than before!

WHAT YOU LEARNED

In this chapter, you learned how to add a whole bunch of game elements. You added varying sidewalk levels to force the player to jump up, gems the player can collect, a scoring system, and high-score tracking. You also learned about using random numbers to add variation to the gameplay and how to use labels to display information for the player.

18

GAME STATE, MENUS, SOUNDS, AND SPECIAL EFFECTS

In this chapter, we'll add the concept of *state* to Schoolhouse Skateboarder. The state of a game is what mode the game is in, such as whether the game is running or has ended and is waiting to start again. Up until this point, the game was always running, and it immediately started over when it ended. Keeping track of the game's state will allow us to add a simple menu system to show when the game is over. We'll also add some sounds to the game and create some special effects using a particle emitter.

TRACKING GAME STATE

First we'll create an enum that lists the various states the game can be in. Add this new enum inside the GameScene class, just after the BrickLevel enum:

GameScene.swift

```
enum BrickLevel: CGFloat {
    --snip--
}

// This enum defines the states the game may be in
enum GameState {
    case notRunning
    case running
}
```

Note that this enum is placed inside the GameScene class because it won't be needed by any other class outside of GameScene. Unlike the enum we created for BrickLevel, this enum doesn't have a raw value. This enum just contains the cases we need to create a GameState data type, and we don't need to associate any values with each case. When the app is first started, the state will be notRunning. While the game is being played, the state will be running. When the game has ended and is waiting to start over, the state will be set back to notRunning. Putting these states in an enum makes it easier to expand the game in the future and add more states. For example, if we added a pause button, we could add a paused case to this enum.

Next, we need a class property to track the current value of the game's state. We'll call it gameState and put it in the GameScene class just after the brickLevel declaration, as shown here:

```
var brickLevel = BrickLevel.low

// The current game state is tracked
var gameState = GameState.notRunning

// Setting for how fast the game is scrolling to the right
```

This new variable, gameState, will track what state the game is in. We set its initial value to notRunning since that's the state we want the game to be in when the app first starts.

When the game starts, we need to set our gameState to running. Add this line to the startGame() method:

```
func startGame() {

    // When a new game is started, reset to starting conditions

    gameState = .running

    resetSkater()
```

And when the game ends, we want to make sure we set the state back to notRunning. Add this line to the gameOver() method:

```
func gameOver() {

    // When the game ends, see if the player got a new high score

    gameState = .notRunning

    if score > highScore {
```

Now that we have a variable to keep track of our game's state, we need to do something with it. If you run the game right now, you'll see that a new game still starts immediately after the current game ends.

To get the game to actually stop, first remove the startGame() method call from the gameOver() method so it doesn't automatically start a new game:

```
func gameOver() {
    --snip--
    if score > highScore {
        --snip--
    }

    startGame() // ← Remove this line of code
}
```

If you run the game now, a new game will not automatically start when the skater falls off the screen. Instead, the bricks will continue moving. To make game updates stop when the game is over, add this code to the update(_:) method:

```
override func update(_ currentTime: TimeInterval) {
    if gameState != .running {
        return
    }

    // Slowly increase the scrollSpeed as the game progresses
```

Now our game loop won't do anything unless the game is running. This is because the method ends at the return keyword and all the following code won't be executed. Run the game again, and you should see everything stop when the skater falls down or gets pushed off the screen. This isn't a very friendly game-over screen, though. We need to add a menu system to tell the player that the game is over and let them know they can tap to start a new game.

ADDING A MENU SYSTEM

We'll add two menu screens to the game: one that appears at the start of the game to instruct the player to tap to play and another that appears at the end of the game to let them know the game is over.

To add the menu screens, we'll create a new class called MenuLayer. Then we'll create one MenuLayer object for each screen, so we'll end up with two MenuLayer objects in total. The class will be a subclass of SKSpriteNode, and we'll use it to display messages on the screen, such as "Tap to play" or "Game Over!" This MenuLayer class will essentially be our menu system for the game. Figure 18-1 shows how our completed menu screens will look.

Figure 18-1: The "Tap to play" menu layer will be shown when the app is first run, and the "Game Over!" layer will be shown once the game ends.

Menu screens usually have multiple options for the user to pick from, but ours will just be used to display simple messages. If we were going to add an option such as the ability to turn sounds on or off, this menu layer would be a good place to do that, too.

CREATING THE MENULAYER CLASS

To make the MenuLayer class, create a new class by right-clicking (or CONTROL-clicking) the *SchoolhouseSkateboarder* folder in the Project navigator and selecting **New File...**. Choose the iOS Source template called Cocoa Touch Class. Name the new class **MenuLayer**, make it a subclass of SKSpriteNode, and choose the default file location to create the new file. Your new class should look like this:

MenuLayer.swift

```
import UIKit

class MenuLayer: SKSpriteNode {

}
```

Just like when we created the Skater class, the first thing we need to do is change the import statement to the following:

```
import SpriteKit
```

Now create a new method inside the MenuLayer class that will allow us to display messages:

```
// Tells the MenuLayer to display a message and to
// optionally display a score
func display(message: String, score: Int?) {

}
```

This method will be used to present messages—such as "Game Over!"— in a menu layer. It will also allow us, if we wish, to display the player's score, which we've defined as an optional. First, let's add the code that creates the main message label. Add this code inside the display(message:score:) method:

```
func display(message: String, score: Int?) {

    // Create a message label using the passed-in message
❶   let messageLabel: SKLabelNode = SKLabelNode(text: message)

    // Set the label's starting position to the left of the menu layer
❷   let messageX = -frame.width
❸   let messageY = frame.height / 2.0
    messageLabel.position = CGPoint(x: messageX, y: messageY)

❹   messageLabel.horizontalAlignmentMode = .center
    messageLabel.fontName = "Courier-Bold"
    messageLabel.fontSize = 48.0
    messageLabel.zPosition = 20
    addChild(messageLabel)
}
```

This code should look familiar because it's very similar to the code we wrote in the setUpLabels() method in the GameScene class to create the score labels. At ❶, we create a label using the message parameter that was passed in to the method as the text to display. Next we determine the starting position of the label. We'll use an action to animate the label moving from the left side of the screen to the center of the screen. In order to do that, we need to first set its position off the screen to the left.

At ❷, we use -frame.width as the x-position to set the label one full screen's width to the left. At ❸, we use frame.height / 2.0 as the y-position to set the label vertically in the center of the screen. We also want this label to be centered horizontally within its frame, so that when we move the label to the middle of the screen, it will be perfectly centered. To do this, we set the label's horizontalAlignmentMode to .center at ❹. Now that we've positioned the label, we set its font, font size, and zPosition and add it as a child of the MenuLayer.

Using Actions to Animate the Label

There's a reason we gave the label an x-position to place it off to the left side of the screen and a y-position to place it vertically in the middle of the screen. We want to add some flair by having the label zoom onto the screen! Add this animation code to the display(message:score:) method:

MenuLayer.swift

```
    addChild(messageLabel)

    // Animate the message label to the center of the screen
❶  let finalX = frame.width / 2.0
❷  let messageAction = SKAction.moveTo(x: finalX, duration: 0.3)
❸  messageLabel.run(messageAction)
}
```

The line at ❶ calculates the final x-position where the label should move in order to end up at the center of the screen. The line at ❷ creates a new object called an SKAction. In SpriteKit, you can use an SKAction to do a huge number of interesting things with nodes—everything from spinning around and fading out to moving along a path. Here we're using moveTo(x:duration:), which creates an action to move a node to a new x-position. We pass in the finalX position that we calculated before and give it a duration value. The duration value tells the action how long the animation should take. We want the label to zoom onto the screen pretty fast, so we set a short duration of 0.3 seconds.

Finally, the line at ❸ tells the message label to run this action. Actions that you create describe what a node should do, but nothing will happen until you tell a node to run that action.

Table 18-1 describes some common action methods.

Table 18-1: Common SKAction Methods

SKAction method	What it does
move(to:duration:)	Moves the node to a new location
moveTo(x:duration:)	Moves the node to a new x-position, keeping the same y-position
moveTo(y:duration:)	Moves the node to a new y-position, keeping the same x-position
move(by:duration)	Moves the node by a given amount from its current location
rotate(toAngle:duration:)	Rotates the node to a new angle
rotate(byAngle:duration:)	Rotates the node by a given angle amount
resize(toWidth:height:duration:)	Resizes the node to a new width and height
resize(byWidth:height:duration:)	Resizes the node by the amounts given

SKAction method	What it does
`scale(to:duration:)`	Scales the node to a new scale; for example, if the node was originally at a scale of `1.0` (the default), scaling it to `2.0` would double its size
`fadeIn(withDuration:)`	Fades in the node
`fadeOut(withDuration:)`	Fades out the node
`playSoundFileNamed(_:waitForCompletion:)`	Plays a sound file, such as a *.wav* file
`sequence(_:)`	Sequences multiple actions together

As you can see, there's quite a lot you can do with an `SKAction`! You'll notice that many of the `SKAction` methods have a *to* version and a *by* version, such as `move(to:duration:)` and `move(by:duration:)`. The *to* version of an action just does the action no matter what the state of the node was originally. For instance, if you want to move a sprite to a new location, say to the middle of the screen, you would use the *to* version and set the new location. The node will move to the location regardless of whether it was originally offscreen, onscreen, or to the left or right of the new location. If you want to make the node move according to where it is already positioned, you would use the *by* version of the action. For instance, if you wanted to make a sprite move `50.0` to the right of its current position, you would use `move(by:duration:)` with an x amount of `50.0`.

Now that we have the message label set up, let's add the code to optionally display a score label so the player can see their final score at the end of each game.

Optionally Showing a Score Label

In our `display(message:score:)` method, the score parameter is optional. So we need to check if it exists before we can display the player's score on the game-over screen. If the score was passed in and is not `nil`, then we'll show a score label that animates in from the right side of the screen. If the `score` parameter doesn't exist, then the score label won't be created. Add this code to the `display(message:score:)` method:

MenuLayer.swift

```
class MenuLayer: SKSpriteNode {

    // Tells the MenuLayer to display a message and to
    // optionally display a score
    func display(message: String, score: Int?) {
        --snip--
        messageLabel.run(messageAction)

        // If a score was passed in to the method, display it
        if let scoreToDisplay = score {
```

```
    // Create the score text from the score Int
    let scoreString = String(format: "Score: %04d", scoreToDisplay)
    let scoreLabel: SKLabelNode = SKLabelNode(text: scoreString)

    // Set the label's starting position to the right
    // of the menu layer
❶   let scoreLabelX = frame.width
❷   let scoreLabelY = messageLabel.position.y - ↵
        messageLabel.frame.height
    scoreLabel.position = CGPoint(x: scoreLabelX, y: scoreLabelY)

    scoreLabel.horizontalAlignmentMode = .center
    scoreLabel.fontName = "Courier-Bold"
    scoreLabel.fontSize = 32.0
    scoreLabel.zPosition = 20
    addChild(scoreLabel)

    // Animate the score label to the center of the screen
❸   let scoreAction = SKAction.moveTo(x: finalX, duration: 0.3)
    scoreLabel.run(scoreAction)
    }
  }
}
```

The code for the score label is practically identical to the code for the message label. The only difference is that the label is first positioned with an x-position just off the right edge of the menu layer ❶ and a y-position that is just below the message label ❷. Just like the messageLabel object, after the scoreLabel object is created and added as a child of the MenuLayer class, it's animated to the center of the screen via an SKAction ❸.

DISPLAYING THE MENU LAYERS WHEN NEEDED

Now that we have the MenuLayer class set up, we need to actually use it to make the menu layers. The first time we want to show a menu layer is right when the application starts. We don't want the game to just automatically start anymore. Instead, we want the player to see a menu screen asking them to tap the screen to start playing. So, in the didMove(to:) method of the GameScene, *remove* the line of code that calls the startGame() method, and add this code in its place to display a menu layer:

GameScene.swift

```
override func didMove(to view: SKView) {
    --snip--
    view.addGestureRecognizer(tapGesture)

    startGame() // ← Remove this line of code

    // Add a menu overlay with "Tap to play" text
❶   let menuBackgroundColor = UIColor.black.withAlphaComponent(0.4)
❷   let menuLayer = MenuLayer(color: menuBackgroundColor, size: frame.size)
```

```
❸ menuLayer.anchorPoint = CGPoint(x: 0.0, y: 0.0)
    menuLayer.position = CGPoint(x: 0.0, y: 0.0)
    menuLayer.zPosition = 30
    menuLayer.name = "menuLayer"
❹ menuLayer.display(message: "Tap to play", score: nil)
    addChild(menuLayer)
}
```

This code makes a new `MenuLayer` object with the message "Tap to play" displayed in its label. Now, instead of the game starting right away, this message will be displayed. The line at ❶ creates a `UIColor` using black as a starting point and then applies an alpha component of 0.4 to it. *Alpha* sets how transparent something is on a scale from 0.0 to 1.0. If we set an alpha of 0.0, then the color would be fully invisible or transparent. An alpha of 0.5 makes a color half transparent, like a sheer fabric. An alpha of 1.0 means that the color is completely opaque—not transparent at all. For the menu layer, setting a partially transparent background color will make it look like the menu text is on top of the game. This line just sets up the `UIColor`. In order to actually make the screen darken, we need to apply the color to the `MenuLayer` object.

The line at ❷ creates a new `MenuLayer` object by passing in the color we created and setting the object's size equal to the size of the scene's `frame`. This makes the menu layer as big as the game scene so it can completely cover it when shown.

The line at ❸ sets the `anchorPoint` of the menu layer node to (0.0, 0.0). As you learned in Chapter 14, these coordinates set the anchor point in the node's lower-left corner. Next we set the `position` of the menu layer to (0.0, 0.0) as well. Because the menu layer and the scene are the same size, we can ensure that the menu layer fits perfectly over the scene by pinning both the anchor point and the position at (0.0, 0.0).

The line at ❹ calls the `display(message:score:)` method on our new `menuLayer`. We pass it the string `"Tap to play"` for the `message` that will animate onto the screen, and we pass `nil` for the `score`. We don't want this screen to display a score, because the player doesn't have one yet. Run the game now, and you should see the "Tap to play" menu layer appear.

There's one other time we need to display a menu layer: when the game ends. Add the following code to the `gameOver()` method:

```
func gameOver() {
    --snip--
    if score > highScore {
        --snip--
    }

    // Show the "Game Over!" menu overlay
    let menuBackgroundColor = UIColor.black.withAlphaComponent(0.4)
```

```
let menuLayer = MenuLayer(color: menuBackgroundColor, size: frame.size)
menuLayer.anchorPoint = CGPoint.zero
menuLayer.position = CGPoint.zero
menuLayer.zPosition = 30
menuLayer.name = "menuLayer"
menuLayer.display(❶message: "Game Over!", ❷score: score)
addChild(menuLayer)
}
```

This menu layer is just like the one we created for the start of the game, except it has a different message ❶ and we pass in the player's score ❷. So when the game ends, the screen will display both the "Game Over!" message and the score the player achieved in that game.

REMOVING THE MENU LAYER

When the player taps on the screen while on the "Tap to play" menu, we want the game to start playing. However, our game is still set up only to make the skater jump when the player taps on the screen. Let's update the handleTap(_:) method so that the skater jumps only when the game is running and, if a menu is being shown, the menu disappears and a new game starts.

Change the handleTap(_:) method to look like this:

GameScene.swift

```
@objc func handleTap(tapGesture: UITapGestureRecognizer) {

❶   if gameState == .running {

        // Make the skater jump if player taps while she is on the ground
        if skater.isOnGround {

            skater.physicsBody?.applyImpulse(CGVector(dx: 0.0, dy: 260.0))
        }
❷   } else {

        // If the game is not running, tapping starts a new game
❸       if let menuLayer: SKSpriteNode = childNode(withName: "menuLayer") ↵
            as? SKSpriteNode {

❹           menuLayer.removeFromParent()
        }

❺       startGame()
    }
}
```

First, we wrap the jumping code inside an if statement that makes sure the gameState is equal to .running ❶. If the game is not running, then the skater shouldn't jump!

Next, we add an `else` block ❷ to handle what should happen when the player taps but the game is not running. Right now we have only two game states, `running` and `notRunning`. So if the game is not running, it must be showing a menu layer.

Inside this `else` block, we need to get a reference to the menu layer by asking the scene for its child node by name. Both times when we created a new `MenuLayer` object, we set its `name` property to `"menuLayer"` so that we could retrieve it by this name using the `childNode(withName:)` method. We do that here with an `if-let` statement ❸. Inside the `if-let` statement, we remove the menu from its parent ❹, which will make the menu disappear.

Finally, to close out this `else` block, we call `startGame()` ❺. That should do it—run the game now, and you should have a fully functioning menu system!

MAKING SOUNDS

While our new menu system has improved our game a lot, we can make it even more fun for players by adding some cool sound effects. Adding sound effects to a SpriteKit game is easy. It takes only one line of code to play a sound, and the right sound effects can really bring a game to life. But first we need to add the sound files to the project. We've prepared a couple of *.wav* files—one to play when the player jumps, and one to play when the player collects a gem.

ADDING THE SOUND FILES

Download the sound files you'll need from the book's web page at *https://www.nostarch.com/iphoneappsforkids/*. Once the download is complete, you'll have a folder named *ch18-sounds* inside your *Downloads* folder with all the files you need.

To add the sound files to your project, you'll need to drag them from Finder into Xcode and drop them in the Project navigator, near *Assets.xcassets*. Once you drop them, an Import Options window will pop up. Make sure **Copy items if needed** is checked, as shown in Figure 18-2.

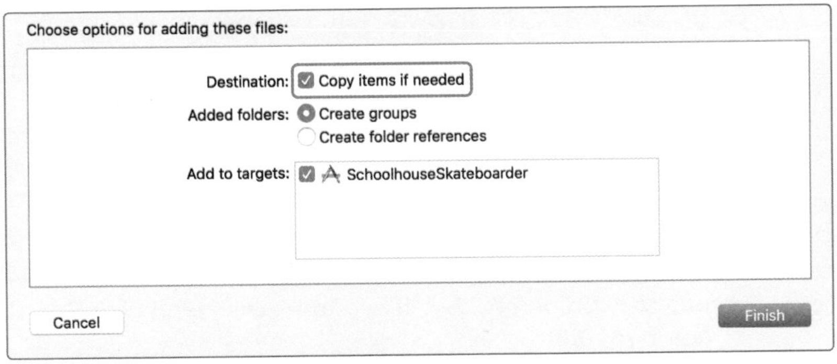

Figure 18-2: Import options for the sound files

You should now see two new files in the Project navigator: *jump.wav* and *gem.wav*. Now that the sound files have been added to the project, they are ready to be used in the game.

PLAYING THE SOUNDS AT THE RIGHT TIME

First let's add the code to play *jump.wav* when the player jumps. Add this line of code to the handleTap(_:) method:

GameScene.swift

```
@objc func handleTap(tapGesture: UITapGestureRecognizer) {

    if gameState == .running {

        // Make the skater jump if player taps while she is on the ground
        if skater.isOnGround {

            skater.physicsBody?.applyImpulse(CGVector(dx: 0.0, dy: 260.0))

            run(SKAction.playSoundFileNamed("jump.wav", ↵
                waitForCompletion: false))
        }
    }
```

Since we already have a spot in the code where the player taps to make the skater jump, all we do is run an action on the scene to play the right sound file. The SKAction method playSoundFileNamed(_:waitForCompletion:) is given the name of the *.wav* file to play. We set waitForCompletion to false. This property would only matter if we were sequencing multiple actions together. Since we aren't in this case, we set it to false. You'll see an example of sequencing multiple actions together when we create a particle emitter in the next section.

To play *gem.wav* when the player collects a gem, add this line of code to the didBegin(_:) method:

```
func didBegin(_ contact: SKPhysicsContact) {
    --snip--
            updateScoreLabelText()

            run(SKAction.playSoundFileNamed("gem.wav", ↵
                waitForCompletion: false))
        }
    }
}
```

Now when the player collects a gem by touching it, in addition to getting 50 extra points, they'll hear the gem sound play. Run the game and see how it sounds.

SHOOTING SPARKS

Now it's time to learn about something that will make our game even more exciting: particle emitters. A *particle emitter* is used in games to create special effects—snow, rain, fire, explosions, and more! You add a particle emitter to a game scene, and it shoots out (or emits) particles. The particles can be any image, such as a snowflake, a blob, or a bit of fire, and the particle emitter will shoot them out in whatever speed, direction, and quantity you tell it to. For example, to create an explosion, you can tell a particle emitter to emit fire particles in all directions at once. Or you can tell a particle emitter to emit snowflakes that drift downward from the entire top edge of the screen. For Schoolhouse Skateboarder, we'll add a particle emitter that shoots sparks out from the bottom of the skateboard whenever the skater lands on the ground, because that'll look cool.

Luckily, Xcode has a fantastic built-in way to create particle emitters. CONTROL-click the *SchoolhouseSkateboarder* folder in the Project navigator and choose **New File…**. Then select **iOS**, scroll down to find the Resource section, choose **SpriteKit Particle File**, and click **Next**.

Xcode will ask you which particle template to use. There are a handful of templates to choose from, and each one will give you a pretty good starting point for the type of effect you want to create. Since we're making sparks for the skateboard, pick **Spark** and then click **Next**.

When Xcode asks for a filename, change it to *sparks.sks*, make sure your project folder is already selected, and then click **Create**.

Now you should see a particle emitter shooting out sparks in every direction! This is the built-in particle editor, and we'll use it to make these sparks look more like sparks that might shoot out from the wheels of the skateboard. First, as shown in Figure 18-3, make sure the utility pane is displayed.

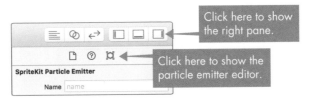

Figure 18-3: Displaying the particle editor utility pane

Part of the fun of the particle editor is that you can play around with the settings and see what interesting emitters you can make. For the skateboard sparks, we've already done this and found some settings that look right. Update the emitter's values in the right pane so they match Table 18-2. For any values not listed in the table, make no changes.

Table 18-2: Particle Emitter Settings to Create Skateboard Sparks

Setting	Value
Emitter, Birthrate	1000
Emitter, Maximum	100
Lifetime, Start	0.3
Position Range, X	75
Angle, Start	180
Angle, Range	10
Alpha, Speed	–3
Scale, Start	0.1

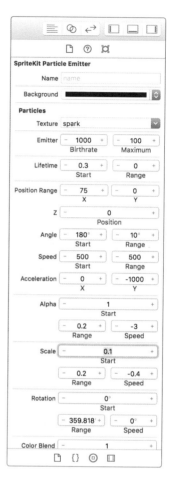

When you're done making the value changes for this emitter, it should look like Figure 18-4.

It's amazing how many different special effects you can create with a particle emitter just by tweaking these settings. Table 18-3 explains what each setting does.

Figure 18-4: Sparks emitter settings

Table 18-3: Particle Emitter Settings

Setting	Description
Name	Can be set so that the emitter may be accessed later via childNode(withName:).
Background	Can be set in the .sks editor to make it easier to see the particle emitter you're working on. This color is ignored when you create the emitter in your game code.
Texture	The image file that should be used as the particles. SpriteKit will provide a basic *spark.png* image as the default when you create a new spark particle emitter, but you can use any image you want.
Lifetime, Start	How long, in seconds, each particle should be visible after it is emitted.
Lifetime, Range	The amount of variation in a particle's lifetime. A value of 0 means all particles have the lifetime specified in "Lifetime, Start," whereas a value of 1.0 means that particle lifetimes are allowed to vary, randomly, by up to 1.0 second.

Setting	Description
Position Range, X	The range of x-positions where the particles should spawn. A value of 0 means the particles will all spawn from the exact same x-position. A value of 100.0 means the particles should be allowed to spawn randomly over an x-position range of 100.0.
Position Range, Y	The range of y-positions where the particles should spawn. A value of 0 means the particles will all spawn from the exact same y-position. A value of 100.0 means the particles should be allowed to spawn randomly over a y-position range of 100.0.
Position Range, Z	The range of z-position spawning for particles. Apple has marked this property as *deprecated*, which means it's an old property that should no longer be used.
Angle, Start	The angle at which to shoot the particles out, in degrees, where 0 is straight to the right, 90 is up, 180 is left, 270 is down, and 360 is right. Any valid CGFloat value may be used for the angle.
Angle, Range	The amount of variation in the emission angle.
Speed, Start	The speed at which the particles should be emitted.
Speed, Range	The amount of variation in emission speed.
Acceleration, X	How much the particles should speed up in the x-direction after they're emitted. A positive value means to accelerate to the right, and a negative value means to accelerate to the left.
Acceleration, Y	How much the particles should speed up in the y-direction after they're emitted. A positive value means to accelerate upward, and a negative value means to accelerate downward.
Alpha, Start	How transparent the particles should be when they're emitted. Valid values are any CGFloat between 0.0 and 1.0, where 0.0 means completely transparent, and 1.0 means completely opaque.
Alpha, Range	The amount of variation in alpha transparency.
Alpha, Speed	How quickly the alpha transparency should change over the particle's lifetime.
Scale, Start	The starting scale, or size, of the particles. A value of 1.0 means normal-sized, not scaled up or down at all. A value of 2.0 means double-sized, 0.5 means half-sized, and so on.
Scale, Range	The amount of variation in particle scale, or size.
Scale, Speed	How quickly the scale of the particles should change.
Rotation, Start	The rotation of the particles. For a texture like the *spark.png* default texture, rotation won't be noticeable. But if you used the *skater.png* image as the texture, you would notice that 0.0 is right side up, and 180.0 is upside down. Any valid CGFloat value is allowed.
Rotation, Range	The amount of variation in particle rotation.
Rotation, Speed	How quickly the rotation of the particles should change.
Color Ramp	How the tint color of each particle should change over the particle's lifetime. You can specify that the particles should start off as green, for example, turn blue, and then end up yellow before finally disappearing.
Blend Mode	Allows you to set how the colors of overlapping particles should be blended together.

You may have noticed that when you chose the Spark template, a new image file was added to the Project navigator, *spark.png*. This is the default image of a single spark that's used by a sparks emitter. You can change the image in the emitter settings and have an emitter that shoots flowers or anything you want. But for now, we'll leave it as sparks.

In the Project navigator, also notice there is a *sparks.sks* file. This file describes the emitter we just created. So to use this emitter in our game, we just have to write some code that references this file. Switch to *Skater.swift* and add the following method inside the Skater class below the existing setupPhysicsBody() method:

Skater.swift

```
func setupPhysicsBody() {
    --snip--
}

func createSparks() {

    // Find the sparks emitter file in the project's bundle
  ❶ let bundle = Bundle.main

  ❷ if let sparksPath = bundle.path(forResource: "sparks", ofType: "sks") {

        // Create a Sparks emitter node
      ❸ let sparksNode = NSKeyedUnarchiver.unarchiveObject ↵
            (withFile: sparksPath) as! SKEmitterNode
      ❹ sparksNode.position = CGPoint(x: 0.0, y: -50.0)
      ❺ addChild(sparksNode)
    }
}
```

This code references the *sparks.sks* file that we created by looking it up in the project's *bundle*—the grouping of files and assets that make up the project—and uses it to create an emitter, or SKEmitterNode, called sparksNode. In order to access the *sparks.sks* file, which is part of the project, we need to get a reference ❶ to the application's main bundle, where all the files in the project will be. Once we have the bundle, we call its path(forResource:ofType:) method ❷ to get the file location, or path, of the *sparks.sks* file. The line at ❸ creates an SKEmitterNode named sparksNode with the help of the *sparks.sks* file we created, by calling NSKeyedUnarchiver.unarchiveObject(withFile:). This function can convert certain files, such as *.sks* files, into Swift objects.

Once the sparksNode is created, we set its position ❹ and then add it as a child of the skater sprite ❺. Since this emitter will be a child of the skater sprite, it will move around with the skater as if it were glued to her. More importantly, it's very easy to position the emitter so that it's on the bottom of the skater sprite. We simply set its position to (0.0, -50.0), which places it on the bottom middle of the skater.

Just like any other SpriteKit node, once we're done with the emitter, we should remove it. This sparks emitter should take only half a second or less to finish shooting a few sparks. After that, we need to remove it so it's not taking up memory and other system resources. Add this code to the new createSparks() method:

```
func createSparks() {
    --snip--
    if let sparksPath = bundle.path(forResource: "sparks", ofType: "sks") {
        --snip--
        addChild(sparksNode)

        // Run an action to wait half a second and then remove the emitter
   ❶ let waitAction = SKAction.wait(forDuration: 0.5)
   ❷ let removeAction = SKAction.removeFromParent()
   ❸ let waitThenRemove = SKAction.sequence([waitAction, removeAction])

   ❹ sparksNode.run(waitThenRemove)
    }
}
```

Earlier, we used actions to animate some labels and play some sounds. There's another cool thing we can do with actions: we can sequence them together. That means we can have a node automatically perform a series of actions, one after the other. We'll make some variables first to store the actions we want to sequence in order to make the code easier to read. The line at ❶ creates waitAction using SKAction.wait(forDuration:), which tells the node to wait for 0.5 seconds before moving on to the next action. The line at ❷ creates our next action, removeAction, which tells the node to remove itself from its parent.

The line at ❸ creates a waitThenRemove action, which is a sequence of those other two actions. To create a sequence action, we call SKAction.sequence() and pass it an array of SKActions. Since we already created waitAction and removeAction, we simply put them in an array using square brackets, like this: [waitAction, removeAction]. We only need two actions in our sequence, but there is no limit to how many actions you can string together this way. Finally, we simply tell the sparksNode to run that sequence of actions ❹, and we're done.

Particle emitters, once created and added to the scene, are always emitting particles. Any actions you perform on an emitter will happen in addition to what the node is already doing, which in this case is emitting sparks. So if you animated a particle emitter to move across the screen, you wouldn't be changing the way the particles behave, you'd just be changing where the particles are emitted from.

Now that we have a way to create sparks for the skateboard, we just need to add the code to decide when to actually call this createSparks() method.

Switch back to *GameScene.swift*, and update the first half of the
didBegin(_:) method to look like this:

GameScene.swift

```
func didBegin(_ contact: SKPhysicsContact) {

    // Check if the contact is between the skater and a brick
    if contact.bodyA.categoryBitMask == PhysicsCategory.skater && ↵
        contact.bodyB.categoryBitMask == PhysicsCategory.brick {

❶      if let velocityY = skater.physicsBody?.velocity.dy {

❷          if !skater.isOnGround && velocityY < 100.0 {

❸              skater.createSparks()
            }
        }

        skater.isOnGround = true
    }
}
```

Since we already have code to determine when the skater hits the
ground, we just added an if statement to check if:

- The skater is *not* already on the ground (notice the exclamation point
  before skater.isOnGround, meaning we're checking if she is not on the
  ground since ! reverses the meaning of a Boolean value).
- The skater is going down, not up.

Since the skater's physics body is an optional and we can't compare an
optional to a number like 100.0, we first need to unwrap the skater body's
y velocity, as shown at ❶. Next, the line at ❷ checks that the skater is not
already on the ground and that her y velocity is less than 100.0. If both of
these are true, then we call the skater's createSparks() method ❸ in order to
show the sparks emitter.

We check which direction the skater sprite is moving by looking at
her physics body's velocity in the dy direction. For velocity, dx means the
horizontal direction (positive values are right and negative values are
left), and dy means the vertical direction (positive values are up and negative values are down). To check if the skater is going down, technically
we should check if her y velocity is less than 0.0. But we are checking if it
is less than 100.0, because sometimes when she first hits the bricks, her y
velocity is slightly positive as she bounces off the bricks. So using a check
for velocityY < 100.0 ensures we'll always see the sparks when she hits the
ground.

If both of the if conditions are met, then sparks will fly off of the
skater's skateboard, as shown in Figure 18-5.

Figure 18-5: Sparks fly!

Run the game now, and enjoy the cool-looking sparks whenever the skater lands on the ground!

NOTE   *Schoolhouse Skateboarder is now complete! Remember that the final project files are available from* https://www.nostarch.com/iphoneappsforkids/, *so you can compare yours to double-check that everything is in the right place.*

WHAT YOU LEARNED

In this chapter, you learned a number of ways to make a game more professional. You learned about game state and why it's important to keep track of what state your game is in. You added a simple menu system to the game and used actions to animate the labels. Then you learned how to add sound effects to your game. Finally, you learned about particle emitters and used one to shoot sparks from the bottom of the skateboard.

RESOURCES

You've come a long way in developing your iOS coding skills, which means you now have what it takes to make your own apps from scratch. The best way to get better at making apps is by making more apps. Think about an app that you'd love to make, and then make it! Choosing something that excites you will make it easy to stay motivated. With every app you work on, there will be something new you haven't had to do before, and thus a new learning opportunity. Once you've explored some app ideas and have written a lot of code, you'll have a better idea of what areas to focus on.

This appendix provides some resources that will help you as you make your own apps, including tips for troubleshooting errors, where to find useful documentation, handy keyboard shortcuts, and information about Xcode versions.

TROUBLESHOOTING ERRORS

We can't cover every possible thing that can go wrong. But if you're having trouble building or running your apps, there are a few steps you can take to figure out what's going on. Here are some tips for finding solutions to any problems you encounter:

- Check the error message that Xcode is giving you. If you switch to the Issue navigator (⌘-5), you can view the current list of errors and warnings. Warnings are in yellow and usually don't have to be fixed (though it is strongly suggested you *do* fix them because they often turn into errors later). Errors are in red, and they must be fixed before the project will build. Sometimes the error message will tell you how to fix the issue, so make sure to read it and to also try to understand what's causing the issue.

- If the cause of the issue isn't clear, it's often helpful to tell Xcode to clean things up and try again. When you build a project in Xcode, it creates temporary files that are used to make future builds faster. Sometimes these files need to be removed so that the build process can create them again from scratch. There are two ways to "clean" in Xcode. You can clean the project with ⌘-SHIFT-K, or you can clean the build folder with ⌘-OPTION-SHIFT-K. Both methods do the same thing, but cleaning the build folder is more thorough. Try one or both of these, and then build the project again and see if the error goes away.

- Search the web for the issue you're having. It's a good idea to search for the exact error message that Xcode is giving you so you can find other people who have encountered the same issue and see how they solved it. These web searches will often take you to a website called Stack Overflow (*http://www.stackoverflow.com/*), which is dedicated to programming questions, errors, and solutions.

- Try closing and reopening Xcode, and if that doesn't help, reboot your computer.

- Read the docs! The next section tells you where to find any documentation you may need.

APPLE DOCUMENTATION

Apple has easily accessible documentation for everything you could hope to know about iOS, Swift, and more. To access it, log in to your Apple Developer Center account and visit these links:

- **The API Reference** (*https://developer.apple.com/reference/*) contains the full documentation of the iOS SDK. Here, you'll be able to research any method, property, or class within the iOS SDK and learn how it is used. To access this documentation from within Xcode, select **Window ▸ Documentation and API Reference** from the menu, or use the keyboard shortcut ⌘-SHIFT-0.

- **Guides and Sample Code** (*https://developer.apple.com/library/content/navigation/*) features hundreds of how-tos and examples, all written by Apple developers, covering every iOS topic under the sun.

- **The Apple Developer Forum** (*https://forums.developer.apple.com/*) is a great place to find answers to many questions.

- **The iOS Human Interface Guidelines** (*https://developer.apple.com/ios/human-interface-guidelines/overview/design-principles/*) is where Apple explains exactly what makes a great app and offers guidance on how to approach designing apps.

- **The App Distribution Guide** (*https://developer.apple.com/library/content/documentation/IDEs/Conceptual/AppDistributionGuide/Introduction/Introduction.html*) is Apple's guide to distributing apps on the App Store.

NOTE *The links to Apple documentation tend to change now and then. You can find an updated list on the book's website,* https://www.nostarch.com/iphoneappsforkids/.

XCODE KEYBOARD SHORTCUTS

You can accomplish everything you need to do in Xcode through a menu item or by clicking an icon. But once you spend a lot of time programming in Xcode, you'll find that knowing some keyboard shortcuts can be a real time-saver. Table A-1 shows a few common ones you might find helpful.

Table A-1: Xcode Keyboard Shortcuts

Shortcut	Action
⌘-B	Builds the project. This is a good way to test that the code is building properly, with no errors.
⌘-R	Runs the project. This builds the project and then runs it in the currently selected simulator (or device, if you have one attached and selected).
⌘-.	Stops the project from running or cancels an in-progress build.
⌘-SHIFT-Y	Shows or hides the debug area.
⌘-0	Shows or hides the Navigator pane on the left side of the screen.
⌘-1 through ⌘-9	Select the various Navigator panes, such as the Project navigator and Issue navigator.
⌘-OPTION-0, -1, and so on	Select the various Utilities panes.
⌘-SHIFT-K	Cleans the project.
⌘-OPTION-SHIFT-K	Cleans the build folder.
⌘-SHIFT-0	Accesses the documentation.

(continued)

Table A-2: (continued)

Shortcut	Action
⌘-/	Comments out the highlighted line(s) of code (or comments them if they are already commented out).
⌘-[	Decreases the indentation level of one or more lines of code.
⌘-]	Increases the indentation level of one or more lines of code.
⌘-F	Finds something in the current pane.
⌘-OPTION-F	Finds and *replaces* something in the current pane.
⌘-SHIFT-F	Finds something anywhere within the entire project by searching across all the project files.
⌘-OPTION-SHIFT-F	Finds and *replaces* something anywhere within the entire project.
⌘-CONTROL-left arrow	Returns to the previously selected file.

IOS SIMULATOR KEYBOARD SHORTCUTS

The iOS simulator also has some useful keyboard shortcuts, as shown in Table A-2. All of these are easily found as menu items in the simulator.

Table A-3: iOS Simulator Keyboard Shortcuts

Shortcut	Action
⌘-1	Zooms to 100% scale (which is good if you have a big computer screen).
⌘-2	Zooms to 75% scale.
⌘-3	Zooms to 50% scale.
⌘-4	Zooms to 33% scale.
⌘-5	Zooms to 25% scale (which is good if you have a small computer screen).
⌘-left arrow	Rotates the device to the left.
⌘-right arrow	Rotates the device to the right.
⌘-SHIFT-H	Simulates tapping the home button on the device.
⌘-K	Toggles the onscreen keyboard on or off. It works only when a control is selected that uses the keyboard, such as a text field.
⌘-S	Takes a screenshot of the simulator's screen and saves it to your desktop. This is useful for creating screenshots of your app for the App Store.

XCODE VERSIONS

The code in this book was built using Xcode 9, so you may want to use that version of Xcode when following along, even if there's a newer version available. To download older versions of Xcode, log in to your Apple Developer Center account and visit *https://developer.apple.com/download/*. At the bottom of that page, click the link **See more downloads**. From there, you should be able to find the download for *Xcode 9.xip*, as shown in Figure A-1.

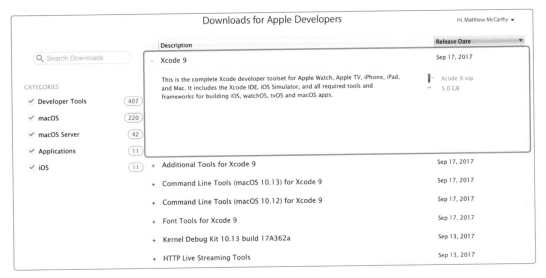

Figure A-1: Finding the download link for Xcode 9

If you'd like to use a newer version of Xcode for the projects in this book, check the book's website (*https://www.nostarch.com/iphoneappsforkids/*) for any changes you'll need to make to the code.

INDEX

repeat-while loops, 52–53
return keyword, 91
return values, 91–93
rotating device, in simulator, 213
running an app
    in simulator, 12–13
    on a device, 14–16

S

saving
    birthdays, in BirthdayTracker,
        173–181
    managed objects, in
        database, 180
    projects, 13
scene
    in SpriteKit, 205, 208
    in a storyboard, 10
Schoolhouse Skateboarder
        (app), 203
    anchorPoint, setting for
        scene, 208–209
    bricks
        adding, 224–225
        animating, 226–230
        leaving gaps, 229–230
        physics bodies for, 245–246
    contacts and collisions, 246–250
    creating the project, 205–206
    ending the game, 254–255
    game loop, 231–233
    game state, 280–281
    gems
        collecting, 267–268
        removing, 264–265
        spawning, 262–264
        updating, 265–267
    gravity, simulating, 235–238, 240
    images
        displaying background,
            207–211
        downloading, 204, 206
        filling the screen, 215
    menus (MenuLayer class), 282
        displaying, 286–288
        message label, 283–285
        removing, 288–289
        score label, 285–286

orientation, setting, 211–213
platforms, adding multilevel,
        258–262
scores
    displaying with labels,
        268–272
    for collecting gems, 275–276
    high scores, 276
    updating, 272–275
skater
    checking rotation of, 255
    jumping, 234–238, 250–251
    physics body for, 244–245
    resetting, 220–221
Skater class
    creating, 218
    instantiating, 219
sounds
    adding to project, 289–290
    downloading, 204, 206
    playing, 290
    sparks, 291–297
    speeding up the game, 257–258
    starting the game, 251–254
scope, 55–57, 103–104
SDK (Software Development Kit), 4
segues, 132, 171–172
selectors, 235
self keyword, 106–107
simulator (iPhone simulator)
    rotating device, 213
    running app on, 12–13
Size Inspector, 11, 127
SKAction object, 284–285, 295
SKEmitterNode, 294–295
SKLabelNode class, 269–273
SKPhysicsWorld class, 240
.sks (SpriteKit scene) files, 206,
        291, 294
SKScene class, 208, 240
SKSpriteNode class
    creating, 210, 218, 225
    subclassing, 218, 282
Software Development Kit (SDK), 4
sound effects
    adding to project, 289–290
    finding, 204
    playing, in SpriteKit, 290

sparks, adding with particle
emitters, 291–297
spawning, in games, 225
SpriteKit, 204
animating via actions,
284–285, 295
debug information, 223
game loop update(_:) method,
231–233
didMove(to:) method, 208, 210,
234, 253
filling the screen, 215
nodes, 223
getting by name, 273
name property of, 271, 273
physics engine. *See* SpriteKit
physics engine
scene size, 215
SKAction, 284–285, 295
SKEmitterNode, 294–295
SKLabelNode, 269–273
.*sks* (SpriteKit scene) files, 206
SKScene class, 208
SKSpriteNode class, 210
subclassing, 218, 282
sound effects, 289–290
spawning, 225
sprites. *See* sprites
SpriteKit physics engine, 239
applying forces, 250–251
categoryBitMask property, 248
collisionBitMask property, 248
contacts and collisions,
246–250, 267
contactTestBitMask property,
248–249
didBegin(_:) method,
249–250, 267
gravity, 240
physics bodies, 240
applying to sprite,
244–245, 263
properties, 242–244, 253–254
shapes, 241–242
physics categories, 247
SKPhysicsBody class, 241–251
SKPhysicsContactDelegate protocol,
249–250

SKPhysicsWorld class, 240
speed, 240
vectors, 240, 250–251
sprites, 204
adding, 210–211, 220, 222,
225, 263
animating, 226–229, 231–233,
284–285
children and parents, 211, 220
color, 286–287
displaying, 210, 220, 263
moving, 284–285
overlapping, 221
positioning, 210, 220–221,
226–227, 263
removing, 226–227, 252,
264–265, 288
zPosition property, 220–221, 225,
270, 283
state, of an object, 95–96
storyboard, 9, 126
adding a navigation
controller, 129
adding view controllers, 127
auto layout, 138–139
elements
adding, 10
positioning, 11–12, 134–136
segues, 132
String data type, 24
strings, 24
concatenation, 25
embedded variables, 49
formatting, 273–274
structs, 117–118
CGPoint, 210
IndexPath, 165–166
use in Schoolhouse
Skateboarder, 247
subclasses, 108–110, 218
subtraction operator (-), 27
superclasses, 108–110
super keyword, 109
Swift, 4
creating file, 142–143
playground. *See* playground
safe language, 59